T0198520

THE WRITER'S
— GUIDE TO —
WEAPONS

A Practical Reference for Using Firearms and Knives in Fiction

WRITER'S DIGEST
BOOKS

Benjamin Sobieck

FOREWORD BY DAVID MORRELL

WRITER'S DIGEST BOOKS

An imprint of Penguin Random House LLC
penguinrandomhouse.com

Copyright © 2015 by Benjamin Sobieck

Penguin supports copyright. Copyright fuels creativity, encourages diverse voices, promotes free speech, and creates a vibrant culture. Thank you for buying an authorized edition of this book and for complying with copyright laws by not reproducing, scanning, or distributing any part of it in any form without permission. You are supporting writers and allowing Penguin to continue to publish books for every reader.

ISBN 978-1-59963-815-7

Edited by Rachel Randall
Interior designed by Laura Spencer and Alexis Brown
Cover designed by Bethany Rainbolt

ACKNOWLEDGMENTS

Excluding anyone from recognition is a sin, but there isn't enough space to list the many writers of fiction and nonfiction upon whose shoulders I stood to write this guide. However, a few people deserve special mention for their assistance with this work.

Exceptional gratitude goes to Corey Graff, James Card, Joe Kertzman, and Steve Shackleford for their time and effort as fact-checkers.

Vast libraries of information helped produce the technical side of this guide. Thanks to the teams at *Gun Digest*, *BLADE*, *Living Ready*, *Deer & Deer Hunting*, *Turkey & Turkey Hunting*, and *Trapper & Predator Caller* for the cumulative centuries' worth of knowledge. Thank you also for the guidance during my tenure at F+W. To James Duncan and Rachel Randall, my editors, thank you for bringing out the best in this guide. To Phil Sexton, the publisher at *Writer's Digest*, goes my appreciation for believing in my crazy ideas in the first place.

I must also recognize my family. This guide is a testament to the firearm, knife, and outdoors knowledge they've passed down.

I saved the best for last: Thank you to Meredith, for the times you left me alone to write and for the times you didn't.

TABLE OF CONTENTS

DISCLAIMER

The information presented in this guide is to be used only as a reference for writing fiction. It is not a guide for the operation, procurement, manufacture, or transfer of firearms or knives. The author and publisher do not condone illegal activity of any kind, nor are they responsible for any damage—intentional or unintentional—to persons or property that may be inspired by this information. Always follow local, state, and federal laws when buying, selling, transferring, possessing, manufacturing, and using firearms and knives or their accessories.

ABOUT THE AUTHOR

Benjamin Sobieck is an online editor and online product manager for a number of weapons and outdoors magazines, including *Gun Digest*, *BLADE*, *Living Ready*, and *Modern Shooter*. Sobieck is also a crime and thriller author, appearing in such anthologies and journals as *Burning Bridges: A Renegade Fiction Anthology*, *Exiles: An Outsider Anthology*, *Black Heart Magazine presents Noir*, and *Out of the Gutter*. He's also worked as a newspaper crime reporter. For more about Sobieck and his crime-fighting creation, detective Maynard Soloman, visit CrimeFictionBook.com.

FOREWORD

Many years ago, when I lived in Iowa, a post-office carrier knocked on my door and handed me a special-delivery letter, for which I had to sign a receipt. The letter came from South Africa. I didn't know anyone there, so with great curiosity I opened the envelope and discovered a message from a combat school. An angry message. The teachers and students had been fans of my novels for a long time, I was informed, but they were fans no longer because my latest book made clear that the creator of Rambo knew nothing whatsoever about firearms.

Two hours later, a different post-office carrier knocked on my door and delivered a second special-delivery letter. Again I signed a receipt, and again I noted that the letter came from South Africa. It was from a combat school as well, but from a *different* combat school. The teachers and students there had been fans of my work also, but they, too, vowed never again to read a word of my wretched prose because it was obvious that I had never fired a handgun in my life and knew nothing about them.

These letters surprised me, not only because they came from so far away and had the same angry message but also because I had, in fact, a lot of experience with firearms, particularly handguns, and did my best to double-check the facts about anything I wrote, especially firearms.

What on earth were these knowledgeable schools complaining about? To my shock, when I looked at the passages they cited, I realized that the schools were right. But it wasn't my fault.

Well, not exactly.

This is what had happened: In my then-recent novel (which I won't name because I don't want anyone looking at the book for the wrong reason, and anyway in most subsequent editions the problem was fixed), I had foolishly decided at the last minute (the very last minute, because the novel was at the galley stage, my final opportunity for corrections) that there were a lot of semi-automatic handguns in the book and for variety maybe I should change one of them to a revolver.

(As an aside, let this be a cautionary tale about not making changes at the galley stage, when a copyeditor will no longer be available to make certain that the changes are consistent with the rest of the text.)

So, presto, a semi-automatic pistol (the ammunition is in a magazine inserted into the weapon) became a revolver (the ammunition is in a rotating cylinder).

But I didn't think to change any other details. Thus, in a major action scene, as my protagonist prepared to scale a wall, he pressed the revolver's safety catch. Later, he released the revolver's safety catch.

Writing those words, I grit my teeth. My chest tenses. My face turns warm with shame. Aarrgh.

Revolvers don't have safety catches (at least none that I'm aware of, but I've learned that if I make absolute statements about firearms, someone will find an exception). There is indeed a button at the side of some revolvers, but its function is to allow the ammunition cylinder to swing open for reloading. When my protagonist pressed that button, in all likelihood he would have caused the cylinder to open, dumping the ammunition onto the ground.

The moral is—when you write about firearms, you can't be too careful.

You can kill a dog in one of your novels, and you'll receive angry e-mails (no need for someone to send a special-delivery letter from a foreign country; these days, an e-mail creates instant gratification). You can make a mistake about a motor vehicle, and you'll definitely hear about it. You can make a mistake about a particular type of horse or the distance between two cities or a sports statistic, and you'll hear about it, and you'll probably receive a one-star review on Amazon because of it.

But no wrath is greater than that of firearms enthusiasts. Even if you've had instruction, Benjamin Sobieck's *The Writer's Guide to Weapons: A Practical Reference for Using Firearms and Knives in Fiction* is going to save you a lot of time apologizing and vowing to do better in response to a barrage of e-mails from irate readers.

Of course, the best way to learn about firearms is to contact a local sporting-goods store and sign up for a course. I'm baffled why some authors who write about firearms don't do this. At the least, they'd discover that a gunshot is *loud* and gives off a distinctive acrid odor—sensory details often omitted from gunfight scenes written by authors whose only experience with firearms is in watching movies.

How many times have you watched an action film in which a villain threatens someone by pulling back the pump-action on a certain type of shotgun and then doing it again, and again, never firing? The repetition apparently is meant to emphasize that he means business. The only problem is that the pump-action on a certain type of shotgun inserts a shell into the firing chamber. The next time the pump is used, the shell in the firing chamber is ejected while a new one is inserted. Thus, in movies that show a character "racking" a shotgun repeatedly without ever firing it, shells ought to be flying onto the floor. Ditto for Western movie characters who repeatedly work the lever on a rifle without firing it, evidently intending to indicate their intense emotions. Again, in the real world, perfectly good ammunition would be flying comically through the air. Ditto for a character who repeatedly racks the slide on a semi-automatic pistol without firing it. Perfectly good ammunition would be accumulating at the character's feet.

I was pleased and amused to see Benjamin Sobieck emphasize these and many other mistakes. "Don't" is often as good an instructional technique as "do." For authors, regardless of their sophistication about these matters, the clarity with which this book explains many kinds of firearms and knives is a gift. The differences between semi-automatic pistols and revolvers, between the types of calibers, between magazines and clips (I once heard someone say he would never read a famous thriller author again because that author referred to a magazine as a clip)—these and similar danger zones for writers who use firearms in their novels can now be entered without fear.

David Morrell

INTRODUCTION
WHY GETTING IT RIGHT MATTERS

Bill Robber, serial check bouncer, just made off with $330 trillion in two-dollar bills from the freshly burglarized First State Bank, thus recouping his lifelong accrual of overdraft fees. Bill's sports car displayed an energy drink decal in the rear windshield, indicating to police that pursuit in typical cruisers was out of the question.

Fortunately, Maynard Soloman, gal-damn detective, watched the whole thing unfold across the street. He popped an antacid and hit the gas on his rattrap RV. The engine belched smoky profanity as the speedometer approached 900 miles per hour. The sheer speed lifted the RV off the ground, causing it to take flight high above rush hour traffic.

Once positioned above Bill's sports car, Maynard gently tapped the brakes. The RV dropped onto Bill's sports car with a devastating crunch.

"Your scam is finished. No one escapes overdraft fees," Maynard said to Bill's mangled figure. "The next bad check you'll have is the inspection when your carcass gets to prison."

Chalk up another victory for Maynard Soloman, the world's crustiest detective.

Other than the slapstick tongue-in-cheekery, does anything seem off about that passage? Like *factually* wrong?

This example has some pretty obvious problems: No one would write about an RV rocketing down the highway at 900 miles per hour—RVs just don't do that. Science has also yet to prove that RVs can fly with any degree of accuracy. And outside of an absurdist comedy or maybe science fiction, there's no way a single person could hold $330 trillion in rainmaking two-dollar bills. That's if a bank would carry that many twofers in the first place.

But you're writing more serious fare: thrillers, mysteries, police procedurals, and the like. To a certain degree, sticking to reality matters quite a bit. Yes, it's true that errors in these genres may not be quite as obvious as those in a passage involving $330 trillion in cash and a flying RV, but shaky clichés, crimes against physics, and mistakes of ignorance still abound in depictions of firearms and knives. Cornea-shattering eye rolls can yank readers out of the story and put the writer's credibility into serious question.

I've read too many otherwise terrific tales tarnished by these grossly inaccurate depictions. In fact, one particular online crime story (which shall remain nameless) got a shotgun so mind-bogglingly wrong that it inspired me to write this guide. And given the number of military veterans, gun owners, knife enthusiasts, outdoors types, and history buffs that make up the readership of the thriller, mystery, and crime genres, it's a safe bet I'm not the only one who has raised an eyebrow.

However, I'm not here to pass judgment on other writers. I had the good fortune to grow up around firearms and knives. I built a career in publishing firearm and knife magazines and books, working with TV shows, and creating digital content at *Gun Digest* and *BLADE*. I sometimes forget that not everyone comes from the same background.

So why should it be a surprise that some stories source their firearm and knife information from popular culture? That's all the exposure some writers have to these weapons. And that's where the trouble starts. Pop culture—be it books, movies, video games, or TV shows—does a D+ job at depicting firearms and knives. They use just enough truth to make the rest believable if you don't know any better.

I don't hold this bad habit against anyone. Instead of wagging my finger at social media and writing forums, I wrote this guide. That's Minnesota Nice for you.

What follows is a guide to the firearms and knives commonly used in thrillers and crime fiction. The information is boiled down so writers unfamiliar with these items can quickly learn the ropes. I offer detailed information, but I won't go all Tom Clancy on you. As such, this guide is by no means an exhaustive look at every firearm, knife, or accessory in existence. It's a practical reference for writers, not an encyclopedia. To paraphrase the late Elmore Leonard, I tried to leave out all the parts writers skip. Get in, get out, and get back to work.

To help me along the way, I'd like to formally introduce you to Maynard Soloman, gal-damn detective. He's a crotchety PI from my own writing who cracks cases out of his decaying RV. Maynard agreed to take a few blows as an example character throughout this guide, where I stick him into scenarios that inaccurately depict firearms and knives. Try to spot the errors as Maynard does battle with his moronic arch nemesis, Bill Robber. Then I'll explain what went wrong and how to fix it. Introduce yourself, Maynard.

"I haven't had health insurance since '86. Please be gentle," Maynard says.

Not to worry, Maynard. There's an ice pack and a case of beer waiting for you at the end of this book. You'll be fine. There's plenty of pain to go around in this guide. Just ask the crime writer who shared his true story of getting shot in Ireland. Or the remains of characters turned to soup by writers using weapons on the Hit List in Part Three. I've also included some of the most baffling myths about weapons in fiction and real life, as well as information about the most popular weapons in the thriller, crime, mystery, and war genres. And if the information in this guide piques your interest, you will find even more firearm and knife information in *Gun Digest* and *BLADE*. I highly recommend them as the next step in your weaponry education.

Finally, I'd like to say that this guide is a labor of love for me, but don't take it as dogma. Push the envelope of creative license all you want. My hope is you'll do so with a better understanding of firearms and knives. Your readers will thank you for it.

TEN GOLDEN TIPS FOR WRITING ABOUT WEAPONS

Lists of writing rules are just asking to be broken. However, here are my Ten Golden Tips for writing about weapons. These will help you get a footing for the rest of the book.

1. **DON'T OVERTHINK FIREARMS AND KNIVES.** That might sound odd coming from this full-length guide, but it's true. This guide is written to be a practical, get-in-and-get-out reference. Figure out what you need to know more about, see how it works, throw it into the story, and be done with it. Unless you're tapping your inner technical writer, just shoot for accurately depicting the weapons in your story. There's no need to expound every single detail of your master criminal's choice revolver. Doing so … slowwwws … down … the … story.

2. **HOPELESSLY LOST? START WITH WHAT LOOKS COOL.** This guide includes sections on matching firearms and knives to characters. That will help a great deal if you don't know what weapon to choose, but if you're *totally* lost, search online for images of firearms and knives. Pick a couple that look cool to you. Then check them against this guide. Are they capable of doing what you want them to do? Do they fit the genre, time period, and style of your story?

3. **YOUTUBE IS YOUR FRIEND.** It's not always possible to get your mitts on a certain firearm or knife. Fortunately, you can join the vibrant community of reviewers on YouTube for a real-world perspective. Watch their videos on weapons and how they work, and use that information as a base for further research.

4. **IF IT'S IN A MOVIE OR ON TELEVISION, IT'S PROBABLY INACCURATE.** No one would take legal advice from TV police procedurals. A person (hopefully) wouldn't attempt surgery after watching a medical drama. It's the same with firearms and knives in movies and television. Hollywood takes a truckload of creative license, but real firearms and knives must be grounded within the realms of physics, technology, and history. Strive to make your weapons as accurate as possible to retain credibility.

5. **BUY A KNIFE OR HIT THE GUN RANGE.** Knives are relatively easy to buy. If a character's knife is central to the story, chances are good that buying it in real life is a possibility (with a few exceptions outlined in this guide). What could be better for writing than having the knife right there? Plus, it'll look nice next to the keyboard. Firearms are a different story, but hitting the gun range is a great place to start.

Many ranges offer gun rentals to shoot on location. If that's too intimidating or not possible, you can start by taking a gun safety course instead. These courses offer hands-on training from professionals, and most offer a state certificate at the end.

6. **STUCK? WRITE AROUND THE WEAPON.** The old writer's trick of maneuvering around challenging grammar and sentence structure also applies to weapons. If you can't determine the exact firearm or knife a character should be outfitted with, avoid it by going generic. Just use *knife, pistol, revolver, rifle, shotgun*, and the like. Remember to keep the use of those items equally generic and consistent, or it will become obvious that you don't know the weapon.

7. **READ A NEWSPAPER.** There's no better (or worse) example of how humans use firearms and knives on each other than the crime report. It's fertile ground for fiction. For example, you could source a weapon for a character based on a real murder. Sure, it's morbid, but it grounds the item's use in reality.

8. **BAD GUYS CAN GET JUST ABOUT ANYTHING.** The illegal trade of firearms and knives means a criminal can use a firearm manufactured in the Czech Republic to knock off a Chicago liquor store if he has the right connections. Don't feel limited when outfitting a "bad guy" with unusual firearms and knives. Unlike the legal market, the back alley offers plenty of variety.

9. **BUT GOOD GUYS CAN'T.** Professional law enforcement and military organizations have good reasons to standardize their firearms and knives. Firearm selection, especially in the military, is determined through rigorous testing. Ammunition is often purchased in bulk. Certain knives might not physically mesh well with other gear. Tossing some obscure firearm or knife into these characters' hands doesn't always make sense. They will require more research to get right. The same goes for everyday, law-abiding civilian characters. Research federal, state, and local laws so they're not walking around with something ridiculously illegal.

10. **SOMEONE WILL SAY YOU'RE WRONG, EVEN IF YOU'RE RIGHT.** Put three readers keen on firearms and knives in a room together, and then ask them for an opinion. The only thing two of them will agree on is that the third is wrong. So if an armchair general, a mall ninja, or an everyday Internet troll starts complaining about the inaccuracy of the well-researched Walther .380 pistol you featured in your story, just wait. Someone else will come along to rip that guy's argument apart. Unless you totally biffed on something, stick to your proverbial guns and ignore the macho knuckle-draggers trying to ruin your day.

[PART ONE]
FIREARMS

FIREARM SAFETY

Anytime you talk about firearms, the first thing that should come up is safety. Any firearm-toting character, good or bad, should be familiar with general safety principles. It's surprising how often they're not followed in fiction, especially by characters who enforce the law.

Please keep that finger off the trigger until you're ready to shoot, unless the character's disembodied hand is ready to blast its way out of a rectangle. (Photo courtesy of *Gun Digest*.)

- **KEEP THE FINGER OFF THE TRIGGER UNLESS PREPARED TO FIRE.** Sure, people could drive with two feet on the gas if they wanted to, but one split second of confusion can end in tragedy. That's why red flags go up when characters, especially law enforcement types, put a finger on the trigger before bolting into a tense scene. However, if a firearm uses a safety (not all do; be sure to research the model), the character would disengage the safety if he thought firing a shot were probable. For example, a stranger walks into Maynard's RV. Maynard would switch the safety off while determining if the stranger is a threat. But he still wouldn't put his finger on the trigger until he was ready to shoot, since the stranger might just be there with a pizza delivery.
- **BE SURE OF THE TARGET AND WHAT LIES BEYOND.** You could also say that what goes up must come down. Projectiles from even the smallest firearm can travel miles. The character shooting is responsible for that shot the entire journey. Characters cracking off random shots are being reckless. And when law enforcement characters shoot at a fleeing vehicle, they're just asking for collateral damage. Warning shots are another problem. If you shoot up, that bullet still has to land somewhere.

- **NEVER POINT THE FIREARM AT PEOPLE OR PROPERTY THE CHARACTER IS NOT WILLING TO DESTROY.** In other words, if a firearm is aimed or even briefly pointed at a character, that character better be someone the shooter is willing to kill. It follows that a character would never check to see if a firearm is loaded by looking down the barrel. Need a visual example of what not to do? Watch Ed Wood's classically awful *Plan 9 from Outer Space* "movie" (that's being generous). The characters aim handguns at each other and themselves with reckless abandon.
- **TREAT EVERY FIREARM AS IF IT IS LOADED.** Unless a character is reckless, he or she would use the same amount of caution with an unloaded firearm as with a loaded one.
- **USE TWO HANDS WHEN POSSIBLE.** Accuracy, and therefore safety, is always compromised when only one hand is used to shoot. Even with small handguns, using two hands is the safest, most accurate way to shoot. Reckless characters, or writers going for flash, might not care. That's okay, but it's worth stating anyway.

SHOTGUNS 101

Shotguns are perfect for close- to mid-range encounters. These ranges depend on what kind of ammunition the character is using with the shotgun. *Shot*, the term for a bunch of BBs (small spheres of lead, steel, or other metal material), is effective at ranges out to 50 yards. A *slug*, which is a large single projectile, is effective out to 100 yards or so.

PUMP-ACTION SHOTGUNS

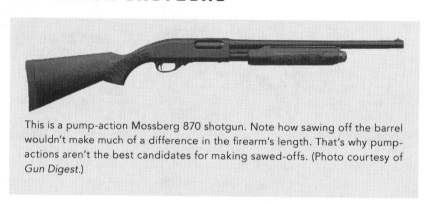

This is a pump-action Mossberg 870 shotgun. Note how sawing off the barrel wouldn't make much of a difference in the firearm's length. That's why pump-actions aren't the best candidates for making sawed-offs. (Photo courtesy of *Gun Digest*.)

Popular pump-action shotguns: Benelli Nova, Ithaca Model 37, Mossberg 500, Remington Model 870, Winchester Model 12

When people imagine a shotgun, they usually picture a pump-action shotgun, sometimes called a slide-action shotgun. The *click-clack* sound of the sliding pump, its most distinguishable feature, is made when the user "pumps" a sliding mechanism underneath the barrel back and forth. A single back-and-forth motion equals one pump.

That pumping motion works the action, which is the mechanism that moves ammunition through the firearm. One back-and-forth pump will transfer one shell (ammunition) from the magazine (a tube under the barrel holding ammunition) into the chamber (the spot at the base of the barrel where the shell is seated to be fired). That same pump will simultaneously eject a shell, if one is present, from the chamber.

I'll repeat that in order to make a point: One back-and-forth pump will simultaneously eject and load one shell. This means that those television characters who unnecessarily and dramatically pump their shotguns during confrontational situations likely ejected unfired shells onto the ground, or they approached the situation with a shotgun that wasn't ready to fire. If that's confusing, just avoid dramatic pumping of shotguns, or any firearm, altogether. You'll be accurate every time.

Advantages

- Pump-action shotguns are among the most popular types of firearms in the world. They're effective for hunting, sport shooting, and defense. It wouldn't be out of place to outfit a character anywhere in the world, from the 1880s through today, with a pump-action shotgun.
- Just about everyone is familiar with the *click-clack* sound of the pump-action. That sound alone can be enough to send others running.
- Pump-action shotguns are considered safer than other firearms to operate. They require extra manipulation in order to fire them. Not only does the operator have to switch off the safety (a button or sliding switch that prevents the firearm from firing), she also has to physically pump a shell into the chamber. If a shell is already in the chamber, it is mechanically impossible to fire the shotgun unless the slide is all the way forward. These extra steps also increase reliability. Because the operator is manually working the action, there is less chance of mechanical failure.
- Pump-action shotguns come in a variety of gauges (not calibers, unless a character is using the relatively weak .410 shotshell) to suit any number of needs. The most common are the 12-gauge and the 20-gauge, although there are several others. The smaller the number, the greater the firepower.

Disadvantages

- An operator cannot fire a pump-action shotgun as quickly as a semi-automatic shotgun, although the pump-action's reliability still makes it a good choice for a character in a firefight.
- In fiction scenarios where stealth is required, a pump-action shotgun is not always the best choice. The *click-clack* sound of the action could give someone away.
- Most shotguns cannot hold as much ammunition as most rifles. Shotgun magazines rarely carry ammunition in amounts beyond single digits. A character might be better off with a high-capacity rifle over a shotgun for that reason.

Inaccurate Example

Bill Robber had Maynard Soloman right where he wanted him.

"What's the combination to the safe? Don't play dumb; you know the one I'm talking about. The one with the secret recipe for Crystal Pepsi," Bill said and aimed his semi-automatic shotgun at the detective.

Maynard raised his hands in the air and said, "1 ... 2 ... 3 ... I forget the rest."

Bill pumped the shotgun and switched the safety off.

"I'll blow your brains out. Start talking," Bill said.

"Seriously? You couldn't guess the rest?" Maynard said.

Accurate Example

Bill Robber had Maynard Soloman right where he wanted him.

"What's the combination to the safe? Don't play dumb, you know the one I'm talking about," Bill said and switched the safety off his pump-action shotgun.

Maynard raised his hands in the air and said, "1 ... 2 ... 3 ... I forget the rest."

Bill poked Maynard in the eye with the shotgun barrel.

"I'll blow your brains out. Start talking," Bill said.

"Seriously? You couldn't guess the rest?" Maynard said.

What Went Wrong?

A couple of things went awry in the inaccurate example.

First, Bill pumped the shotgun for dramatic effect, which likely dropped an unfired shell onto the ground. Remember: Pumping a shotgun simultaneously loads a shell from the magazine into the chamber to be fired and ejects a shell, fired or unfired, from the chamber. Bill's a paint-fumed nincompoop, but even he wouldn't be that stupid. Better to write the intimidation in other ways, as I did with Bill prodding Maynard in the eye.

Second, a semi-automatic shotgun does not need to be pumped. It's a completely different type of shotgun.

SEMI-AUTOMATIC SHOTGUNS

Popular semi-automatic shotguns: Beretta Xtrema2, Browning Auto-5, Mossberg 935, Remington Model 1100, Winchester Super X3

A semi-automatic shotgun has no pump. Instead the action (the mechanism that cycles ammunition through the firearm) uses gas or a mechanical device to capture force from the recoil generated by shooting the firearm. It uses this force to simultaneously eject and load consecutive shells each time the shooter pulls the trigger. You just load and shoot; no pumping required.

The shooter manually loads the first shell into the chamber by working the charging handle (sometimes called a *cocking handle*). This handle functions similarly to the slide on a pump-action shotgun, except it's a small tab or knob situated near the chamber (the place where a shell is seated to be fired).

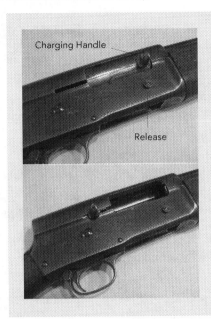

This photo demonstrates how manually moving the charging handle back exposes the chamber, moving a shell from the magazine into the chamber. Or the operator might manually drop a shell in. Pressing the release (or just letting go in some models) snaps the charging handle forward, readying the firearm for shooting. With slight variations, this is how the first shell is loaded in all semi-automatic and fully automatic shotguns and rifles. (Author's photo.)

To fire the first shot, the shooter pulls the charging handle back manually. This seats a shell into the chamber from the magazine (the tube underneath the barrel where shells are held in reserve). The shooter could also manually drop a shell into the chamber. Then the shooter pushes a release button or switch so the charging handle snaps forward. The shell is ready to be fired. Some models don't have a release. The shooter would just pull back the charging handle and let go. Write around that detail if you're not sure.

The semi-automatic action takes over only after the first shell is fired. This is because recoil to drive the action isn't produced until a shot is fired. Only one shell will fire per pull of the trigger. The shooter cannot hold down the trigger and have the shotgun continuously fire. That's why it's called a *semi*-automatic. A *fully* automatic shotgun would allow the operator to continuously fire so long as the trigger is pulled.

Outside of the military, video games, and a few hardcore firearms collectors, it is rare to encounter a fully automatic shotgun. If a scene calls for one, treat it like a semi-auto. The difference is it would fire continuously so long as the trigger is pulled. Full-autos are also heavier, since they have to carry more shells in their magazines.

Like pump-action shotguns, semi-autos use a magazine located under the barrel to house ammunition. Pump-actions and semi-autos look similar because of this, but some high-capacity semi-automatic shotguns use detachable drums (a pancake-shaped ammunition magazine).

Advantages

- Semi-automatics can fire rounds faster than any other type of shotgun, except for fully automatics. They're ideal for firefights.
- Once loaded, semi-autos are simple to operate. Just switch off the safety, aim, and pull the trigger. Keep pulling until the ammunition runs out.
- Just like pump-action shotguns, semi-automatic shotguns come in a variety of gauges (not calibers, except for the relatively weak .410) to suit any number of needs. The most common are 12- and 20-gauge, although there are many more. Remember, the smaller the number, the greater the firepower.
- Like pump-action shotguns, semi-automatic shotguns are among the most commonly owned firearms. They're perfect for hunting, shooting sports, and defense.

Disadvantages

- Because they contain more moving parts, semi-automatic shotguns are considered less reliable than other shotguns. Failure by some component of the action may cause ammunition to jam. Writers can use a well-timed jam to their advantage.
- Most shotguns cannot hold as much ammunition as most rifles. Shotgun magazines rarely carry ammunition in amounts beyond single digits. A character needing to crank out a lot of shots would likely choose a rifle over a shotgun.

Inaccurate Example

Maynard loaded shells into his semi-automatic shotgun's magazine, then squeezed the trigger. He held it down as the body of Bill Robber absorbed shot after bloody shot.

When the smoke cleared, what was left of Bill and his belongings spackled the floor, walls, and ceiling. Maynard spat a nugget of Bill's gore from his lips, grinned, and pumped the shotgun.

"Now to collect my money," he said and peeled from the bloody wall the twenty bucks Bill owed him for gas.

Accurate Example

Maynard jacked the first shell into his semi-automatic shotgun's chamber, then squeezed the trigger. He pulled it again and again as the body of Bill Robber absorbed shot after bloody shot.

When the smoke cleared, what was left of Bill and his belongings spackled the floor, walls, and ceiling. Maynard spat a nugget of Bill's gore from his lips and grinned.

"Now to collect my money," he said and peeled from the bloody wall the twenty bucks Bill owed him for gas.

What Went Wrong?

Two functions of the shotgun are in conflict in the inaccurate example. Maynard doesn't pump the shotgun between shots as he shoots Bill. He just pulls the trigger. A paragraph later, he pumps the shotgun. The shotgun must be either an automatic or a pump, but not both.

For the purposes of this example, let's say it's an automatic. Is it a semi-auto or a full-auto? The trigger pulling needs to match. If Maynard fires a semi-automatic shotgun, as in the accurate example, he'd pull the trigger "again and again." He wouldn't hold it down, since semi-autos fire once per trigger pull.

A somewhat sneakier error is in the magazine loading. Loading the magazine isn't enough to start firing with semi-autos. The shells in the magazine need to get into the chamber somehow. That means working the charging handle. The accurate example takes this into account when Maynard "jacked the first shell."

SINGLE-SHOT AND DOUBLE-BARREL SHOTGUNS

This decked-out 20-gauge Stoeger is an example of a side-by-side double-barrel shotgun. Although fiction doesn't often dress these shotguns up with extras, don't let that stop you from doing so in a story. (Photo courtesy of *Gun Digest*.)

Popular single-shot and double-barrel shotgun brands: Browning, Ithaca, Rossi, Savage Arms, Winchester

As their names suggest, single-shot and double-barrel shotguns can hold only one or two shells, respectively. Triple-barrels and quad-barrels do exist, but they're uncommon.

The majority of single-shot and double-barrel shotguns are loaded by "breaking" open the action. This is called a break-action. The shooter uses a lever or release that cracks open the action (it looks as if the gun is on a hinge) and exposes the chamber(s) (the spot where ammunition is seated to be fired). The shooter places shells directly into the chamber, then closes the action.

Double-barrel shotguns can be split into two categories: over-under and side-by-side. With an over-under, one barrel sits on top of the other. With a side-by-side, the two barrels are horizontal to each other.

Double-barrel shotguns sometimes feature two triggers, known as double triggers. Each barrel gets its own trigger. Other versions have a single trigger controlled by a switch that designates which barrel is being fired.

Some, but not all, single-shot and double-barrel shotguns use a hammer (a lever located behind the action that moves the firing pin). When the hammer is pulled back, the shotgun is cocked (ready to fire). When the hammer is forward, the shotgun is unable to fire. An operator may manually move the hammer forward without firing it. To do so, he or she would simultaneously pull the trigger and carefully guide the hammer into its forward position.

Advantages

- Single-shot and double-barrel shotguns are among the most reliable firearms because they contain the fewest number of moving parts.
- Because of their simple design, single-shot and double-barrel shotguns are lighter in weight than other shotguns. They're a good choice for characters who spend a lot of time on their feet.
- Just like other shotguns, single-shots and double-barrels come in a variety of gauges to meet a number of needs.

Disadvantages

- These shotguns lack a magazine (a place inside the firearm where ammunition is held in reserve). That means they can't put out a high rate of fire. In a firefight with a lot of lead in the air, the shooter will be reloading often.
- The light weight of single-shots and double-barrels means they don't absorb as much recoil (the energy exerted on the shooter upon firing a shot). They "kick" the shooter harder when fired. Heavier shotguns absorb more recoil, lessening the kick.
- The addition of a second trigger on a double-barrel shotgun could confuse a character during a tense situation. The character might pull a trigger that's already been fired. Or conversely, the character might fire unintentionally.

Inaccurate Example

Bill Robber unloaded the double-barrel shotgun into Maynard's generous gut without mercy. *Bang. Bang. Bang.*

He cocked the hammer back, reloaded, and continued firing until the daylight peeked through the meaty window scooped out from the detective's motionless body.

Accurate Example

Bill Robber unloaded the double-barrel shotgun into Maynard's generous gut without mercy. *Bang. Bang.* He paused only to break open the shotgun and reload. The downtime between the gore gave the detective a moment to get the last laugh.

"Hey, Bill. What's the difference between a full-time writer and a part-time writer?" Maynard said.

"I don't know, what?" Bill said and finished reloading the next two shells.

"Unemployment."

What Went Wrong?

The math needs to work in any scene involving firearms. A double-barrel shotgun can fire two shots before reloading. Bill fired three times in the inaccurate example.

Bill's reloading method is suspect, too. This particular double-barrel shotgun uses a hammer (not all do). A hammer is cocked prior to pulling the trigger, not when reloading. Bill should be described as breaking open the shotgun to reload instead.

SAWED-OFF SHOTGUNS

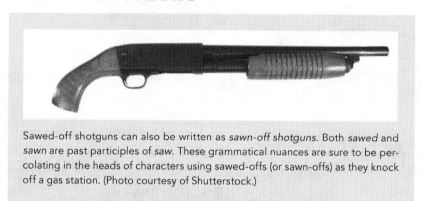

Sawed-off shotguns can also be written as *sawn-off shotguns*. Both *sawed* and *sawn* are past participles of *saw*. These grammatical nuances are sure to be percolating in the heads of characters using sawed-offs (or sawn-offs) as they knock off a gas station. (Photo courtesy of Shutterstock.)

The sawed-off shotgun isn't a type of firearm. It's simply a shotgun in which the barrel has been modified—or "sawed off"—to become less than 18 inches long.

Some shotguns are legally manufactured this way, so they're not "sawed off" per se. Any civilian qualified to purchase firearms can legally own these short-barreled shotguns. They are considered National Firearms Act (NFA) or "Class III" firearms. This means that a character is required to register the gun with the Bureau of Alcohol, Tobacco, Firearms and Explosives (ATF) and to pay a $200 tax, plus get permission from the chief law enforcement official for his or her jurisdiction. This requirement, which also applies to fully automatic firearms, has been in place since 1934.

However, a character might skirt these regulations and literally saw off the barrel of a shotgun. It's illegal to do so, and it's why sawed-off shotguns have a reputation for criminal activity. A character would not be able to buy an illegally modified sawed-off shotgun at a legitimate retailer or pawnshop. And despite the ability of some law enforcement officers and gun collectors to obtain legally manufactured sawed-off shotguns, the rule of thumb for fiction is that they are otherwise illegal.

Any type of shotgun could become a sawed-off shotgun. However, single-shot or double-barrel shotguns are most ideal, because no pump or magazine stands in the way of shortening the barrel.

The firepower of a shotgun doesn't increase after it becomes sawed off. Ammunition determines firepower, not barrel length. Nothing about a sawed-off shotgun makes it more powerful than its long-barreled counterpart.

Advantages

- Sawed-off shotguns are lighter and less bulky. They're easier for a character to transport or conceal.
- A shorter barrel means a character has better maneuverability without sacrificing firepower.
- Sawed-off shotguns are ideal for close-range combat. The shorter barrel allows for a wider shot pattern (the term for the cloud of BBs that exits the shotgun upon firing) at close ranges. This means a target character a few yards away could be hit by more BBs.
- It's possible for a physically powerful character to use a sawed-off shotgun with one hand, given its lighter weight.

Disadvantages

- A sawed-off shotgun is a major indicator that its user could be a criminal.
- A character firing a sawed-off with one hand is probably underestimating the recoil (the force exerted on the shooter from firing the gun). Shotguns are designed for two-handed use. When used correctly, recoil is directed through the stock into the shooter's shoulder. Shooting with one hand means wilder recoil and decreased accuracy. It's not impossible to shoot a sawed-off with one hand; it's just challenging.
- A shorter barrel equals a reduced effective range. Longer barrels increase accuracy, since they give projectiles more time to spin before they exit the firearm. Shorter barrels have the opposite effect. A rule of thumb is to reduce the range of shot (BBs) to 25 yards. Shooting slugs from a sawed-off isn't a good idea except at close ranges out to a few yards.

Inaccurate Example

"My puny shotgun just won't cut it," Bill Robber said to the mirror. "Maynard's beer gut is too bloated for the slugs to get through. And his sleuthing skills are keeping my gluten-free bottled water smuggling operation from reaching shelves. I need more firepower."

"Then cut the barrel off to really make that shotgun hum. Maggots will feast on the flavor of your rage," said Bill's split personality, Ted.

Accurate Example

"My puny shotgun just won't cut it," Bill Robber said to the mirror. "Maynard's beer gut is too bloated for the BBs to get through. And his sleuthing skills are keeping my gluten-free bottled water smuggling operation from reaching shelves. I need more firepower."

"Maybe it's time you upgrade from a .410 to a 12-gauge shotgun," said Bill's split personality, Ted.

What Went Wrong?

The major mistake is the shotgun upgrade. If Bill needs more firepower, cutting the barrel isn't going to change anything. Trading in his .410 for a 12-gauge is the better bet.

Bill's complaint about the slugs failing to penetrate Maynard's gut isn't quite right. A hit from a shotgun slug (a single, solid projectile) is going to hurt. Granted, BBs hurt, too, but Bill shouldn't be concerned if he's making hits with slugs. They're devastating.

On that note, Bill might be firing from too far away to make the BBs count. It's possible to catch a BB from a shotgun and not suffer a serious injury. Instead of upgrading his shotgun, Bill might also consider moving closer to his target.

SHOTGUN AMMUNITION

Shotgun ammunition is most often called *shells*, but *rounds* or *cartridges* are also appropriate. *Bullets* is not. To get more specific, *shotshells* and *slugs* refer to the two types of shotgun ammunition explained in this section.

Popular shotgun ammunition brands: Federal, Hornady, Remington, Winchester

LEAD SHOT   STEEL SHOT

1. Tube
2. Shot
3. Wad
4. Powder
5. Primer
6. Base Wad
7. Head
8. Cushion (lead only)

Anatomy of shotgun ammunition. Both lead and steel shot variations are shown, although the former is most popular. Steel or other nontoxic shot is normally required by law for use in hunting over or near water. (Photo courtesy of *Gun Digest*.)

SHOTSHELLS

When people think of shotgun ammunition, they usually think of shotshells. Shotshells contain shot, also called BBs. *Shot* is more technically accurate than *BBs*, but this guide will use the term *BBs* for simplicity's sake.

A number denotes the size of the BBs in the shotshell. The smaller the number, the larger the BBs. For example, 3 shot contains larger BBs than 6 shot. 00 shot has even larger BBs and goes by the nickname *buckshot*. That's why novelists often use buckshot to really mess up characters.

The cloud of BBs that exits the barrel is called a *pattern*. Patterns are usually described as wide (the BBs are spread out), tight (the BBs are close together), or some variable along those lines. The farther the pattern travels, the more the BBs move away from each other. A typical maximum shotshell range is 50 yards. Beyond that, the pattern becomes unreliable.

A shooter can tweak the pattern using a choke. A choke is a replaceable, legal modification inserted into the end of the barrel. It makes the pattern wider or tighter. A permanent *jug choke* could also be carved out of the inside of the barrel.

When an exceptionally wide pattern is needed at close ranges, such as one able to cover the width of a person, a character might "saw off" the barrel of the shotgun (as mentioned earlier). Doing this significantly widens the pattern as the BBs exit the barrel, but as already noted, it's also illegal.

Fiction writers sometimes use the term *magnum* to describe ammunition. A magnum shotshell contains more gunpowder and BBs. It's usually longer, too. Some shotguns won't take magnums (or longer shells in general) because they mechanically won't fit.

Smaller BBs won't likely pass through a character who's been shot—they'll stay inside the character. A single small BB doesn't pack much punch, since the kinetic energy of the shotgun blast is dispersed over many small projectiles. But this doesn't mean smaller BBs in a group are weak. Characters shot at close range may die with a direct hit.

Buckshot, the larger type of BBs, might pass through a character who's been shot at close range. Its size means a hit from a single BB could cause serious injury. However, because the BBs are larger, there are fewer of them in a shotshell.

Advantages

- Shotshells are among the most commonly sold ammunition in the world because of their use in hunting, shooting sports, and defense.
- Spot-on accuracy isn't as important when using shotshells. Scopes are generally not used in tandem with this ammunition.
- Shotshells are usually tailored to specific purposes. For example, there are shotshells for hunting birds, for defense, and for shooting near water (these use nontoxic BBs instead of lead). As its name implies, buckshot is designed for large game, such as deer. Thrillers and crime fiction correctly use buckshot as a choice for killing characters, although any shotshell can be lethal.
- Fewer restrictions exist for purchasing shotshells over the counter compared to other ammunition.
- A character firing any shotshell at close range will inflict severe damage on the target. Guaranteed.

Disadvantages

- Characters may have a difficult time obtaining buckshot. In some areas, it's prohibited. Compare fictional settings with their real-world counterparts and check out local laws.

- For targets more than 50 yards away, characters would have a difficult time shooting effectively; the pattern would spread out too much. It'd be better to give that character a rifle.
- As with most ammunition, shotshells are not interchangeable between gauges or calibers. A 12-gauge shotshell is too large to fit into a 20-gauge shotgun. Likewise a 20-gauge shotshell may fit into a 12-gauge shotgun, but it won't fire. In fact, it may slip down the barrel and become jammed. Therefore, characters using a 12-gauge shotgun should not use 20-gauge shotshells. Sounds obvious, but it happens in the real world.
- Just because accuracy isn't as important doesn't mean characters don't need to aim. Making a hit still requires experience. A complicated shot will still be out of reach for inexperienced characters.

Inaccurate Example

Bill Robber hauled the shotgun to the roof of the office building. He waited for Maynard to finish visiting his long-lost daughter, Nevaeh, at the strip club across the street. Although Bill was twelve stories up, he still recognized the gal-damn detective's distinctive waddle through the scope.

Bill pulled the trigger, sending a storm of 6-shot BBs into Maynard, killing the detective instantly.

"Sorry to ruin your reunion, Maynard, but you should've known better," Bill said to himself as he packed up the shotgun. "*Nevaeh* isn't *Heaven* spelled backward. It's *stripper* spelled forward. And I'll be seeing you in hell."

Accurate Example

Bill Robber hauled the rifle to the roof of the office building. He waited for Maynard to finish visiting his long-lost daughter, Nevaeh, at the strip club across the street. Although he was twelve stories up, Bill still recognized the gal-damn detective's distinctive waddle through the scope.

Bill pulled the trigger, delivering a hot bullet right into Maynard's neck.

"Sorry to ruin your reunion, Maynard, but you should've known better," Bill said to himself as he packed up the rifle. "*Nevaeh* isn't *Heaven* spelled backward. It's *stripper* spelled forward. And I'll be seeing you in hell."

What Went Wrong?

Assuming that the top of a twelve-story office building is about 50 yards up, a shotgun with BBs was a poor choice to give Bill. A rifle is a better pick for that kind of precision and distance.

Using a scope to fire BBs from the shotgun was also a bad call. Outside of a few limited hunting applications, firing shotshells isn't a precision sport. Sure, it's possible to toss a scope onto a shotgun to fire shotshells, but it is not common and the writer who uses it risks looking amateurish.

One final point about the BBs: Using 6 shot to take a character out at a distance isn't a good call. These small BBs will spread out, rendering the pattern ineffective. Better to go with buckshot. If Bill and Maynard were close to each other, using 6 shot would make more sense.

SLUGS

An inside view of a shotgun slug. (Photo courtesy of *Gun Digest*.)

Unlike shotshells, shotgun slugs contain a single lead projectile instead of BBs. That projectile is called a *slug*, hence the name. They are generally effective out to 100 yards but can travel beyond that with limited accuracy. It's appropriate to refer to shotgun slugs as *shells* or *slugs*, but don't use *bullets* or *shotgun bullets*.

Slugs are used exclusively for larger targets, such as big game. They are never appropriate for shooting birds, small game, or sporting clays. In fiction, they're suitable for shooting characters, and because of how large they are, slugs are absolutely devastating. Sure, being shot with any firearm can be lethal, but slugs hold a special spot in the pantheons of stuff that hurts. Unlike BBs, they will usually pass through a target character, especially if the shooter is up close.

The accessories on a shotgun that shoots slugs are similar to that of a rifle. It's common to use a shotgun scope for better accuracy. It's not required, but shotguns used to shoot slugs may have a special rifled barrel with winding grooves inside that spin the slug as it travels out the barrel, just like rifles or handguns do. This spin helps stabilize trajectory and increase accuracy.

When writing, think of slugs like rifle ammunition, only less elegant. In the projectile world, they're the burly, meat-headed neighbor playing classic rock while working on cars.

Like rifle and handgun bullets, slug entry wounds (the spot where the projectile enters a target) are smaller than exit wounds (the area where the projectile leaves the target as it passes through). This is because the slug expands into a mushroom shape upon impact. Because of their size, slugs get pretty big as they expand. The exit wounds on a character would be obvious for this reason.

Advantages

- Slugs don't require a special type of shotgun. They also allow a shotgun to function similarly to a rifle: The same shotgun that fires shotshells (BBs) can switch over to slugs.
- Unlike shotshells, slugs pack a real punch at distances beyond 50 yards, the effective range of most BBs.
- Accuracy increases when slugs are used in tandem with a shotgun scope.
- A hit from a shotgun slug isn't something a character could shrug off. Any shotgun firing slugs, from the smallest to the largest, will pack a wallop.

Disadvantages

- Shotgun slugs probably wouldn't be a sniper's first choice. For picking off target characters with precise shots in complicated scenes, go with a rifle.
- Slugs deliver quite the recoil. They kick like a mule. Characters who are not in great physical shape might not want to pull the trigger.
- Because of this recoil, if a character shoots a sawed-off single-shot shotgun using slugs with one hand, make sure to write in that character's trip to the dentist.

Inaccurate Example

"We'll wait here for Bill to walk his dog. If he comes in close, I'll cover him with BBs," Penny Flyswatter told Maynard Soloman as they sat in their hiding spot at the city park. She pumped her 12-gauge shotgun twice and checked her scope. "We need to take out Bill Robber once and for all."

"And if he's far away, I'll clean his gal-damn clock with a bullet," Maynard said. He took one of Penny's shells and loaded it into his own 20-gauge with a quick *click-clack* of the pump.

"Between the two of us, Bill won't stand a chance," Penny said. "Although we really shouldn't discuss our plans to kill someone out loud in a public park."

Accurate Example

"We'll wait here for Bill to walk his dog. If he comes in close, I'll cover him with BBs," Penny Flyswatter told Maynard Soloman while they sat in their hiding spot at the city park. She loaded her shotgun and added, "We need to take out Bill Robber once and for all."

"And if he's far away, I'll clean his gal-damn clock with a slug," Maynard said. He loaded a shell into his own 12-gauge with a quick *click-clack* of the pump.

"Between the two of us, Bill won't stand a chance," Penny said. "Although we really shouldn't discuss our plans to kill someone out loud in a public park."

What Went Wrong?

At first glance, this scenario doesn't appear to be too bad. However, there's plenty that went wrong under the surface.

In the inaccurate example, Maynard and Penny designated one shotgun for shotshells (BBs) and one for slugs. There's nothing technically wrong with that *if* they're using the same gauge shotgun, but they're not. If they were both using either 12-gauge or 20-gauge shotguns, they could share ammunition.

Now for Penny's scope. If she's planning on firing shotshells (BBs), a type of ammunition best suited to targets 50 yards away or closer, a scope doesn't make much sense. A scope magnifies targets. It's not necessary if Penny plans to shoot Bill at close range. In fact, a scope can make it more difficult to aim at close ranges. She'd be better off without it.

Penny also pumped her shotgun twice, which is a mistake. Once is fine when loading ammunition. Unless she fires a shot, which she didn't, that second pump will just dump an unfired shell onto the ground.

Maynard said he'll "clean his gal-damn clock with a bullet" from his shotgun. *Bullet* is the wrong usage. Gun-savvy writers call the projectile a slug instead.

Maynard could just as easily switched to a rifle in the accurate example, too. That would make the *bullet* usage kosher.

RIFLES 101

Rifles work best over longer distances and in tactical situations. They offer power and precision. Rifle calibers abound, but most practical for fiction (sorted least to most powerful) are the .17, .22, .223, .243, .270, .300, .308, .30-06, 7mm, .338, and .50. The larger the number, the greater the firepower. A .50 has more firepower than a .22.

SEMI-AUTOMATIC RIFLES

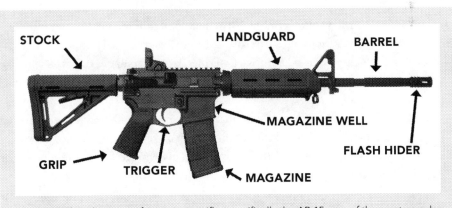

Here's a look at the parts of a semi-auto rifle, specifically the AR-15, one of the most popular civilian rifles. The terms in this image would be similar for other rifles. (Photo courtesy of *Gun Digest*.)

Popular semi-automatic rifles: Colt AR-15, Browning BAR, Ruger 10/22, Springfield Armory M1 Garand

A semi-automatic rifle functions much the same way as a semi-automatic shotgun—one pull of the trigger equals one shell fired. A character cannot hold down the trigger to continuously fire; only fully automatic rifles can do that, and they are covered in their own section in a few pages.

Generally speaking, a shooter would load a semi-auto rifle in one of three ways. The most common, and of most use to writers, is to insert a detachable magazine of ammunition into the firearm. A second method is to load *cartridges* (another term for *shell* or *round*) one at a time into a magazine built into the firearm (called an internal magazine). The least common way is to insert a clip of several cartridges bundled together into an internal magazine.

The shooter then works a charging handle (a small knob or tab) back and forth one time to move a cartridge out of the magazine and into the chamber (the spot inside the firearm where a cartridge is seated to be fired). Only after the first cartridge is fired does the rifle's semi-automatic action take over. It harnesses energy from the recoil from each shot to simultaneously unload and reload ammunition.

Some fully automatic rifles, usually leftover military models, are modified to function as semi-automatics only. This makes them more marketable, since the law places many restrictions on fully automatics. That's a point worth considering if a character doesn't have access to a black market yet needs an aggressive-looking firearm.

Advantages

- Semi-automatic rifles enjoy far fewer restrictions than fully automatics. Because of this, a variety of calibers (not gauges) are available for any number of needs.
- Compared to bolt-action and pump-action rifles, semi-automatics can fire shells faster. However, the increase in speed is not usually that great because recoil can negate it. The operator has to aim again.
- Scores of modifications for semi-automatic rifles can be had. This is especially true in recent years, with the popularity of the AR-15, a firearm suited to accessories and modification. Characters needing an especially customized firearm might choose a semi-automatic rifle.

Disadvantages

- As with any automatic firearm, semi-automatic rifles contain moving parts prone to failures and jams. By comparison, a bolt-action rifle is much more reliable. But, as I've mentioned before, a well-timed mechanical failure may come in handy at some point in your writing. The most common problem is fired cartridges becoming jammed inside the rifle when they are supposed to eject.
- Semi-autos are prohibited in some areas and situations. Adjust your setting based on real-world regulations.
- Converting a semi-auto rifle to a fully automatic version requires a ton of gunsmithing know-how that is out of reach or too onerous for most people. Such a conversion is like switching a car's manual transmission with an automatic one. It's not easy, and it's also illegal. Characters in settings prior to May 19, 1986, (the date the Firearm Owners Protection Act went into effect) would have a less challenging time making

the conversion, since there was still a legal market for homemade fully automatics. But nowadays? Forget it. Unless a character has an extensive understanding of firearms or outside (criminal) help, no number of illegal kits over the Internet or mail are going to make conversion as easy as one, two, three.

Inaccurate Example

Through the scope, Bill Robber could see the damage his rifle inflicted on Maynard Soloman. The first two shots shattered each of the sleuth's knees, sending him to the ground. The third demolished a hip. Each pull of the trigger ejected another red and yellow chunk from Maynard's body.

Bill lit a cigarette and reloaded his assault weapon's clip with a quick pump. With Maynard down for the count, he could relax and enjoy using the detective for target practice.

"I'll be dipped—I knew I should've brought something more than a screwdriver to this gunfight," Maynard said before dying. "Well, you win some, you lose some."

Accurate Example

Through the scope, Bill Robber could see the damage his rifle inflicted on Maynard Soloman. The first two shots shattered each of the sleuth's knees, sending him to the ground. The third demolished a hip. Each pull of the trigger ejected another red and yellow chunk from Maynard's body.

Bill lit a cigarette and replaced his rifle's magazine with a fresh one. With Maynard down for the count, he could relax and enjoy using the detective for target practice.

"I'll be dipped—I knew I should've brought something more than a screwdriver to this gunfight," Maynard said before dying. "Well, you win some, you lose some."

What Went Wrong?

The first paragraph of the inaccurate example suggests Bill is firing a semi-automatic rifle. Each pull of the trigger appears to fire one shot.

However, things get complicated in the second paragraph. Bill is suddenly reloading his "assault weapon's clip with a quick pump." What is an assault weapon? Is it a fully automatic rifle? A semi-automatic rifle? Or something else? *Assault weapon* doesn't have a set definition. *Semi-automatic rifle* and *fully automatic rifle* do, though, and they won't confuse readers like *assault weapon* will. Pick one, say what it is, be consistent, and avoid using vague terminology.

Also, the vast majority of semi-automatic rifles use detachable magazines—*mags* for short—instead of clips. Unless Bill's rifle model specifically uses clips, *magazine* is the better term. And reloading that rifle wouldn't involve pumping any part of the firearm unless the rifle model is specifically a pump-action. Although there are pump-action rifles out there, my experience as a reader is that some writers reload every firearm with "a quick pump" a la pump-action shotguns.

This highlights two important things. First, a lot can go wrong in only seven words. Second, it's a good idea to choose a specific firearm to write about to avoid inconsistencies—even if the exact gun model is never revealed. For example, I might have a Colt AR-15 in mind when writing about a generic semi-automatic rifle. That gives me details about the rifle to stick to throughout the story.

FULLY AUTOMATIC FIREARMS

Popular fully automatic firearms: Avtomat Kalashnikov 47 (AK-47), Fabrique Nationale FAL, Colt M16, M4, Thompson submachine gun (Tommy gun)

A fully automatic firearm is capable of firing more than one time per pull of the trigger. The action (the mechanism that cycles ammunition through the firearm) captures force from the recoil to continuously move cartridges in and out of the chamber. A detachable magazine usually feeds the ammunition. A long belt of ammunition is another option.

Much like semi-automatic rifles, preparing a fully automatic to fire requires the operator to insert a detachable magazine (not a clip) loaded with ammunition into the firearm. Then the operator works the charging handle (a small tab or knob located near the chamber) back and forth one time to move a cartridge from the magazine into the chamber (the spot inside the firearm where the cartridge is seated to be fired). The gun is ready to fire.

Fully automatic firearms fall into one of two categories: submachine guns and machine guns. The primary difference is in their ammunition. Machine guns use rifle ammunition and are more powerful. Submachine guns use pistol ammunition and are less powerful.

Does that mean submachine guns are actually amped-up pistols? That's true in some cases but not all. It usually depends on the size of the firearm. Small models approaching pistol sizes might be called *machine pistols*. Larger models leaning toward rifle sizes might be called *submachine guns*. There isn't a clear line in the sand, though. The best bet is to stick to the *submachine gun* term.

Since they use the same type of ammunition, the term *fully automatic rifle* can be used interchangeably with *machine gun*. If you're unsure whether *machine gun* or *submachine gun* is the right term to use, go with *full-auto* or *fully automatic* instead.

Fully automatic firearms are *highly* restricted, and they're difficult to obtain—even when you fill out the proper paperwork and pay the fees. In the United States, civilians may only possess fully automatics that were made before May 19, 1986.

So why are there videos of people online shooting "new" full-autos? If they're within the law, they're using pre-1986 parts and housing them inside new bodies. Remember, function matters with firearm laws, not form. (Check out the upcoming section on firearm laws for a more thorough rundown of automatic firearm restrictions.)

Some fully automatic firearms feature toggles that adjust the rate of fire. Depending on the model, a character could switch between fully automatic, a burst of only a few shots, a semi-automatic mode, and back again. Firearms with this toggle are said to be *select-fire*.

Advantages

- If a character needs to put the fear of God into someone, he or she should bring a fully automatic firearm to a fight. Its mere presence is intimidating.
- Fully automatic firearms crank out more shots in a shorter period of time than any other firearm.
- An automatic firearm will often inflict multiple wounds due to the high rate of fire.
- Modern fully automatic rifles (machine guns) can be effective at long ranges. A character would need a lot of experience to shoot accurately, though.
- Outfitting a character with a fully automatic firearm says something about her. There's a good reason the character has it, and that reason probably isn't to protect herself when she picks up the kids after soccer practice.

Disadvantages

- Accuracy is a problem with fully automatics. The stereotype for these firearms is a shooter holding down the trigger and spraying an area with bullets. That's the worst way to depict a full-auto if you're trying to be accurate. The constant bucking and jerking of the recoil would send bullets flying every which way. The most effective way to fire fully automatics is in short bursts. Doing so keeps clusters of bullets on target and recoil in check, but it takes experience to get the technique right.
- Legal restrictions make fully automatic firearms difficult for civilians to purchase or possess. Characters in law enforcement or the military are most likely to use them. Criminals may find their own means of obtaining them as well. Again, check out the section on firearm laws to understand what's possible and what's unrealistic.
- There's no mistaking the sound of a fully automatic firearm's rapid fire. This distinct sound isn't helpful for a character trying to keep his activity on the down low.

- More moving parts means more chances for things to go wrong. Fully automatic firearms are highly susceptible to jamming, and they require considerable maintenance to function properly.
- Fully automatic firearms can empty their magazines in a few seconds. Unless a character has preloaded magazines on hand, plan on her taking a couple of minutes or more to reload the mag with ammunition. Remember that loaded magazines carry considerable weight. Stuffing a few into a pocket means those pants will be around the character's ankles if a belt isn't present.
- Of all the different firearms, fully automatics have the steepest learning curve. Machine guns and submachine guns aren't something a person masters in an afternoon. Characters either need experience or the ability to figure out their operation quickly.

Inaccurate Example

Bill Robber, chronic check-kiting enthusiast, kicked open the door to the crowded First City Bank of Overdraft Fees. He opened up with his submachine gun and let the lead fly for a solid minute. Two dozen bodies folded onto the concrete.

Maynard Soloman managed to dodge Bill's death rain by locking himself in the bathroom. But that didn't prevent Bill from finding him.

"Come on out, Maynard. I'm not leaving any witnesses," Bill said.

"Go to hell, you dewdroppin' four-flusher," Maynard said from behind the bathroom door, dropping his signature old-timey insults—and something else into his pants.

Bill held down the trigger. A cloud of bullets dissolved the bathroom door and drained the warmth from Maynard's insides. The gal-damn detective said a prayer as his life ended perched against a toilet.

A SWAT team answered the prayer a few seconds later. Bill hosed the officers in lead from his machine gun before making off with $27 and a handful of breath mints.

"Totally worth it," Bill said to himself in the mirror of his getaway car.

Accurate Example

Bill Robber, chronic check-kiting enthusiast, kicked open the door to the crowded First City Bank of Overdraft Fees. He opened up with his machine gun and let the lead fly. Two dozen bodies folded onto the concrete in a matter of seconds.

Maynard Soloman managed to dodge Bill's death rain by locking himself in the bathroom. But that didn't prevent Bill from finding him.

"Come on out, Maynard. I'm not leaving any witnesses," Bill said and popped a fresh magazine into the machine gun.

"Go to hell, you dewdroppin' four-flusher," Maynard said from behind the bathroom door, dropping his signature old-timey insults—and something else into his pants.

Bill held down the trigger. A cloud of bullets dissolved the bathroom door and drained the warmth from Maynard's insides. The gal-damn detective said a prayer as his life ended perched against a toilet.

A SWAT team answered it a few seconds later. Bill raised his gun to shoot but only heard a single click. Out of ammo.

The officers spared no time shooting Bill to death.

What Went Wrong?

Consistency is a big problem in the inaccurate example. Is Bill using a machine gun or a submachine gun? It's written both ways. It's an important choice. He needs to demolish the bathroom door Maynard is hiding behind. A machine gun, the more powerful of the two, is the better bet for handling that task.

This scenario also presented a classic case of the magic machine gun that never runs out of ammunition. It's assumed Bill did a lot of shooting in the beginning, having killed two dozen people. He needed to reload before "dissolving" the bathroom door to kill Maynard. Bill probably needed to reload again just as the SWAT team arrived. Since he only had a few seconds, it's unlikely he had the time. That's why the SWAT team killed him in the accurate example.

Did you notice the click when Bill ran out of ammunition? It only happened once. That's more accurate than writing in multiple clicks as the trigger is pulled, a common trope in fiction when the ammo runs dry. Without getting too technical, that click sound comes from the gun attempting to fire. The only way it can reset itself to click again is to actually fire. But if the ammunition is out, that can't happen. The result is just one click.

BOLT-ACTION RIFLES

Bolt-action rifles are generally used for precision shooting. (Photo courtesy of *Gun Digest*.)

Popular bolt-action rifles: Browning A-Bolt, McMillan TAC-50, Remington Model 700, Springfield Model 1903, Winchester Model 70

A bolt-action rifle uses a sliding metal cylinder (bolt) to move shells in and out of the chamber (the spot inside the firearm where the shell is seated to be fired). The operator manually shifts the bolt-action (it looks like a metal knob on the side of the gun) up and back to eject a shell from the chamber. Then the operator moves the knob forward and down to seat the next shell from the magazine (the place where ammunition is held in reserve) into the chamber. With the bolt-action in this forward-down position, the rifle is ready to fire.

If the bolt is not in the forward-down position, it's mechanically impossible for this type of rifle to fire.

Bolt-action rifles use either an internal or detachable magazine. Internally, shells rarely exceed single-digit capacities. A magazine with up to six shells is pretty common, depending on caliber. Detachable magazines have a much greater capacity.

To fire the first shot, the operator would first insert a magazine or load shells into an internal magazine, then manually work the bolt. After switching off the safety, the gun is ready to fire. The operator would work the bolt between each consecutive shot to unload and reload.

Remember: There is nothing automatic about a bolt-action rifle. The operator must manually work the action at all times. Also, bolt-action rifles don't have hammers, but they do have a safety button or safety switch. On some models, the safety must be off for the bolt-action to move freely, meaning the character can load and reload only if the safety is off. Even with the safety off, it is mechanically impossible for the rifle to fire unless the bolt is in the forward-down position.

Advantages

- A bolt-action rifle is more reliable than other rifles. It has fewer moving parts than an automatic rifle. It's also dependent on the shooter (rather than the recoil) to work the action. Unless the shooter loses a hand between shots, the action is going to cycle ammunition through the rifle.

- A case could be made that bolt-actions are more accurate than their semi-automatic counterparts. There's plenty of room for debate, but characters needing to fire over long distances would likely choose a bolt-action rifle. Sniper characters are great candidates for bolt-action rifles.
- Compared to other rifles, bolt-action rifles have fewer restrictions placed on them, so characters will have an easier time obtaining one.
- The popularity of bolt-action rifles is worldwide. You are virtually guaranteed that every rifle caliber is available as a bolt-action. This should make it easier on writers looking for a generic rifle type to use as a default.

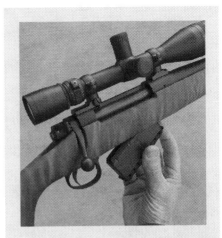

Some detachable magazines are flush with the stock of the rifle. This detail might not be clear if you simply peruse Internet photos of rifles when researching for a story. Double-check the model's specs to be sure. (Photo courtesy of *Gun Digest*.)

Disadvantages

- Characters who need to put out a lot of lead might shy away from bolt-action rifles. They're slower to reload and to re-sight between shots.
- The fact that the safety must be off in order to move the bolt could be a concern. This counterintuitive setup could confuse characters new to bolt-actions. Even worse, they might forget to switch the safety on when the action is in the forward-down position. Accidents convenient to the plot could happen this way.
- Despite their reliability, bolt-action rifles can still become jammed when reloading. When inserted at the right moment, these jams can be critical to a story.

Inaccurate Example

Maynard Soloman bolted into the shop with the XXX sign above the door, rifle in hand.

"Which one of you latrine dippers is making gal-damn moonshine in here?" Maynard said to a woman next to a window.

"Uh, we're not that kind of store. You've got the wrong place," the woman said. "Are you here to rob my store?"

"No, but I'm not leaving here without arresting someone for something, or I don't get paid," Maynard said. He worked the bolt on his rifle to load the first round.

"I'm not going anywhere," the woman said and produced a revolver.

Maynard took aim and shot the revolver out of her hand, then quickly pulled the trigger again to send the woman through the window.

Accurate Example

Maynard Soloman bolted into the shop with the XXX sign above the door, rifle in hand.

"Which one of you latrine dippers is making gal-damn moonshine in here?" Maynard said to a woman next to a window.

"Uh, we're not that kind of store. You've got the wrong place," the woman said. "Are you here to rob my store?"

"No, but I'm not leaving here without arresting someone for something, or I don't get paid," Maynard said.

"I'm not going anywhere," the woman said and produced a revolver.

Acting quickly, Maynard took aim and shot the woman's shoulder, forcing her to drop the revolver. Without skipping a beat, he reloaded and pulled the trigger again. The woman slumped to the ground as the window shattered behind her.

What Went Wrong?

Aside from Maynard's botched moonshine raid, let's start with how he entered the shop without having a shell in the chamber. He waits to load when he needs to accent a point. If he's anticipating a firefight, it's best to be ready for it. I reinforce this point throughout this guide only because it happens quite a bit in fiction.

When Maynard fires in the inaccurate example, he doesn't pause to reload. It's as if his rifle will continue to fire with each pull of the trigger after working the bolt one time. That's incorrect. The bolt-action must be worked each time between shots.

Shooting a gun out of a hand is a trope from schlocky Western movies. That should tell you something about the realism (or lack of it) in this scene. The better bet is to have a character hit the hand or arm holding the gun. Those body parts are larger targets and easier to hit. A real-life scenario on this topic is presented in the true crime section.

This example also rolls out the "character hit by gunfire flies through window" trope. Remember Newton's Third Law of Motion: Every action has an equal and opposite reaction. If Maynard's shot packs enough punch to send the woman through the window, it should knock him backward with the same amount of force. He should slam against a wall behind him. He doesn't.

This is corrected in the accurate example. Instead of the woman flying through the window, she slumps onto the ground.

What about the window shattering? In the accurate example, I assumed the bullet broke the window when it passed through the woman instead of remaining inside her. That choice was up to me as the writer, but it highlights an important point. Keep track of those bullets. They don't dissipate into the air. Ask yourself if the bullet remains in the target character or continues traveling. If it does keep going, does it hit some other part of the scene?

PUMP-ACTION RIFLES

This is a short section because pump-action rifles play a relatively small role in thrillers and crime fiction.

Pump-action rifles are most common with smaller calibers, such as the .17 and the .22. The most popular pump-action rifle caliber is the .22. It's not a high-power caliber, but a shot from one could still wreck someone's day. To put its firepower into perspective, I use a pump .22 with a scope for my family's annual squirrel hunt. (Yes, that's really a thing. Yes, we make the finest buffalo squirrel wings on this side of the Mississippi. But that's a story for another day.)

Unless your character is young or is hunting small game, you will probably be better off using larger caliber semi-automatic, fully automatic, and bolt-action rifles for characters looking to do some damage.

Pump-action rifles are sometimes called slide-action rifles, and they function similarly to pump-action shotguns. They usually use a tube magazine that runs underneath the barrel to store ammunition. One pump simultaneously ejects a fired cartridge from the chamber and replaces it with a fresh one from the magazine. Capacities can be quite high, into the teens and beyond. That's one of the biggest advantages of pump-action rifles.

And, as stated earlier, pumping one of these rifles for dramatic effect doesn't make sense.

Finally, don't take any of these points to mean that pump-action rifles are off-limits to you as a writer. They're still fine to include. Just don't drop them into intense tactical situations if you can help it.

LEVER-ACTION RIFLES

Lever-actions, such as this Winchester 1886, are commonly found on older or classically inspired rifles. For all practical purposes, write them similar to pump-actions. The only difference is the lever used to work the action. (Photo courtesy of *Gun Digest*.)

When writing, think of lever-action rifles as the grown-up version of pump-action rifles. They function similarly, except they use a lever instead of a pump.

The key difference is the ammunition. Lever-action rifles, including the famous Winchester Model 94 (see the Hit List section of this guide), can get into the midpower calibers, such as the .30-30.

Lever-action rifles aren't as prominent in thrillers and crime fiction (although they're standard fare in Westerns), so they're not explored in detail here. Writers might still appreciate knowing that the external hammer automatically cocks as the lever is worked. As with pump-action firearms, dramatic hammer cocking (or dramatic lever working) for intimidation is usually unnecessary and will empty unfired ammo onto the ground.

Handguns are best applied at close ranges. They're portable and powerful but lack accuracy due to their short barrels. It might be hard to believe, but it's actually difficult to accurately shoot beyond 20 yards or so. Don't believe me? Hit up a gun range and prepare to be humbled.

Many types of handguns are available, but a writer can't go wrong outfitting a character with a .22, .25, .32, .38, 9mm, .40, 10mm, .357, .45, .44, or .50 (sorted from the least to most powerful caliber).

PISTOL

Popular semi-automatic pistols: Beretta 92, Colt 1911, Glock 17, Springfield XD, Walther PPK

A pistol is a handgun that uses one or more stationary chambers (the spot inside a gun where a cartridge is seated to be fired). Pistols can be single-shot, semi-automatic, or fully automatic (a.k.a. *machine pistols*). Semi-automatics are the most popular pistols in thrillers and crime fiction, and for this reason this section focuses on semi-autos.

It's important to understand that the word *pistol* is not synonymous with *revolver*, which is covered in a different section of this guide. This is one time to forgo the

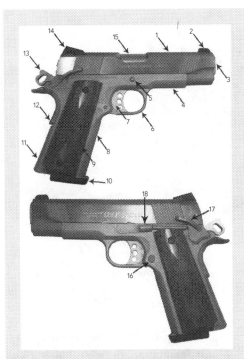

PARTS FOR COLT 1911-STYLE PISTOL

1. Slide
2. Front Sight
3. Muzzle
4. Frame
5. Takedown Pin
6. Trigger Guard
7. Trigger
8. Frontstrap
9. Stock Panel
10. Magazine
11. Backstrap
12. Grip Safety
13. Hammer
14. Rear Sight
15. Ejection Port
16. Magazine Release Button
17. Safety
18. Slide Release/Stop

A schematic of pistol components on a Colt Model 1911. Every model is different, but the terms and parts are similar. The style of handgun shown here is popular in fiction and emulated by many companies other than Colt. (Photo courtesy of *Gun Digest*.)

dictionary definition and go with modern usages to prevent confusing readers. If you need another word for *pistol*, use *handgun*.

Pistol ammunition is usually stored in a detachable magazine that slips in and out of the handle (grip). This is sometimes incorrectly referred to as a *clip*. In the vast majority of cases, the correct term is *magazine*. A clip bundles ammunition together for insertion into a magazine. A magazine holds ammunition and is either detachable or built into a firearm.

The operator of this pistol is working the slide-action. Pulling the slide back and letting go is called "racking the slide." This loads the first round from the magazine into the chamber. (Photo courtesy of *Gun Digest*.)

A semi-automatic pistol's action (the mechanism that cycles ammunition through a firearm) simultaneously ejects and reloads one shell after each shot. When writing, you'll most likely want to use one of two semi-auto actions:

1. The slide-action pistol uses a sliding mechanism fitted over the barrel (to the untrained eye, it looks like the top half of the gun). It slides backward and forward as the pistol is fired, powered by the recoil of the shot being fired. After inserting the magazine, chambering the first shell involves pulling the slide back and releasing so it snaps forward. This is called "racking the slide." After that shell is chambered, the operator can continuously fire without pausing. Most modern pistols, such as the ubiquitous-to-fiction Glock, use a slide-action, and most writers will opt for a slide-action for their characters' semi-auto pistols.

2. Another type of semi-automatic pistol uses arms and levers instead of a slide-action: toggle-lock actions. This action is more common with older pistol models, such as the Luger.

Luger pistols are some of the most well-known toggle-lock pistols. The most notorious (but not exclusive) users of Lugers were the Nazis, fiction's favorite bad guys. (Photo courtesy of *Gun Digest*.)

Derringer is a generic term you'll hear used for a small pistol. Derringers are ideal for characters who need a backup firearm, since they are easy to conceal. Spies or stealthy characters might also opt for a derringer. Just remember that the shorter the barrel, the harder it is to hit a target. Derringers don't offer much for accuracy beyond a few yards.

Many thriller and crime fiction characters cock a pistol's hammer back for dramatic effect. (I discuss this in greater detail in the Top Weapons Myths section.) While this is mechanically possible at times, it doesn't make sense from a practical standpoint, especially with most modern handguns.

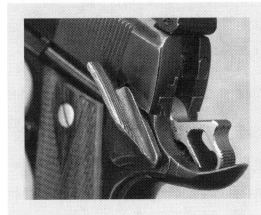

The hammer on this single-action 1911 is cocked. That happens automatically as the operator racks the slide, which loads a cartridge into the chamber. It'll happen again as a round is fired. There's no need for a character to cock it manually for dramatic effect. To do so would require de-cocking the hammer after loading the gun, then re-cocking it for dramatic effect. If the hammer wasn't cocked in the first place, why aim the gun at someone? (Photo courtesy of *Gun Digest*.)

Advantages

- Pistols are easy to conceal and transport.
- Pistol magazines usually offer more shots than revolvers. Characters needing a handgun capable of firing many times would choose a pistol over a revolver.
- Pistols with detachable magazines are quicker to reload than revolvers. Popping a magazine in and out takes only a couple of seconds.
- Scores of pistol designs are available in a variety of calibers to suit any number of purposes.

Disadvantages

- With semi-auto pistols, more moving parts equals more chances for something to go wrong, such as a shell becoming jammed in the chamber. Although pistols have come a long way in reliability, a revolver's simpler operation is less prone to complications.
- Handguns in general, and especially semi-automatic pistols, are subject to more restrictions than their long-barreled counterparts, making them more difficult to obtain legally.
- It's difficult to accurately fire any handgun, including pistols. The shorter the barrel, the less rifling (spin) the bullet receives as it exits the pistol. Less spin equals a less-stable trajectory and reduced accuracy. Extensive training and practice is necessary to accurately shoot any handgun even at close ranges.
- Semi-automatic pistols have a steeper learning curve compared to relatively simple revolvers. Characters unfamiliar with them won't necessarily figure out how to use one.
- Reloading a pistol with a fresh magazine is one thing. Reloading the magazine is a different animal. Shells must be fed into the magazine one at a time. This can take a minute or more. A character in a tight spot better have preloaded magazines ready to go in a firefight.

Inaccurate Example

"You're going to tell me what I need to know right now," said Bill Robber. He popped a fresh clip into the business end of his Glock and took aim at Maynard Soloman, gal-damn detective.

"When you get to be my age, hindsight is fifty-fifty," said Maynard into the pistol barrel only inches away. "I have no idea where you lost your keys."

Bill cocked the hammer on the Glock.

"I saw you go through my dirty clothes at the Laundromat," he said.

"I was searching for evidence. And loose change. But I didn't take your gal-damn keys, you ditch-diggin' Neanderthal," Maynard said.

Bill switched the pistol's safety off with his thumb.

"This is your last chance before I blow your brains out," Bill said.

Accurate Example

"You're going to tell me what I need to know right now," said Bill Robber. He popped a fresh magazine into the grip of his Glock and took aim at Maynard Soloman, gal-damn detective.

"When you get to be my age, hindsight is fifty-fifty," said Maynard into the pistol barrel only inches away. "I have no idea where you lost your keys."

Bill racked the slide on the Glock.

"I saw you go through my dirty clothes at the Laundromat," he said.

"I was searching for evidence. And loose change. But I didn't take your gal-damn keys, you ditch-diggin' Neanderthal," Maynard said.

Bill pressed the barrel into Maynard's nostril, indenting the detective's cauliflower nose.

"This is your last chance before I blow your brains out," Bill said.

What Went Wrong?

Let's go through this one chronologically. Bill popped a "fresh clip" into the Glock in the inaccurate example. Semi-automatic pistols use detachable magazines, not clips. He also inserted the clip into the "business end" of the pistol. That's a slang term for barrel. Bill should stick the *magazine* into the handle (a.k.a. grip) instead.

Some pistols have external hammers that a shooter would cock, but Glocks do not. They also don't have safety switches. A bit of research ahead of time would've taken care of those errors.

Also, *Glock* is sometimes used as a generic term to describe any modern semi-automatic pistol. Don't do that. Glock is a specific brand that offers unique pistols.

Bill's process of loading the Glock in the corrected version is a great example of how to get most semi-automatic pistols ready. Pop a magazine in and rack the slide, then pull the trigger when ready to shoot.

But I think the real lesson here is to stay close to your laundry at a Laundromat. Otherwise a cheapskate private detective might help himself to it.

REVOLVERS

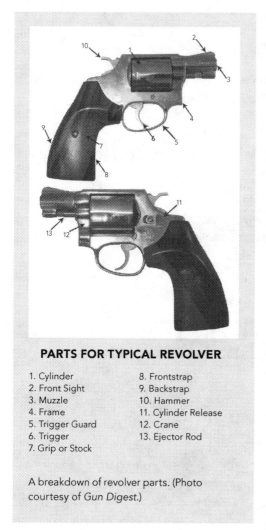

PARTS FOR TYPICAL REVOLVER

1. Cylinder
2. Front Sight
3. Muzzle
4. Frame
5. Trigger Guard
6. Trigger
7. Grip or Stock
8. Frontstrap
9. Backstrap
10. Hammer
11. Cylinder Release
12. Crane
13. Ejector Rod

A breakdown of revolver parts. (Photo courtesy of *Gun Digest*.)

Popular revolvers: Colt Detective Special, Ruger Single Six, Smith & Wesson Model 10, Smith & Wesson Model 29 (a.k.a. the "Dirty Harry" revolver), Taurus Judge

A revolver is a handgun that has a cylinder with multiple chambers that rotates as the firearm is fired—picture the classic cowboy handgun. Pulling the trigger or cocking the hammer rotates the cylinder. Unlike pistols, revolvers don't eject their shells automatically after firing. They remain in their chambers until they're removed manually by the shooter. That can be helpful for characters not wanting to leave empty casings behind.

Whereas many pistols use safeties, it's less common for a revolver to have one. A character likely wouldn't switch the safety off a revolver before firing.

There are three styles of cylinders (actually four if you count a few old revolvers, but those aren't used very often, so they won't be covered here).

The first is the iconic swing-out cylinder. The cylinder swings out from the revolver to the side to be loaded or unloaded. This is what most modern revolvers use. It's the one most people picture when imagining revolvers.

The swing-out cylinder is the most popular type of revolver. (Photo courtesy of Shutterstock.)

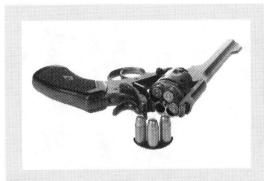

Top-break cylinder revolvers crack open forward for loading and reloading. Unless there's a reason to use one specifically, it's probably easier to write in the common swing-out cylinder revolver instead. (Photo courtesy of Shutterstock.)

The top-break cylinder revolver opens forward and down on a hinge to load or unload the chambers. It's not as common as the swing-out style, although it's been around since the 1870s or so.

Finally, the cylinder on a fixed-cylinder revolver doesn't move away from the handgun at all. Instead, ammunition is loaded and unloaded via exposed chambers accessible along the side of the revolver. This is most common with much older revolvers.

If in doubt about what kind of cylinder a revolver is using, write around anything related to it. Stating exactly how a shooter reloads a revolver is not as important as keeping a consistent shot count (don't have eight shots come from a six-shooter). Chances are good, though, that most writers will use swing-out cylinder revolvers.

Speed loaders remain the most popular tool in fiction—and in reality—to quickly load a revolver. (Photo courtesy of Shutterstock.)

Revolvers do not use or contain magazines for loading ammunition. Cartridges can be inserted into their chambers one at a time by hand, dropped into place all at once with a speed loader (a device that drops shells into all empty chambers of a revolver at once), thumbed in with a speed strip (a flexible strip that drops shells into the chambers two or three at a time), or placed in with a moon clip (similar to a speed loader, except it's a frame that holds the shells together and drops with the cartridges into the chambers).

Unloading revolvers involves exposing the chambers and manually removing the shells. This can be done with fingers, gravity (tip the revolver so the shells fall out), or an ejector.

The most iconic image of a revolver is that of the cowboy and the "six-shooter." Yes, revolvers often come with six chambers, but there are many variations. These include five, seven, eight, and more. In other words, don't assume that all revolvers fire six times.

If the hammer (a metal tab above the grip) must be cocked prior to firing each shell, the revolver is single-action. Single-action revolvers are more common with older models (such as most Old West revolvers). Most modern revolvers are double-action. The hammer can be cocked before pulling the trigger, but it isn't required. Just pulling the trigger is enough. Some revolvers don't even have a hammer. Those are called hammerless revolvers.

Moon clips are similar to speed loaders and are often overlooked when writing revolvers. These thin frames hold cartridges together for quick loading. Be sure to write *moon clip* when referencing them. If you write *clip*, readers will wonder if you meant *magazine*, which revolvers don't use. (Photo courtesy of *Gun Digest*.)

On the topic of hammers, let's jump back to dramatic cocking again, which is the act of working a firearm's action purely for effect or posturing. Of all the firearm types, revolvers stand the best chance of getting away with dramatic cocking. Still, there is no practical purpose for a revolver to be cocked for dramatic effect. The gun is already aimed at someone. Why isn't it ready to fire in the first place?

With double-action revolvers, there is at least one practical reason to cock the hammer first, even though it's not required: to make a steadier, more controlled shot. Cocking the hammer in this way makes it easier to pull the trigger, which is usually set to a high level of resistance.

Advantages

- Because of their simple design, revolvers are considered more reliable than their pistol counterparts. Reliability is the number-one advantage of using a revolver over an automatic pistol.
- Revolvers offer a mild learning curve. A character could learn how to operate one in no time.

The Writer's Guide to Weapons

- Pistols might be quicker to reload than revolvers but only if the detachable magazine is already loaded with ammunition. Loading up one of these magazines takes considerable time. Revolvers don't use magazines. A character with a revolver wouldn't worry about blowing through preloaded magazines.
- Revolvers are easy to conceal and transport.
- Given their lengthy history, a revolver isn't out of place in settings from the mid-1800s through today. Revolvers can be the default for a character when the writer isn't clear whether semi-automatic pistols would be available in that setting.

Disadvantages

- Compared to pistols, revolvers don't offer much ammunition capacity. Characters might choose a pistol with a generous magazine over a revolver for an intense firefight.
- Revolvers tend to be bulkier than their sleek pistol counterparts. They can bulge out from clothing when concealed.
- Even with speed loaders, revolvers usually take a longer time to reload than pistols using detachable magazines. The difference is only a matter of seconds, but it's worth considering for fight scenes.
- Handguns in general are subject to more restrictions than their long-barreled counterparts, making them more difficult to obtain. Revolvers are usually subject to fewer regulations than semi-automatic pistols.
- As with any handgun, it takes extensive training and practice to shoot accurately with a revolver.

Inaccurate Example

Maynard Soloman whipped the revolver out of its holster. Taking aim with his six-shooter, he shot out each of the windows of Bill Robber's dilapidated shack in the woods. *Bang. Bang. Bang. Bang. Bang. Bang.*

"Got your attention yet, Bill?" Maynard said. He fired another warning shot for good measure. "I'm here to take you to the hoosegow. Your little Nigerian princess Internet scheme is finished."

Bill stumbled out the front door of the shack with his hands in the air. Maynard instinctively planted his pistol's scope on Bill's chest.

"Okay, you caught me, Maynard. But before you haul me off, I should probably give back all the money I swindled," Bill said.

"Nice to see you've had a change of heart," Maynard said. He lowered the revolver and flicked the safety back on. "Where's the loot?"

"It's in a bank not far from here. I just need some money to help get it out," Bill said.

Maynard pulled out a wad of cash. "Great. Is this enough?"

Accurate Example

Maynard Soloman whipped the revolver out of its holster. Taking aim with his six-shooter, he shot out each of the windows of Bill Robber's dilapidated shack in the woods. *Bang. Bang. Bang. Bang. Bang.*

"Got your attention yet, Bill?" Maynard said. He fired another warning shot for good measure. "I'm here to take you to the hoosegow. Your little Nigerian princess Internet scheme is finished."

Bill stumbled out the front door of the shack with his hands in the air. Maynard instinctively planted his revolver's sights on Bill's chest.

"Okay, you caught me, Maynard. But before you haul me off, I should probably give back all the money I swindled," Bill said.

"Nice to see you've had a change of heart," Maynard said. He holstered the revolver. "Where's the loot?"

"It's in a bank not far from here. I just need some money to help get it out," Bill said.

Maynard pulled out a wad of cash. "Great. Is this enough?"

What Went Wrong?

Not every revolver fires six shots, but this example pegs the gun as a "six-shooter." That means Maynard couldn't fire seven times (six for the windows, one for the warning shot) in the inaccurate example. Keep the shot count consistent. That goes for any firearm.

As the Myths section of this guide explains, warning shots aren't a good idea from a legal standpoint—you never want to be the first to pull the trigger unless it's to stop a threat. Writers playing things closer to reality should keep that in mind. In this case, Maynard isn't the brightest bulb, so the warning shot matches his character.

The inaccurate example uses *revolver* and *pistol* interchangeably. A dictionary might say this is correct based on historical usage, but I say this only confuses the reader, since the modern usage of those words splits them into separate categories. Walk into any gun shop and ask to see a pistol. You'll never be shown a revolver.

It's possible to mount a scope on a revolver, but it can look amateurish to feature one unless there's good reason. Stick to using *sights*, which are built into the revolver instead. Scopes and sights are covered in their own section.

RIFLE AND HANDGUN AMMUNITION

Bullets fired during gunplay can become downright magical in thrillers and crime fiction. From ricocheting into conveniently placed targets to penetrating any material under the sun, they're like mini-superheroes. In reality, there's nothing supernatural about them. They're just pieces of metal flying through the air, and they're limited by the same physics as a baseball in flight.

Popular rifle and handgun ammunition brands: Federal, Hornady, Remington, Winchester.

Ammunition for rifles and handguns is called *shells*, *rounds*, or *cartridges*. We'll refer to them as cartridges in this section to be consistent. Some people refer to rifle and handgun ammunition as *bullets*, but that's not technically accurate. A bullet only refers to the thing that comes out of the barrel. When you look at an actual unfired cartridge, you'll notice that the bullet is only the metal projectile seated at the top of the cartridge.

Other parts of the cartridge are the brass casing (the metallic jacket that comprises the lower part of the cartridge), gunpowder, and primer (found inside the casing and hit by the firing pin to ignite the gunpowder). The cartridge itself refers to the entire thing.

Cartridge sizes are specific to the caliber of the firearm. The cartridges cannot be swapped between different kinds of firearms unless the firearm shoots the exact same caliber and size cartridge. Caliber numbers are an expression of width. A .22, for example, means the bullet has a diameter of $22/100$ of an inch. A .50 caliber fires a bullet that's a half-inch in diameter. Because of this, larger calibers of ammunition gener-

BASIC CARTRIDGE ANATOMY

Rifle

Bullet

Cannelure

Metal Casing

Powder

Primer
(firing pin
hits here)

Handgun

Primer
(firing pin
hits here)

Anatomy of rifle and handgun ammunition. (Photo courtesy of *Gun Digest.*)

ally inflict more damaging wounds than smaller calibers. A .22 will drill out a third nostril. A .50 will take the head clean off.

Some calibers are developed using the metric system, so they don't use inches as specified above. In this case, a 9mm's bullet has a diameter of 9 millimeters. The 10mm's diameter is 10 millimeters. When researching ammo and firearm calibers, writers might stumble on something like "9 × 19mm." The first number is the bullet's width. The second is the length, useful for noting variations within the caliber. It's still acceptable to write *9mm* instead of *9 × 19mm*. Just don't put a period in front, as in *.9mm*. That's a common mistake. For length variations within English measurements, there's usually a word tacked onto the caliber number. For example, a .22 Long Rifle denotes a lengthier version of the .22. A .22 Short is the stubbier version. In either case, it's appropriate to skip the length information when writing.

No matter the caliber, bullets themselves are measured in grains. The higher the grain, the heavier the bullet. Gunpowder and other ammunition features are also measured in grains. One grain is equivalent to 64.79 milligrams ($\frac{1}{7,000}$ of a pound). One ounce is equal to 437.5 grains. This detail may also be more than you need for your story, but it's good to know.

Let's take a second to discuss entry and exit wounds. Entry wounds are smaller than exit wounds. A small, clean hole is made where the bullet enters a target. The bullet will then expand into a mushroom shape (or explode entirely, as with hollow-point bullets, explained later in this chapter). The exit wound will usually be larger and messier, since the jagged mushroom shape is wider than the original bullet.

When researching rifle and handgun ammunition for thrillers and crime fiction, writers will often come across two terms: *centerfire* and *rimfire*. It's helpful to understand a little bit about each.

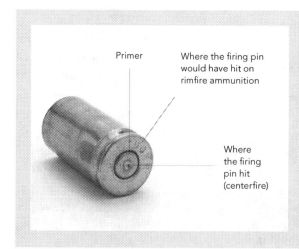

Primer

Where the firing pin would have hit on rimfire ammunition

Where the firing pin hit (centerfire)

This photo depicts where the firing pin hit this 9mm primer. It's obvious this is centerfire ammunition because the firing pin hit the direct center of the primer. If the firing pin had hit the rim, it would be apparent that the ammunition was rimfire. Either way, the mark from the firing pin is like a firearm's fingerprint. This detail is useful for writing *CSI*-type scenarios in which a character matches fired ammunition to a particular firearm. (Photo courtesy of Shutterstock.)

Centerfire ammunition means the firing pin (the device integral to the firearm that strikes the primer inside the cartridge and ignites the gunpowder) hits the center of the primer. Centerfire primers are often used with thicker casings and can support greater pressure and therefore greater firepower. In this case, when a character examines the mark left by a firing pin on a spent cartridge, the mark will likely appear in the center of the primer if a more powerful firearm was used. That's a great way to work in a clue at a crime scene.

Rimfire ammunition means the firing pin strikes the rim of the cartridge's casing instead of a primer in the center. A thinner casing is used in this case, which means it can support less pressure and therefore less firepower. It's most often used in such lighter calibers as the .22 and the .17.

Here are some other common terms you may come across in your research and writing:

MAGNUM. When describing ammunition, thriller and crime fiction writers sometimes use the term *magnum*. This means the cartridge has extra gunpowder and/or a heavier bullet, and therefore greater firepower. There isn't an industry standard for what constitutes magnum ammo; it's up to the manufacturer. If there's any consistency, it's that magnum ammo packs more punch than nonmagnum ammo within the same caliber. A .22 magnum cartridge is more powerful than a standard .22 cartridge.

HOLLOW-POINT BULLETS. This means the tip of the bullet is missing by design. Such bullets explode upon impact, breaking into smaller pieces inside the target. For this reason, it is unlikely for a hollow-point bullet to pass through its target. Hollow-point bullets are usually used when collateral damage caused by a bullet passing through a target is a risk. It's often said the Geneva Conventions banned hollow-point bullets for wartime use because of the increased suffering they can cause. However, the ban actually went through in 1899 at the Hague Peace Conferences. Whether they increase suffering is debatable, since being shot by any ammunition type is typically pretty horrific.

The ban doesn't prohibit characters from using hollow-point bullets, however. It only applies to state militaries of signatories at war with another state signatory. Although the ban and its implementations changed through the years, it's best not to outfit military characters with hollow-point ammunition. They'd likely use full metal jacket bullets (explained next) instead. Other characters, from civilians to police officers, are free to use hollow-point bullets when the law does not restrict their use (usually for hunting).

FULL METAL JACKET. This means the lead bullet is coated in metal (usually copper). This design makes it more likely to pass through a target. It's said this type of ammunition is designed to wound rather than kill, because it doesn't break apart as it travels through a target. While there is some truth to that, shot placement is the real concern. A full metal jacket bullet to a vital area will still kill a character. This type of bullet has been around since the late nineteenth century.

ARMOR-PIERCING AMMUNITION. The mythology of armor-piercing ammunition would have us believe that these bullets are able to penetrate bulletproof vests and other gear. What armor-piercing *actually* means is pretty vague.

One type of armor-piercing ammunition involves bullets coated in Teflon. The Teflon reduces wear on the barrel, making the bullet able to withstand greater pressures and therefore allowing it more of a punch from the gunpowder. This boost in kinetic energy *might* be enough to penetrate body armor, such as bulletproof vests. Whether Teflon-coated bullets actually can do so depends on variables such as range, trajectory, environmental conditions, the type of bulletproof vest, and more. In that regard, they're no different from any other bullet that, under the right conditions, could bust through a bulletproof vest. *Armor-piercing* is a misnomer.

Because of legal restrictions, Teflon-coated bullets went virtually extinct in the 1990s. It's unlikely a character from the 1990s onward would use them. Confine their usage to 1960s through 1980s settings.

The other type of armor-piercing ammunition relates to the materials used in the bullet itself. As grade-school science classes (hopefully) made clear, harder materials cut softer materials. A bullet made of something harder than what it's hitting stands a better chance of penetration. Use a bullet made of hardened steel, among other materials, and it might plow through the materials used to armor buildings, vehicles, and people.

There's no guarantee, though. Any number of variables, from the thickness of the target material to the range at which the shot is taken, will determine whether the ammunition will actually pierce the armor.

For example, armor-piercing bullets fired from a mile away lose most of their kinetic energy, reducing the chance of deeply penetrating the target. Conversely, standard ammunition (not armor-piercing) fired at a closer range might transfer more kinetic energy into a target, causing penetration.

For these reasons, I don't recommend using the term *armor-piercing* when describing bullets or ammunition in a story.

I also don't recommend using the term *cop-killer ammunition*. It's sometimes used as an umbrella term that includes armor-piercing ammunition, but once again the name doesn't mean anything. All sorts of ammunition are tossed into the "cop-killer" category. Hollow-point ammunition is one, although I've never understood the reasoning there. Hollow-point bullets aren't designed to pass through targets, much less police vests or body armor. Sure, a cop *could* be killed with hollow-point bullets, but there's nothing exceptional about that when any bullet could do the same thing. Police officers aren't like werewolves—a special type of bullet is not necessary to kill them. They're human beings like anyone else.

So, as with armor-piercing ammunition, I don't recommend depicting cop-killer ammunition in a story. Some better adjectives for this type of ammunition include *high-velocity*, *magnum*, *high-powered*, and *full metal jacket*. They're vague enough to allow for penetration of various materials but still grounded firmly in reality.

Inaccurate Example

Maynard Soloman examined the carnage of the crime scene. He leaned down and inspected an empty bullet, noting a mark on the rim of the brass.

"What do you think?" said Captain Penny Flyswatter from the far side of the room.

"I think this is the work of Bill Robber. He had himself a big ol' gun, too," Maynard said, nodding at the fresh corpses. "Bill fired three times. Hollow points."

"But there are four bodies. How do you figure?" Captain Flyswatter said.

"A shot went through one of the first three, then hit the fourth victim. If I know Bill, he won't stop at four," Maynard said and took a bite from his sloppy sub sandwich. "You don't mind if I have lunch in here, right?"

Accurate Example

Maynard Soloman examined the carnage of the crime scene. He leaned down and inspected an empty casing, noting a mark in the center of the bottom of the brass.

"What do you think?" said Captain Penny Flyswatter from the far side of the room.

"I think this is the work of Bill Robber. He had himself a big ol' gun, too," Maynard said, nodding at the fresh corpses. "Bill fired three times. Full metal jackets."

"But there are four bodies. How do you figure?" Captain Flyswatter said.

"The shot went through one of the first three, then hit the fourth victim. Lucky shot. If I know Bill, he won't stop at four," Maynard said and took a bite from his sloppy sub sandwich. "You don't mind if I have lunch in here, right?"

What Went Wrong?

All sorts of things are suspect in this example.

An "empty bullet" isn't a thing. A bullet is the projectile. The brass casing is what's empty and left on the floor.

In the first example, Maynard noted a "mark on the rim of the brass." That points to rimfire ammunition. As mentioned previously, rimfires are used with light calibers, such as the .17 and .22. That doesn't sound conducive to the "big ol' gun" Bill apparently used. Centerfire ammunition would be in line with a "big ol' gun," since it's used for more powerful calibers. Maynard would notice a mark from the firing pin in the center of the primer, as he does in the corrected example.

If hollow-point bullets were used, the likelihood of one passing through a victim and killing another is low. Hollow-point bullets are designed to explode upon impact and not pass through.

Seeing three shots and four bodies led Maynard to make an educated guess that the shooter used full metal jackets in the corrected version. That type of bullet can pass through targets.

Finally, eating a sub sandwich at a crime scene is just a bad idea. It can be forgiven, though, since Maynard is one helluva clueless detective.

A QUICK WORD ABOUT "SELF-GUIDED" BULLETS

Rifle and handgun bullets adjusting in midair to hit targets would seem to be the stuff of science fiction. But in 2012, Sandia National Laboratories brought the concept into reality.

Sandia's projectile uses fins—sort of like a miniature airplane—to change trajectory. Sensors on the nose of the bullet lock in on a separate laser beam focused on a target.

This doesn't mean the bullet can make hard turns, a la *The Fifth Element*. Rather the adjustments keep the bullet's trajectory in check.

An article on Sandia's website (share.sandia.gov) states, "Computer simulations showed an unguided bullet under real-world conditions could miss a target more than a half mile away (1,000 meters away) by 9.8 yards (9 meters), but a guided bullet would get within 8 inches (0.2 meters), according to the patent."

How writers choose to embellish this technology is up to them. It's still helpful to know a scene referencing "self-guided" bullets isn't so far from reality these days.

HOLSTERS AND CONCEALED CARRY

There's a lot to know about holsters, but one takeaway you must not miss is Bianchi's Law. It's a concept in the firearms world that goes like this: "The same gun, in the same place, all the time."

Assign one (or more) holster to a specific part of a character's body, and then don't veer from that selection. It takes practice to build the muscle memory required to draw a handgun smoothly from a holster. So avoid writing wandering holsters.

Also, one-size-fits-all holsters do not exist. A holster might be designed to work with several firearm models, but that doesn't suggest universal compatibility. Let's take a look at some key aspects of holsters that will help make your writing accurate and clear.

RIGHT- OR LEFT-HANDED?

Assigning a holster actually starts with determining if the character is right- or left-handed. This matters because the best way to draw a handgun is usually from the "strong side." For example, a right-handed character would be drawing the handgun from the right side of the body, where the character likely has the best strength and dexterity.

If that right-handed character positioned the holster on the left instead of the right, that would be called a "cross draw holster."

The strong side is the best choice, though. And the best part of the body to attach that holster to is the hip. In his book *Gun Digest Book of Concealed Carry Second Edition*, renowned firearms expert Massad Ayoob says, "The strong-side hip is the odds-on choice for weapon placement. … It is also the standard location for law enforcement officers in uniform. This is probably not coincidental. Many ranges, police academies, and shooting schools will allow only strong-side holsters. The theory behind this is that cross draw will cause the gun muzzles to cross other shooters and range officers when weapons are drawn or holstered."

TYPES OF HOLSTERS

There are as many variations of holsters as there are handguns. This section of the chapter boils down everything for the sake of practicality.

All holsters can be put into one of two categories: retention or automatic locking.

Retention holsters offer a snug fit and are used for either revolvers or pistols.

Auto-lock holsters, designed for pistols, use an internal lock that must be pressed to release the handgun. There's an audible click as the handgun is holstered and locked in place. Law enforcement characters might use this to prevent someone from grabbing their handguns.

Within those categories, holsters are classified by how they're worn.

Hip holsters, as mentioned, are the most popular. As the name suggests, they secure to a belt and lie against the hip. Hip holsters can be moved along the belt to other places, such as the back. Holsters designed specifically for wearing at the back are called small-of-back holsters.

The IWB holster gives characters a fresh take on the "Is that a pistol in your pocket or are you just happy to see me?" cliché. (Photo courtesy of *Gun Digest*.)

Some hip holsters are designed to sit on the inside of the pants instead of the outside. These are called inside-the-waistband (IWB) holsters. IWB holsters are perfect for concealed carry. They allow clothing to lie or tuck over the holster. This greatly reduces the visibility of the handgun, provided the holster doesn't cause the clothing to bulge. However, IWB holsters are more difficult to draw. Clothing must be moved out of the way (lifting up a shirt, for example) to access the holster. An inexperienced character would have a tougher time making a smooth draw with an IWB.

While hip holsters have the edge in real-world effectiveness and popularity, shoulder holsters (which are strapped to the shooter's shoulder with the firearm positioned against the ribs) dominate in fiction and film. Ayoob acknowledges this in his book:

"Ah, yes, the shoulder holster is a part of the whole noir scene, in movies and novels alike. … The mid-twentieth century saw Mickey Spillane's classic 'hard-boiled private eye,' Mike Hammer, carrying a .45 automatic in a shoulder rig. … [Another] popular paperback private eye of the 1960s, Shell Scott, was armed by author Richard S. Prather with a snub-nose Colt

Detective Special .38 in a clamshell shoulder holster. … The late Ian Fleming equipped [James Bond] with a Beretta .25 in a chamois shoulder holster in the early novels."

Unlike hip holsters, shoulder holsters should not be attached to the strong side of the body. Shoulder holsters are cross draw only. A right-handed character would draw from a shoulder holster secured to the left side of the body.

Shoulder holsters secure to the body using a "rig" or harness. When writing, factor in that the character is wearing something underneath the rig. A shoulder holster against bare skin is going to leave a mark. Toss a jacket or coat over the top, and now the handgun is concealed. Just remember that a character would have to open that garment to access the holster.

Women often prefer shoulder holsters. Females tend to have narrower chests than males. This allows for a shorter, easier reach to access the holster.

Shoulder holsters are also popular with people who do a lot of sitting, because a hip holster could get in the way. Consider a disgruntled and well-armed tollbooth operator. (Now there's a character idea!)

Pocket holsters are inserted into, suitably enough, the pocket. Because of their positioning, they use retention to secure the handgun, not auto locks, and are positioned on the strong side of the body. Pocket holsters can be awkward to use without the right pair of pants. That's why they're sometimes inserted into a vest, a jacket, or coat pockets instead.

In fiction, handguns are sometimes fired through the pocket. Reality actually backs this up, but it's not a great idea. I didn't feel like testing this out, but Ayoob did. He had students at his firearm school give it a try. In his book, he says, "Three of the participants used [pistols] for firing through coat pockets. All three specimens went five shots for five tries without a malfunction. The shooters did notice that it was distracting to have trapped, hot casings burning their hands and wrists inside the pockets."

In other words, in reality it's possible, but not comfortable, for a pocket shot. Have at it, writers. Just watch out for those hot casings.

Ankle holsters secure to their namesake. A pant leg typically conceals them unless a character sports ankle holsters as a fashion statement while wearing shorts … and probably socks with sandals, but I digress. In fiction and reality, the ankle holster is best suited for a smaller secondary handgun (i.e., the "backup gun," usually in a smaller caliber such as the .22 or .38). It's also ideal for those who do a lot of sitting.

It takes practice and training to make a smooth draw from this type of holster, as well as the ability to bend down to the ankles. Bulkier characters who are unable to bend over to tie their shoes wouldn't go with an ankle holster. But move that ankle holster up the leg, and it becomes a thigh holster that can be worn inside or outside the clothing.

HOLSTERS FOR WOMEN

Female characters can use any style holster, but a few holsters are specifically designed for them by taking advantage of accessories typically worn or carried by women.

New to the market in recent years are purse, brassiere, under-the-skirt (basically a re-tooled thigh holster), undershirt, and waistband holsters. Each is designed for concealed carry and is perfect for stealthy characters.

AMMUNITION HOLSTERS

Characters would be wise to carry some spare ammunition. Fiction often doesn't account for where this ammunition comes from, though. It just appears. Not so in real life.

For pistols, spare magazines can be kept in holsters or pouches separate from or built into the handgun holster. Products like the Snagmag allow for a magazine to be clipped into the inside of a pocket, sort of like a pen cap hooking into a notebook.

Magazines can also be kept loose in bags, pockets, and purses, but doing so isn't always practical. Treat spare magazines like handguns in your writing. They need to be accessible and secure.

Spare revolver ammunition is a little trickier, since it doesn't come in the convenient "ammo burrito" of a magazine. In that case, a few speed strips (a length of flexible material holding cartridges in a single-file line that can be thumbed into the chambers two or three at a time) in a pocket or pouch will do. Moon clips and speed loaders are other options, although they can be bulky and produce a bulge. Depending on the ego of the character, this might not be a bad thing.

Bandoliers, a strap lined with cartridges, are typically used for rifle or shotgun ammunition, although they could carry rounds for handguns, too. They can carry dozens of cartridges, but they're heavy as a horse, so make sure the character wearing the bandolier is strong enough to do so.

Speed loaders are always an option, but don't forget about speed strips when writing a revolver reload. (Photo courtesy of *Gun Digest*.)

CONCEALED CARRY

This concealed carry section is small and comes at the end of the holster section. Why? Because holsters are a huge part of concealed carry and are as important as the handguns themselves.

Whenever a holstered handgun is hidden from view on a person, it's considered concealed carry. There are special laws that regulate concealed carry. Read up on them in the section about must-know firearm laws later in Part One.

It's time for another example ...

Inaccurate Example

Maynard Soloman yowled in pain as Bill Robber's bullet tore through his right hand. He clutched the wound against his burly chest.

"Aw, nuts, that's my gal-damn bingo blotter hand," Maynard said. "How am I supposed to win that turkey dinner now? I'm no leftie."

With the little dexterity that remained, Maynard stretched out his stubby arm and used his shredded hand to grab the revolver holstered to his right shoulder. He nailed Bill in the chest with two dead-on shots.

Accurate Example

Maynard Soloman yowled in pain as Bill Robber's bullet tore through his right hand. He clutched the wound against his burly chest.

"Aw, nuts, that's my gal-damn bingo blotter hand," Maynard said. "How am I supposed to win that turkey dinner now? I'm no leftie."

With the little dexterity that remained, Maynard stretched out his stubby arm and used his shredded hand to grab the revolver holstered to his right hip. He nailed Bill in the chest with a lucky shot.

What Went Wrong?

In the corrected example, Maynard holstered his revolver at the hip instead of his shoulder. This simple change solved two problems at once.

First is the issue of Maynard's dimensions. He sports a burly chest and stubby arms. Thus, a shoulder holster is probably not a good choice for him. Replacing it with a hip holster remedies the situation. Always consider a character's physical traits before assigning any piece of gear.

Second is the positioning of the shoulder holster. Since Maynard is right-handed, he'd strap the holster to his left shoulder, not his right. Again, the hip holster secured to his right side solves that problem.

One gray area concerns whether Maynard could successfully fire the revolver with a wounded hand. It's not explicit in this example, but, as other sections of this guide reveal, Maynard is elderly. Firing a revolver with an uninjured hand is difficult enough. In this instance, I reduced the shots fired from two solid hits to a single lucky one. It goes to show that all weapons usage depends on the character's condition. It's something to consider every time a gun is fired or a knife is used.

SUPPRESSORS, SILENCERS, SCOPES, AND SIGHTS

SUPPRESSORS AND SILENCERS

Thrillers and crime fiction depict silencers unrealistically all the time. Television shows, books, and movies often show these supernatural devices reducing a controlled explosion of gunpowder from a handgun, rifle, or shotgun to the sound of a gerbil fart. The truth is nothing like fiction.

Let's start with the name: *silencer*. *Suppressor* is the more accurate term. *Silencer* became adopted colloquially, and it's easy to see why. These tubular modifications, screwed into the end of a barrel, reduce the sound of a shot being fired. But reduced is not silenced. They "suppress." That's why they're more accurately called suppressors.

Before I dive into how exactly that works, let me clarify something—I don't think it's necessarily *wrong* to use the term *silencer*. It's just *technically* inaccurate. Still, the usage of *silencer* is so common that it might confuse readers to use *suppressor*. So if writers want to use *silencer* because it's simpler, I won't suppress them, but I still think it's valuable to understand why *suppressor* is the more accurate term.

How Suppressors (Don't) Work

Generally speaking, the sounds suppressors muffle are the sharp, high-pitched cracks from the shot. The rest of the noise will still echo all across that "dark and stormy night."

The ignition of gunpowder inside a cartridge produces a powerful blast of gas. It's that gas that makes gunshots so noisy. If the gas is contained inside something as it exits the barrel, like the tube of a suppressor, much of the explosive noise is reduced.

Reduced—not eliminated. The best suppressors capture the most gas, but there's yet to be a model that contains all of it. Some gas still manages to escape and make noise.

Even if a suppressor contains 100 percent of the gas, that gunshot is still going to make noise. That's because of a little thing called the sound barrier. The speed of sound is 1,126 feet per second (fps). That's pretty slow in the land of firearms. Most ammunition can easily hurry past 1,126 fps. The ammunition in the .270 rifle I use for deer hunting clocks in around 3,000 fps. An object traveling faster than the speed of sound will create noise. The best suppressors in the world can't bend the laws of physics.

Do Suppressors Actually Make a Difference?

None of this is to say suppressors don't make a difference. They certainly do. A noticeable reduction in noise occurs when a suppressor is used. However, the reduction is not always huge, and the resulting shot won't involve the *joot* sound Hollywood so often employs.

Nothing I write can tell that story quite like a trip to YouTube. There you'll find many side-by-side comparisons of suppressed and nonsuppressed firearms, but one of the best I've found is at tinyurl.com/suppressor-comparison. It demonstrates much of what's explained in this section.

The videos also highlight a noise many writers don't consider: the normal function of the firearm itself. Even a fictional suppressor that absorbs every bit of the shot's sound can't cover up the click of the firing pin, the cacophony of the action cycling ammunition, and the various other metallic workings of the firearm. A firearm is a mechanical object that makes mechanical sounds. Total silence can't be achieved so long as moving parts are involved.

So, does it make sense to outfit a character with a suppressor? That depends on the scene. If total silence is required, a suppressor isn't going to cut it. For characters trying not to be noticed amidst other background noises, suppressors will do the trick.

In the real world, outside of the military and law enforcement, suppressors are often used for special hunts near residential areas as a courtesy to those living nearby.

The Secret to Successful Suppressors: Subsonic Ammunition

Subsonic ammunition is designed to stay under 1,126 fps. This is most often associated with .17 and .22 ammunition, although calibers all the way up to the .50 can be subsonic.

Pairing subsonic ammo with a suppressor will drastically reduce the noise. The shot doesn't produce much gas, and the bullet isn't breaking the sound barrier. That's the secret to using suppressors. Writers looking to add some realism to a covert operation might have their characters use suppressors *and* subsonic ammunition.

There's a trade-off, though: Subsonic speeds reduce the amount of force the projectile exerts on a target, called "stopping power." When it comes to putting a character down, stopping power is a good thing. Not enough stopping power means a character may need some extra coercing to die. Firing from closer ranges will always be the better bet. Point blank is ideal.

One final note: Subsonic ammunition is slow—but only in terms of firearms. It doesn't mean the shooting character needs to fire ahead of a moving target (called *leading the target*) any more than normal.

The Writer's Guide to Weapons

Legality of Suppressors

Suppressors are considered Class III devices under the 1934 National Firearms Act and require ATF registration, just like fully automatic firearms. Law enforcement and military organizations are exempted, and they often have access to better suppressors that trap more gas than civilian models. That still doesn't mean they don't make noise, though.

The law might not matter to some characters, but it's important to understand this bit of trivia anyway.

DIY Suppressors

Erotica isn't the only genre with some wild ideas about pillow positioning. Thrillers and crime fiction do, too. According to many novels, you can just hold a pillow against a firearm's barrel and pull the trigger in perfect silence.

Remember that trapping the gas coming out of the barrel is key to reducing noise. A pillow is soft and full of fluff. While it can trap the breath of a hospital patient who "knows too much," it's not going to lock in gas escaping a metal tube at 3,000 fps. The gunshot will still make noise.

The same goes for using socks, hats, gloves, blankets, grocery bags of food, pumpkins, roadkill, cheeseburgers, pog collections, pickle jars, phone books, and the rest. For any fictional DIY (do-it-yourself) suppressor to reflect reality, it must be able to lock in gas while allowing a projectile to pass through without affecting accuracy. So when you are writing about one, make sure you use your imagination.

Here are a few items that, once modified, have a chance of actually working as DIY suppressors. Steps to create them aren't included in this guide, since manufacturing suppressors, even crappy homemade ones, requires special licensure from the federal government (another thing to keep in mind when writing).

- flashlight
- oil filter
- PVC pipe
- aluminum pipe
- water balloon (one-time use only, of course)

Insert these DIY suppressors into the writing instead of pillows, and the story's street cred will go way up.

Can Revolvers Be Suppressed?

It's been said that revolvers cannot be suppressed. There's a tiny gap between the cylinder and the barrel. Gas, and therefore noise, escapes through the gap, negating any benefit a suppressor might offer.

It's also been said that the amount of gas escaping is minimal and that a suppressor is still beneficial.

Then someone else said there are certain revolver models that don't have that gap. A suppressor would work just as well on those revolvers as it would on a pistol.

Yet a fourth person said that whomever ordered pizza needs to pay for it, because the delivery guy is about to leave.

Yes, things get confusing in a hurry when talking about suppressed revolvers. The only real gap at play is one of agreement. There isn't any clean, fully agreed-upon answer.

Having said that, does it make sense to write about suppressed revolvers?

Yes. In my opinion, I think you should go for it. The majority of gas created by a revolver shot exits the barrel like any other firearm. That means a suppressor would still help. If presented with a choice, though, assign the character a suppressed pistol instead. There's no reason to enter into this argument unnecessarily. Leave that to the voicemails of authors of gun guides.

Inaccurate Example

Maynard Soloman knew Bill Robber was in either room 237 or 217 at the Ov rlook Ho el (the hotel's neon sign was neglected, possibly to avoid a copyright infringement). The trick would be to shoot him without waking anyone up. At this late hour, the hotel was completely booked.

Maynard snapped a silencer onto the end of his .50 caliber Desert Eagle pistol before slipping into the first room through the window. Bingo. Looking up from the pillows of his king-sized bed, Bill appeared to be surprised.

"Did you say your prayers tonight?" Maynard said and shined a flashlight into Bill's eyes with his free hand.

Bill started to say something, but Maynard didn't let him respond. He held a pillow against the silencer for good measure, then pulled the trigger until the drapes in the room matched the dingy red carpet.

It would be hours before hotel staff found Bill's body. Plenty of time for Maynard to cross three state lines in his RV and make a clean escape.

Accurate Example

Maynard Soloman knew Bill Robber was in either room 237 or 217 at the Ov rlook Ho el (the hotel's sign was neglected, possibly to avoid a copyright infringement). The trick would be to shoot him without waking anyone up. The hotel was completely booked.

Maynard screwed a silencer into the end of his 9mm Beretta 92 pistol before slipping into the first room through the window. Bingo. Looking up from the pillows of his king-sized bed, Bill appeared to be surprised.

"Did you say your prayers tonight?" Maynard said and shined a flashlight into Bill's eyes with his free hand.

Bill started to say something, but Maynard didn't let him respond. He pulled the trigger until the drapes in the room matched the dingy red carpet.

The hotel lit up as the other guests woke in a panic. People flooded the hallways. Rats bolted from the toilets. Staff canceled the continental breakfast.

Security guards arrived at room 237 in a matter of seconds. They tackled Maynard and dialed 911.

What Went Wrong?

Given he's at a crowded hotel, Maynard required total silence in this scenario. Unfortunately a suppressor can't offer that, not even with the addition of a pillow pressed against it. That's why Maynard's plan went to ruin in the accurate example. This correction might've gone differently with a couple of alternatives. Maynard could've smothered Bill with a pillow or strangled him with a cord, provided I gave him more time to surprise his target.

Maynard did head in the right direction by switching from a .50 caliber Desert Eagle to a 9mm Beretta in the accurate example. Assuming he had the choice, Maynard would leave the .50 at home. Even with a suppressor, it's a noisy hand cannon that's not cut out for stealth. The 9mm makes much less noise and is a better fit. Here again is a general ranking of handgun calibers sorted by least to greatest firepower, a good indicator of noise: .22, .25, .32, .38, 9mm, .40, 10mm, .357, .45, .44, and .50.

Also, Maynard should screw in the silencer instead of snapping it in place.

Left unchanged in the accurate version was the *silencer* reference. As mentioned previously in this section, the term is so popular that using *suppressor* would probably cause more confusion than it's worth.

SCOPES AND SIGHTS

A scope on a handgun? With some larger hunting revolvers, this makes sense. With a bit of creativity, a scope could be mounted to a pistol—but it's not common. (Photo courtesy of *Gun Digest*.)

Scopes and sights help increase accuracy, but they're not the last word in shot placement, as you'll see. The terms *scope* and *sight* are sometimes used interchangeably. In some cases this is accurate, but I think it spares confusion to follow this rule: Use *scope* when referring to a telescoping lens. Use *sight* when referring to hardware that lacks a telescoping lens.

It generally takes more time to line up a shot with a scope than it does with a sight. First, when you look through a scope, it can take a second to find the target. A scope may need to zoom in or out, depending on the distance from the target, while a sight requires the user to simply look, aim, and shoot. There's no need to find the target in the scope first. That's why sights are quicker.

Most firearms come with sights built into them, while a scope is an adjustable, telescoping lens mounted on top of a firearm. Scopes are best for characters needing to make an accurate, long-distance shot; they are challenging to use at close ranges. If a character using a scoped firearm comes upon a target up close, he might have to shoot without any visual aid.

The lines used for aiming when looking through a scope are called a *reticle*. The classic crosshairs, commonly used in thrillers and crime fiction, are a type of reticle. However, scores of reticles exist. Some even help determine range and ballistics information using a few quick calculations. For a comprehensive rundown on types of reticles, head to www.gundigest.com/reticlebook for a free PDF from *Gun Digest*.

Sights are pieces of hardware fixed to a firearm and used to line up shots. They don't contain a telescoping lens. Sights are most effective for mid- to close-range targets. It's not impossible, but it is difficult for a character to make a long-range shot with a sight. Some sights are pieces of metal, such as a bead. Others are strips of colorful fiber optic.

Some sights are tubes mounted on top of a firearm like a scope. The difference is they don't magnify the target. Instead they use batteries to illuminate a reticle, which is useful for low-light conditions. They might also display a red dot inside the tube used for aiming. This is known as a red dot sight. A shooter might use one for faster aiming, since the battery-powered red dot is so bright.

A variation of the red dot sight is the red dot scope, which sports a telescoping lens. Don't confuse red dot sights and scopes with laser sights. Laser sights are a popular choice in fiction, and they should not be written interchangeably with red dot sights and scopes. The classic image of law enforcement officers covering a suspect in red or green cherries is courtesy of laser sights, not red dot sights. When writing laser sights, remember these tips:

- Think of laser sights like laser pointers attached to a gun.
- They're useful for low-light conditions or as a backup when the shooter cannot see into the regular sight or scope.
- Laser sights can act as a useful distraction for tactical or intimidation purposes, too. Nothing says, "You're screwed," or "I'm watching you," like a meandering red dot. That's something traditional scopes and sights can't offer.
- Red laser sights are the most popular, but green versions are catching up. Some say green sights work better in daytime conditions.
- Laser sights require batteries, and batteries add weight to the firearm that can throw off an otherwise comfortable aim. These sights are also expensive. That means more experienced or well-heeled characters would likely use laser sights over less experienced or less affluent ones.
- Laser sights are available to the public, as well as law enforcement and the military.
- Most laser sights are accurate out to around 20 yards. The laser can project beyond that, but it's not as effective for the shooter's aim. As explained in the Ballistics section of this book, bullets don't actually travel in straight lines like a laser.
- Laser sights are most commonly installed on pistols and rifles. Fiction sometimes pairs them with scoped sniper rifles. This isn't practical for aiming purposes, so just use the scope in your writing.
- Laser sights were first used by law enforcement in 1984. They didn't gain widespread use until around 1994. If a story takes place prior to 1984, don't write in a laser sight.

Inaccurate Example

Maynard Soloman got to work setting up his perch high above the busy city street. He loaded up his sniper rifle and studied the traffic below.

Some shady clients had paid him $50 (they had a coupon) to assassinate the newest appointee in the department of transportation, Undersecretary of Parking Tickets Dick Move. Needing to pay off the impound lot where his beloved RV sat, Maynard enthusiastically accepted the job.

Once Undersecretary Move's motorcade appeared one block away, Maynard switched on the red dot sight on his rifle. Through the scope, he could see the red dot hovering on Move's forehead.

"This is for towing my RV last week," Maynard said as he pulled the trigger.

Accurate Example

Maynard Soloman got to work setting up his perch high above the busy city street. He loaded up his sniper rifle and studied the traffic below.

Some shady clients had paid him $50 (they had a coupon) to assassinate the newest appointee in the department of transportation, Undersecretary of Parking Tickets Dick Move. Needing to pay off the impound lot where his beloved RV sat, Maynard enthusiastically accepted the job.

Once Undersecretary Move's motorcade appeared one block away, Maynard took aim with his red dot scope.

"This is for towing my RV last week," Maynard said as he pulled the trigger.

What Went Wrong?

The inaccurate example commits a pile of blurry errors in record time.

The red dot sight is being confused with a laser sight. A laser sight projects a red dot onto a target, sort of like a laser pointer. A red dot sight displays a red dot inside a tube used for aiming and does not project onto a target.

However, neither piece of gear is appropriate for a sniper scenario. Maynard is perched a block away from his target. That's out of range for a laser sight, which is only effective out to 20 yards or so. Maynard needs more than a red dot sight, too, since that type of device doesn't magnify targets. Remember the rule of thumb to spare confusion: A scope magnifies a target; a sight does not.

Since this scene seems intent on using some sort of ruby-themed aiming device, a red dot scope is used in the corrected version. It's identical to a red dot sight, except it sports a telescoping lens. It could magnify Maynard's target a block away.

If this is confusing, another route is to treat weapons depictions like grammar snags and just write around them. Simplify Maynard's setup by giving him a standard rifle scope. Then it's as easy as having him line up the crosshairs as the motorcade approaches.

BALLISTICS

Ballistics is the science behind how a bullet travels. From hunting to forensics, ballistics is essential to firearms in reality. It's a little different with fiction: Writers either spend a lot of time on ballistics or none at all. The reason is the science itself. Taking the time to explain everything that goes into ballistics stops the story. But even if ballistics plays a minimal role in your story, it's important to understand how it functions. When you're finished with this section, have some morbid fun and sketch out how a scene's ballistics might work given the shooter and the target character.

THE LIFE OF A BULLET

To understand ballistics, it's important to break down what's happening when a bullet is fired.

Gunpowder (call it propellant for some *CSI* flavor), measured in grains, is full of potential energy. When the gunpowder ignites, the potential energy transfers into the bullet (or projectile, again for that science feel), where it becomes kinetic energy.

The kinetic energy moves the bullet out of the barrel. As the bullet starts its journey, it increases in velocity, usually measured in feet per second.

Several factors influence the path the bullet takes, which is called a *trajectory*. These factors include the angle of the barrel, air temperature, elevation, and especially wind. I'll give you a shortcut for figuring in those factors a little later.

Eventually the kinetic energy wears off, velocity decreases, and gravity tugs the bullet back to earth. This descent is called *drop*.

Should the bullet collide with something before it returns to earth, such as a character, the projectile sheds its kinetic energy into whatever it hits. It's that transfer of kinetic energy that creates wounds or holes in characters or targets. How much kinetic energy is transferred is called *stopping power*, and it's measured in foot-pounds.

That's why a character who is shot point blank is going to hurt a lot more than one who is shot on the outskirts of a firearm's range. There's more kinetic energy, or stopping power, being transferred into the target.

Make sense? Ballistics is more about the transfer of energy and environmental factors than the bullets themselves.

STRAIGHT AS A BULLET? MORE LIKE A SOFTBALL

One assumption some writers make is that bullets travel in perfectly straight lines. However, kinetic energy doesn't play fair. It doesn't expend itself evenly across the bullet's trajectory. Like Maynard Soloman at a family reunion, it can't wait to get the hell out of there. A bullet's kinetic energy expends a massive amount of itself to begin with, then tapers off depending on a number of factors. Because of this, the bullet actually rises a little bit as it initially exits the barrel. It then levels off for a short time before gravity gradually drags it down.

This means bullets form an arc as they travel, not a straight line. Some bullets arc more or less than others depending on the cartridge, but all abide by the same principle.

To visualize this for writing, think of throwing a softball with an underhand toss. The softball doesn't make a straight line. It rises slightly, then returns to earth, forming an arc. It's the same way with bullets.

When thinking about ballistics, picture a softball being thrown underhand. The ball rises slightly, then drops. Despite appearances, bullets don't travel in perfectly straight lines. (Photo courtesy of Shutterstock.)

AIMING

Visualizing that arc is helpful when writing. Picture it spread out across a firearm's effective range. Here's a quick reference for those.

- **EXTREME RANGE (300 TO 2,000 YARDS):** rifles specifically designed for extreme distances (.338 and .50 calibers)
- **LONG RANGE (100 TO 300 YARDS):** intermediate to large caliber rifles (.243, .270, .30, .30-06, .30-30, .300, .308, 7mm)
- **MID-RANGE (25 TO 100 YARDS):** small to intermediate caliber rifles (.17, .22, .22-250, .223, .243, .270), shotguns firing slugs (out to 100 yards), shotguns firing BBs (out to 50 yards), submachine guns, machine guns
- **CLOSE RANGE (25 YARDS ON DOWN):** pistols, revolvers, submachine guns

Now think about where the target falls along that arc. Is it near the beginning of the arc? The character shooting wouldn't need to compensate much for drop when aiming.

Is the target in the middle of the arc? The shooter would aim slightly higher.

Is it at the end of the arc, near the bullet's maximum range, when drop becomes most severe? The character shooting would need to aim higher, perhaps a few inches, to adjust for drop.

Put into an example, let's say Maynard Soloman is firing a rifle at a target character 200 yards away. Maynard wants to make a hit in the heart. Where should he aim?

Since 200 yards is about where Maynard's shot starts to drop, he'd aim a couple of inches above the heart. The writing would reflect that if such a description were important to the story.

STOPPING POWER: MAKING THE HIT

Stopping power is an important concept. It can impact whether a character dies or is merely wounded. Where the target is positioned along the arc determines how much kinetic energy is exerted from the bullet (stopping power).

Spots earlier in the arc offer the greatest stopping power and therefore the most damage.

Spots later in the arc have the least stopping power and inflict less damage.

That's why small calibers aren't cut out for long-range kills. They don't pack much stopping power near the end of their journey.

Granted, taking a bullet at any range from any firearm can be lethal. Remember this axiom: Any firearm can be lethal, but no firearm is always lethal.

BALLISTICS TABLES

The key to putting all of this together is ballistics tables. They'll help you visualize those arcs. (You can download a sample ballistics table at www.WritersDigest.com/guns-knives, originally excerpted from *Gun Digest 2015*, edited by Jerry Lee.) Such tables are rich in information, but there are a few things to look for when using them.

First, find the cartridge on the left side. Cartridges are divided by centerfire and rimfire, rifles and handguns.

Then check out the energy at various distances. That's the bullet's stopping power. A higher number means more damage.

Finally, look at the trajectory across the distances. It's measured in inches. A plus (+) sign means the bullet is rising. To be dead on, the shooter would need to compensate by aiming lower.

A minus (–) sign means the bullet is falling, so the shooter should aim higher. A trajectory of -5.7 means the shooter needs to aim 5.7 inches higher to stay on target.

OTHER FACTORS

Have a solid grasp on ballistics now? Sorry, it's time to throw a wrench into the works.

The ballistics tables don't account for wind, elevation, temperature, sight height, and angle. In the real world, those things matter quite a bit. *Gun Digest* publishes entire books on how to figure that stuff out.

Here's a tip. Use common sense and a bit of imagination to compensate for those variables as much as possible.

Wind blowing from the left will move bullets to the right. Shots travel farther in higher elevations because there is less air resistance. Bullets tend to hit lower on targets far away when the temperature is cooler.

Those are a few rules of thumb. If a full-blown *CSI* treatment is required, it's time to get a dedicated ballistics book that will go in-depth on these nuances.

PSST ... HERE'S THE SHORTCUT

I promised earlier there'd be a shortcut. Every writer and any person interested in this topic needs to get the ballistics calculator from Winchester. It's one of the best resources for ballistics information, and it's free.

Head to this URL to download the calculator for use on desktop computers: tinyurl.com/winchester-calculator.

It's also available as an app for the iPhone. Just search for "Winchester Ballistics Calculator" in iTunes. It'll be the first thing to pop up. As of this writing, the calculator is not in the Android store.

The calculator is a breeze to use, even for beginners. Select the type of bullet, the caliber, the range, and environmental conditions such as wind direction and air temperature. Then hit "shoot." The calculator spits out a line graph showing the arc of the bullet, the drop, velocity, and more.

This is priceless information for writing scenes where trajectory plays a role. It visually reveals why a character might make a hit to the vitals or miss completely. Plus, because it gives you the drop, you could accurately describe where the shooter aims. Based on the drop, a character might aim at a target's hat to put a bullet between the eyes.

Other app calculators, such as iStrelok and Bullet Drop, are more advanced and cost money.

SEND IN THE STICK FIGURES

Got the bullet's arc? Know where the characters are in the scene? Compensated for environmental factors? It's time to send in the stick figures.

Grab a pencil and paper (you kids still know what those are, right?). Sketch out the bullet's arc for the range specific to the scene. Draw in the characters and role-play how the ballistics would impact the written depiction.

WHAT ABOUT SHOTGUNS?

This section focuses on rifle and handgun ballistics for a reason. Ballistics don't matter as much with shotguns. Patterning BBs matters more, and that's explained in the section on shotgun ammunition.

Shotgun slugs, on the other hand, do require some ballistics figuring. They're featured in that Winchester app. The rule of thumb, though, is that they drop a few inches at 100 yards, then nosedive into the ground like old television sets into a gravel pit. At 200 yards, for example, slugs can drop as much as 4 feet.

That's why I don't recommend characters use slugs beyond 100 yards. It's just not practical.

A QUICK WORD ABOUT BULLETPROOF VESTS

All this talk about kinetic energy makes it the perfect time to talk about bulletproof vests.

They work by absorbing the kinetic energy (stopping power) of a bullet. They use a web of durable fibers—such as Kevlar—woven together inside a synthetic cushion, which is then layered. Others use panels of strong resins, such as Kraton.

Both materials work the same way, trapping kinetic energy from the bullet and dispersing it into the material instead of the person wearing the vest. Imagine a soccer ball getting trapped in goal netting instead of flying into the crowd. It's sort of like that.

That doesn't mean 100 percent of the energy is stopped. Some shots will still cause internal injuries, break ribs, or knock down the person wearing the vest. A lucky shot might even run straight through the vest if it has enough kinetic energy. The term *bulletproof* is a little misleading because of this risk. Some say *bullet-resistant* is the more accurate term. I say either is fine when writing, with the safest bet being *ballistics vest*.

OTHER COMMON FIREARM ACCESSORIES AND THEIR UNCOMMON USES

Most of what writers require from firearms is summed up in their operation. Thank goodness for that, because there are a million different ways firearms can be modified and accessorized. But every now and then, a scene calls for a certain accessory. Here's a roundup of some common ones and their not-so-common uses.

BAYONETS

Historically bayonets cornered the market on close-quarter brawls. That was the case up until World War II, when bayonets became shorter, resembling knives more than swords. That allowed them to mesh better with firearm designs used during the war, which favored mobility over the longer rifles of World War I and prior conflicts.

Decreasing the size from a small sword to a long knife also increased bayonets' utility outside of combat. A trusty bayonet can serve scores of purposes, from cutting rope and opening meal tins to prying open boxes and pounding stakes.

Consider that divide in bayonet history when determining their use in a story. World War I marked the last of the large-scale bayonet charges, usually as the enemy retreated. By World War II, they were all but gone.

Military personnel from WWII and beyond either skipped bayonets entirely in favor of proper knives or used knives that doubled as bayonets. Although bayonets played a significant role during hand-to-hand combat in the Falklands War in the 1980s, modern military firearms hardly account for their presence anymore. Some modern firearm features, such as grenade launchers, can't be used if a bayonet is present.

Does that mean there isn't a role for a bayonet in a modern setting? Of course not. You can do a lot more with them than stab a character outright. Writers might consider these other purposes:

- for corralling or detaining other characters (sort of like a cattle prod)
- as a deterrent against someone grabbing the firearm

- as a spare knife for use as a tool
- for intimidation purposes
- for roasting marshmallows in a pinch (hey, sometimes a character just needs a s'more)

It's sometimes said a bayonet can affect the trajectory of a shot. This might be true in some cases, since it can alter the balance of a firearm, but it's probably not enough to concern a fiction writer.

And don't forget: Bayonets aren't just for rifles. They work well attached to shotguns and handguns, too. Get creative.

BIPODS AND TRIPODS

Bipods consist of a pair of folding or stationary supports used for stability, usually affixed to the barrel. This helps with accuracy, most often when shooting rifles (they can be paired with any type of firearm).

Tripods are used for heavier firearms, such as large machine guns, and are mounted closer to the middle of the firearm.

Other than offering stability, bipods and tripods also indicate the character is likely familiar with operating a firearm. This can be useful for quickly establishing character.

CAMOUFLAGE

There are two effective ways to camouflage a firearm: You can paint it, or you can use tape.

Paint is permanent, so it would follow that the environment of the scene never changes.

Tape is temporary and can be changed when conditions—such as the climate or seasons—change.

Either way, remember that camo isn't for concealment alone. It's also for establishing character. Someone who camouflages his weapon probably knows how to take care of business with a firearm.

COLLAPSIBLE STOCKS

Collapsible stocks fold or slide to lengthen or shorten the firearm. In the real world, they're a feature for the comfort of the shooter. In fiction, they're usually there for looks. (Photo courtesy of *Gun Digest*.)

Collapsible stocks gained a lot of attention in the federal Assault Weapons Ban (AWB) when they were banned on new civilian firearms made between 1994 and 2004. Collapsible stocks adjust to shorten or lengthen the part of the firearm shooters hold against their shoulder when they fire. They can fold (called a *folding stock*) or push inward. The latter is most popular since it allows for a custom fit on the shooter. In fiction, collapsible stocks are most often depicted as a sniper is setting up a rifle (think the shooter on the rooftop opening a briefcase of gun parts and assembling the weapon). There's no reason to avoid that, since it seems fiction is mostly interested in these stocks for looks. A character might also use collapsible stocks to conceal a long firearm under clothing or in a hiding place. Law enforcement characters, especially SWAT members, might find that shortening their stocks make it more convenient to get in and out of vehicles.

In reality, using a collapsible stock is primarily a comfort thing. Just don't include one in a story on a firearm made between 1994 and 2004.

FLASHLIGHTS

Flashlights, either mounted onto a firearm or held separately in tandem with a handgun, are useful for illuminating a dark scene. No surprises there, but writers should keep in mind another use: disorienting other characters.

Blinding someone with light is a control technique used by law enforcement. As Scott Wagner points out in his excellent book *Own the Night: Selection & Use of Tactical Lights & Laser Sights*, there's even a snappy saying for that tactic: illuminate, identify, and incapacitate.

Flashlights can attach to any firearm, from rifles to pistols. Some have a built-in on-off switch, while others are toggled with a pressure switch installed in the grips that activates with a squeeze. It's sufficient to describe a character simply turning the light on rather than detailing which system is being used.

Heavy flashlights carried separately also make great melee weapons.

GRENADE LAUNCHERS

Modern grenade launchers (tubes that fire explosive projectiles) are usually mounted below a firearm's barrel. This is most common with rifles well suited to customization, such as the U.S. military's M16 or its civilian equivalent, the AR-15.

While grenade launchers are perfect for turning legs into stumps or disabling vehicles with explosive power, they're much more versatile than that.

Flares, buckshot, tear gas, smoke bombs, and even less-lethal crowd control sponges all can be fired from grenade launchers. The legality of grenade launchers depends on the state in which they're being used and what's being fired. The launcher itself is usually easier to obtain legally than the ammunition it uses.

Grenade launchers dating back to World War I slipped into the end of a rifle barrel. The blast from a blank cartridge set off the grenade. However, the shooter could not quickly shift to firing regular rifle ammunition, so this setup was deemed ineffective. Following World War II, grenade launchers mounted beneath the barrel gained in popularity.

No matter the style, grenade launchers can be a lot of fun to write.

HOLLOW STOCKS

Rifles and shotgun stocks (the part the shooter presses against his or her shoulder) are often solid, but some have hollow butts (insert juvenile joke here). This means that the end of the stock is empty inside. A character with some time and motivation could use it for the storage of small items.

Need some perspective? Creek Stewart, a survival instructor I worked with at *Living Ready* magazine, managed to pack an entire emergency kit into a hollow stock. Some rifles, such as the .22 caliber AR-7, can be completely taken apart and stored inside the stock. On top of that, the AR-7's lone stock can float in water.

Hollow stocks are ripe for fiction. It's a wonder they don't show up more often.

PISTOL GRIPS

Some rifles and shotguns allow for pistol grips instead of the standard stock. This means the shooter's trigger-pulling hand grips a handle fashioned like the ones used on pistols.

That doesn't mean the shooter would hold the rifle or shotgun with one hand like a pistol. It's just a design element.

In fiction, I get the feeling pistol grips are mentioned as a way for a character to show off or look tough, likely influenced by other pop-culture depictions. Is there any practical benefit to them in reality? The jury is out.

A pistol grip on a Mossberg 500 Cruiser shotgun. (Photo courtesy of *Gun Digest*.)

Some say pistol grips are more ergonomic and make shooting at closer ranges easier. Others say they increase the shooter's maneuverability.

Here's my take: Pistol grips are for looks or comfort but don't necessarily add anything to performance.

As far as uncommon uses go, pistol grips are sometimes hollow. That means a clever character could store important items inside.

SLINGS

The primary purpose of a sling is to strap a rifle or shotgun to the shooter. The uses don't stop there, though. Any unorthodox ideas writers can come up with for a short length of rope can be applied to a sling.

Small pouches of important items, spare ammo, and even a knife sheath could be secured along the sling.

Slings are also useful for increasing accuracy. Threading a hand in and around them stabilizes the arm.

Out of ammo? A character could also use the sling to strangle the opposition.

SPARE AMMUNITION FOR SHOTGUNS

If a character's shotgun just won't cut it in the capacity department, she can carry extra ammunition in several ways without stuffing shells into her pockets.

One of the most popular is an extended magazine (the tube under the barrel where the shells are held in reserve). Law enforcement and military agencies often use these extra-long magazines. State laws may dictate how many shells civilians can have in a shotgun. For example, I insert a wooden rod into the magazine of my pump-action shotgun when hunting regulations limit the total number of shells I can have in the firearm at one time. This homemade plug restricts the amount of ammunition that can be loaded into the magazine.

Saddles are another common choice. These plastic clips usually hold three to five shells, secured to the stock.

A shell caddy, basically a small box secured to a belt, can contain up to eight or more shells.

Similar to saddles are elastic shell holders. These bands slip onto shotgun stocks and hold three to five shells. They don't last as long as saddles because they tend to wear out.

Now for some uncommon uses: Spare ammunition offers a chance to swap in different ammunition types. A character might load shotshells (they fire BBs) into the magazine, then stick slugs (they fire a single, solid projectile) into a saddle. Or he might alternate shells as he loads them: for example, shotshell-slug-shotshell-slug. The same could be done for flare rounds (used for signaling help), less-lethal beanbag loads (they fire bean bags instead of BBs or slugs, but not the fun kind you had as a kid), and other variants.

A character might carry these different types of ammo to react to changing situations. This can give the writer more flexibility, too.

SPARE AMMUNITION FOR RIFLES AND PISTOLS

Generous magazines aren't just for shotguns. Rifles and pistols with detachable magazines can enjoy their benefits, too. Using bigger magazines, those firearms can up their capacity to 20, 30, 50, 100, or more.

Rifles with magazines built inside them are out of luck in this department unless they use tubes to hold ammunition similar to a shotgun. This feature is often used in pump-action and lever-action rifles. Then it would be acceptable to write in an extended tube magazine, although most models are already maxed out without this addition.

Rifles can also use elastic bands that hold shells and slip onto the stock. These bands aren't as popular for lighter rifles, such as the .17 and .22, because their shells are so small.

There's not much room for uncommon uses with these accessories. Maybe writers out there will come up with some others.

SPARE AMMUNITION FOR REVOLVERS

Sorry, characters with revolvers, but there's not much you can do about ammunition capacity. A character might carry speed loaders, speed strips, and moon clips—explained in the section on handgun ammunition—separately to avoid manually reloading.

IMPROVISED AND CUSTOM FIREARMS

This guide considers three categories of improvised firearms: zip guns, custom, and plastic (including 3-D printed).

ZIP GUNS

Zip guns are firearms assembled from everyday objects. The "zip" comes from how fast they're thrown together—in a zip. They fire regular ammunition from a store, though, not homemade cartridges.

I'm not going to outline steps to make zip guns, since that's treading on some gray legal territory. I'll stick to the parts that anyone with a basic understanding of physics and projectiles could deduce. I don't recommend any writer (or anyone at all) try making a zip gun, not even for research purposes. There are better ways to lose a finger.

The manufacture of firearms, even sloppy ones, is subject to federal and state regulations. When writing fiction, assume zip guns are illegal, then research the setting to prove they're not (if that's important to the plot). They aren't always 100 percent illegal; it depends on the state they're made in, on the barrel length of the gun, the parts used, whether the gun is for personal use, and other factors.

Firing a zip gun can be dangerous. The shooter risks injury from exploding gunpowder that the guns' homemade parts cannot contain. Also, if the striker (usually a small pin or nail) doesn't hit the primer (the part of the cartridge that ignites the gunpowder when struck) hard enough, several seconds could go by before the zip gun fires.

These downsides, however, could be a benefit for establishing characters or settings. Zip guns speak to the desperation of the characters using them.

For a zip gun that does work, .17 and .22 caliber cartridges are the best bets for ammunition. They're inexpensive and offer little recoil. Shotgun shells, especially the .410, work well, too, since they tend to fit into homemade components, such as metal pipes.

While it's possible to use other types of ammunition, none of them are good choices. Unless machined specifically for firearms, the DIY materials used to make a zip gun probably cannot withstand firepower of that magnitude. Regardless of the ammo used, consider zip guns for short ranges only.

The making of a zip gun requires placing a cartridge into a tube and figuring out how to hit it hard enough that it fires. It's very basic and very dangerous, and typically involves these parts:

- a tube for use as a barrel, able to seat a firearm cartridge on one end
- a striker capable of hitting the cartridge's primer hard and fast, usually a screw or nail
- some way to hold the zip gun (can also be the barrel)
- guts and a few spare fingers

The *character* (not the writer, please) would seat the cartridge in the tube, then strike the primer with the striker. The latter might be built into a cap that slips over the tube to make it easier to use.

CUSTOM FIREARMS

A big step up from zip guns are custom firearms. These can be made in any of three ways: by modifying an existing firearm, assembling one from manufactured parts, or creating one from scratch.

There are many legal "mods and builds" (*mods* is short for modifications; *builds* are firearms made from manufactured parts). Any firearm might be re-equipped for better grip, extra hardware, a bigger scope, and other performance enhancers. In recent years, the AR-15 rifle took the cake as the king of custom mods. I've listed many of those modifications in the previous section of this book.

Illegal mods used for fictional purposes usually focus on converting semi-automatic rifles into fully automatics. As stated earlier, such a conversion is illegal and difficult to do. Despite seemingly functioning in identical ways, semi-autos and full-autos require different hardware to function. There's no switch you can throw to make the conversion. While writers can do what they please in fiction, reality suggests that a character would be better off buying a fully automatic firearm rather than trying to make one herself.

Another illegal mod seen in fiction is the shortening of the barrel of a shotgun by sawing it off. This allows a wider shot pattern at closer ranges. These sawed-off shotguns are illegal, but that wouldn't stop a character in fiction. Feel free to go wild with that modification, but read the sections on shotguns to determine the disadvantages and misconceptions of sawed-offs.

PLASTIC FIREARMS (INCLUDING 3-D PRINTED)

Plastic handguns are typically used in fiction for characters slipping past a metal detector. That's fine for fiction, but the reality is much different.

For starters, any plastic handgun is still going to need a metallic firing pin (a sliver of metal that strikes a cartridge's primer—the part that ignites the gunpowder when hit). Depending on the metal detector, this small pin could pass or fail inspection.

Even if the plastic gun's firing pin skipped detection, few people consider the ammunition. It will certainly contain metal, as ammunition made entirely of plastic doesn't exist. There's no getting around that. Thus the challenge to writers: How would a character get the ammunition past a metal detector?

The legality of plastic firearms is why this is all worth considering. The federal 1988 Undetectable Firearms Act (UFA) prohibits civilian possession and manufacture of firearms able to avoid metal detectors. The UFA can trace its origin to the introduction of the Glock 17 in 1982. The 17 broke new ground by incorporating several plastic parts into a high-performance design. This development led some to believe that a 100 percent plastic firearm was on the horizon. The UFA passed in 1988 in anticipation of that. Its passage certainly didn't hurt the popularity of Glock handguns; in fact, it probably helped. The Act was set to expire in 2013 but was renewed at the end of that year through 2023.

The renewal passed in anticipation of yet another burgeoning technology in firearms: 3-D printed handguns. These are new to thrillers and crime fiction, as well as to the real world.

The parts for these firearms are "printed" using a machine loaded with moldable plastic. The organization Defense Distributed fired the first working model, the Liberator, in early 2013.

Despite being made of plastic, the Liberator is not the undetectable handgun of lore. It still contains a metal firing pin and uses metallic ammunition. Under what category it falls in the eyes of the UFA might depend on the federal government's interpretation of "undetectable," since lawmakers across the board are struggling for ways to govern this burgeoning technology. The proliferation of 3-D printers on the consumer market will make things even fuzzier in the years to come. When writing, forget the laws. This is an area largely unexplored by thrillers and crime fiction, or anyone for that matter. Have fun with it. For example, what would happen if a certain character—good or bad—could print a handgun at home? What about knives or other tools of destruction?

As far as performance is concerned, printed plastic weaponry has a long way to go. The field is too young to say whether it's reliable, accurate, and safe to use. The fact that firearms manufacturers aren't sprinting to the technology is in itself telling.

That said, I don't believe that a 100 percent undetectable plastic handgun exists. If it does, I haven't heard of it, and I'd bet that's how its owner prefers things. Keep that in mind when assigning a plastic handgun to a character. A fictional world might employ reliably undetectable firearms, but it's important to understand the reality of them, too.

MUST-KNOW FIREARM LAWS

Firearm laws might not matter to the criminal characters in your fiction, but they can impact weaponry and the overall plot. While state and local regulations vary, there are four significant federal laws to consider before selecting a firearm for a character.

THE NATIONAL FIREARMS ACT (1934)

The year 1934 should be a line in the sand when outfitting characters with firearms. Whereas characters prior to that year could get their mitts on anything so long as they had the money, 1934 marked the beginning of modern gun control.

In that year, the National Firearms Act (NFA) became law. It levied a $200 tax on so-called "gangster guns." These included machine guns, submachine guns (Tommy guns, for example), shotguns with shortened barrels less than 18 inches (such as sawed-off shotguns), rifles with barrels less than 16 inches long, and suppressors (also known as silencers). These are all known collectively as "NFA firearms" or "Class III firearms."

Under the Act, NFA firearms must be registered with what is now the Bureau of Alcohol, Tobacco, Firearms and Explosives (ATF). A local law enforcement official also has to sign off on the purchase or transfer of NFA firearms. These requirements remain today.

Surprisingly the Constitutional objections to the NFA had more to do with the Fifth Amendment—the right not to incriminate oneself—than the Second. After the NFA went into effect, anyone attempting to register a Class III firearm could be incriminating themselves, since possessing an unregistered firearm is a crime. The United States Supreme Court settled this Fifth Amendment matter in 1968 in *Haynes v. United States*. Parts of the NFA were ruled unconstitutional, making the Act difficult to enforce.

THE GUN CONTROL ACT (1968)

The *Haynes v. United States* decision led to the passage of the Gun Control Act (GCA) of 1968. It changed the NFA to satisfy Fifth Amendment concerns. It also broadened a number of restrictions regarding prohibited firearms and individuals.

Most significantly for this guide, the GCA established the Federal Firearms License (FFL) system to regulate sales and transfers of firearms. Holders of an FFL facilitate transactions between buyer and seller, including the physical transfer of the firearm. Their role is to make sure the transaction is legal.

Since that point, it takes three people for a firearm to legally change hands: the buyer, the seller, and the FFL representative. Consider that the rule of thumb when writing in legally purchased firearms, although exceptions exist in the real world.

THE FIREARM OWNERS' PROTECTION ACT (1986)

In 1986, the Firearm Owners' Protection Act (FOPA) amended the Gun Control Act to end production of fully automatic firearms for civilian use in the United States. No fully automatic firearm made after May 19, 1986, may be possessed, bought, sold, or transferred by U.S. civilians. Fully automatic firearms made before May 19, 1986, were grandfathered in and must be registered. They are highly regulated.

That's important to remember when assigning full-autos to characters. Unless a character is in the military, belongs to a law enforcement organization, "knows a guy," or is engaged in criminal activities, new full-autos are off-limits.

FOPA does not prohibit removing the fully automatic action—the part that fires ammunition—and placing it inside the body of a gun made after May 19, 1986. However, such a gun must still be registered.

BRADY HANDGUN VIOLENCE PREVENTION ACT (1994)

In 1994, the Brady Handgun Violence Prevention Act went into effect. This created the National Instant Criminal Background Check System (NICS), administered by the Federal Bureau of Investigation (FBI). This marked the birth of "background checks" for firearms.

Under the Act, FFL holders are required to check the NICS to see if a person is eligible to buy a firearm. Prohibited persons include:

- anyone sentenced to more than one year of prison.
- convicted felons.
- fugitives.
- users/addicts of controlled substances, as determined by certain court convictions.
- those committed to mental institutions or found to be mentally defective by a court.
- anyone unlawfully residing within the United States.
- people in the United States on a visa and who are not immigrants.
- dishonorably discharged members of the military.
- those who have renounced U.S. citizenship.

- anyone convicted of a misdemeanor (or more serious wrongdoing) related to domestic violence.
- persons with a restraining order with regard to harassment, stalking, or threatening of an intimate partner or children.

If it matters to the story, the FBI goes into detail on these prohibitions at www.fbi.gov/about-us/cjis/nics/general-information/fact-sheet.

WHY THESE LAWS MATTER

Consider these four federal laws before outfitting a character with any firearm. If setting is important to the story, the types of firearms available may depend on where the weapon falls within these important pieces of legislation.

For example, a Tommy gun would be easier to obtain prior to 1934, when the National Firearms Act went into effect. Tommy guns were introduced in 1921. So between 1921 and 1934, it's most likely that a character would be able to buy a Tommy gun off the shelf hassle-free.

On the other hand, the FN SCAR, a machine gun introduced in the 2000s, wouldn't be hanging on the wall of a sporting goods store. It was made after May 19, 1986, and therefore isn't available to civilians.

Keep in mind that some legal semi-automatics, such as the popular AR-15, may look like fully automatics. It's also possible to modify fully automatic firearms to function as legal semi-automatics for resale, as is the case with many civilian AK-47s. Both of these instances are legal.

However, it is difficult, and illegal, to convert a semi-automatic into a fully automatic. Characters would need an advanced knowledge of firearms and extensive access to parts to make a successful conversion. It's not something that can be accomplished by walking into a sporting goods store.

Remember, when it comes to determining legality, form doesn't matter as much as function. On that note ...

1994 ASSAULT WEAPONS BAN

In September of 1994, the Assault Weapons Ban (AWB) went into effect. It prohibited the manufacture of firearms with a certain combination of "military-style" features in the United States for a period of ten years. These features included magazines capable of holding more than ten rounds, collapsible stocks, threaded barrels able to take screw-on accessories like suppressors, and others.

It prohibited only the manufacture of new firearms that have those characteristics. Those made before and after the ban (it expired in 2004) were exempt. That means characters wouldn't necessarily be limited by the AWB. They'd simply obtain a firearm equipped with the features they want and also made outside of those years

THE CASTLE DOCTRINE AND STAND YOUR GROUND LAWS

Recent high-profile news stories, such as the trial of George Zimmerman for the shooting death of Trayvon Martin, have put "Stand Your Ground Law" and "Castle Doctrine" at the forefront of national gun law discussions. For crime fiction, especially procedurals, these concepts can play an important role.

The Castle Doctrine can trace its roots back to English Common Law. Under this principle, a person has no obligation to retreat when threatened at home. A lethal act of violence on an intruder would therefore be justified. The Castle Doctrine is used as inspiration for state laws across the country. It's not a singular rule or law. It's a concept. And each state interprets it differently. Some require an attempt to retreat before force is justified, while others place an emphasis on the intruder's intent.

Stand Your Ground expands the Castle Doctrine beyond the home. "Stand Your Ground" is a generic term for these laws. It's not one law copy-pasted from state to state. The laws vary, but the primary theme is a presumption of reasonableness on behalf of the shooter. In the same way that a person is considered innocent until proven guilty for other allegations, the presumption under Stand Your Ground laws is that the shooter was justified in using lethal force outside the home. A legal obligation to retreat, the type of threat presented, and other factors are dictated in individual state laws to help further define that reasonableness.

If the case goes to court, that presumption of reasonableness means the shooter goes free if a majority of evidence shows that he or she acted in self-defense. The case may also be dropped at an earlier stage in the legal process for the same reason.

Clumsy legalese is what keeps lawyers in business, so here's an example.

> Maynard Soloman, gal-damn detective, is gathering clues to a mass murder of circus clowns at a city park. The coulrophobic Bill Robber jumps out from behind a tree and demands Maynard hand over some particularly damning evidence. Seeing that his life is in mortal danger, Maynard draws his revolver and shoots the unarmed Bill to death. The district attorney charges Maynard with murder. But because that state has a version of its own Stand Your Ground law, and because most of the evidence suggests he acted in self-defense at the moment of the shooting, Maynard is found not guilty.

Stand Your Ground laws bring out intense debate about firearm policies. One of the chief criticisms is that they allow people with bad intentions to kill others without consequence. Supporters say they allow reasonable people to defend themselves without complication.

Regardless of your own opinion, Stand Your Ground laws are worthwhile to research if a plot point depends on legal consequences. Look up state statutes about self-defense to help. Just don't expect them to be labeled explicitly as Stand Your Ground.

STOP THE THREAT: FIREARMS AND SELF-DEFENSE IN GENERAL

When it comes to firearms and self-defense, one overarching principle hovers above all others. Everyone from law enforcement to the military considers it. It's this: "Stop the threat."

It's not "Shoot to kill." That invokes a sort of bloodthirstiness.

It's not "Defend life and limb." That's morally ambiguous.

It's just "Stop the threat." Someone or something is attempting to cause injury. Use the firearm to prevent that from happening. Listen for this phrase when law enforcement and military members are interviewed about violent encounters. It's interesting how often it's used.

With that in mind, one shot too many—after the threat has been stopped—can cross the line from defense into murder. That's because self-defense laws are written to address disparity of force.

That means it's considered self-defense so long as the attacker could overcome the individual with the firearm, even if the attacker is unarmed. One person versus five, for example. A small female attacked by a large male. A person in a wheelchair up against a more mobile attacker.

So long as that disparity exists and the threat is imminent, a self-defense situation is at hand. But the moment the disparity no longer exists, the person with the firearm must not pull the trigger again. If so, the situation changes from self-defense to murder.

Writers would do well to keep this in mind when crafting scenes involving self-defense and firearms. Immobilizing an attacker so you're no longer in danger is one thing. Continuing to fire until the attacker is dead is another.

Time for a real-world example.

On Thanksgiving Day 2012, two unarmed teenagers smashed a window and entered the home of Byron David Smith, 64, in Little Falls, Minnesota. Fearing for his life, Smith, home by himself, shot and killed both teenagers. Audio equipment Smith had set up in light of other break-ins recorded the incident.

Smith shot the teens as they descended a staircase toward him. He was well within the bounds of Minnesota law to do so, which allows for lethal force in the home when a life is threatened or a felony is being committed.

The situation took a major turn when Smith continued firing after the injured teens stopped posing a threat to him.

From an April 26, 2013, article in the *Star Tribune*:

> [Prosecutors] said he also had an audiotape of the killings that recorded Smith telling [the male teenager] "You're dead" in the seconds after he was shot. He later taunted [the female teenager] after shooting her several times, calling her "bitch" as he fired a shot beneath her chin and into her cranium, prosecutors said.

After stopping the threat from the teens, Smith should have dropped everything and dialed 911. He didn't. His actions crossed the line from self-defense into murder. In April 2014, Smith was found guilty of several murder charges and sentenced to life in prison.

That the teens were unarmed and that Smith's home had a history of break-ins both likely played upon the jury's conscience. Neither were the deciding factors, though. After hearing the verdict, Morrison County Sheriff Michel Wetzel summed why.

"This isn't a case about whether you have the right to protect yourself in your home. You very clearly do," Wetzel said in an April 30, 2014, *Star Tribune* article. "Rather, this was a case about where the limits are, before and after a threat to you or your home occurs."

This is why fiction with an eye to the real world should keep the "Stop the threat" principle in mind at all times. Laws vary by state, but this principle is a constant theme. Once the threat is gone, put the gun down. That goes for knives, fists, feet, and any other method of inflicting injury.

For a thorough look at the law and self-defense, I highly recommend the books by Massad Ayoob published by *Gun Digest*.

WARNING SHOTS: NOT A GOOD IDEA

Warning shots are staples of thrillers and crime fiction. As if brandishing a firearm wasn't enough, proving a character is willing to use it ups the ante. Protagonists do this most often. Maybe that's because antagonists just shoot other characters outright, but that's beside the point.

Consider the "Stop the threat" principle from the previous section. The law doesn't look kindly on using a firearm in an encounter for any other purpose than to stop the threat. Does a warning shot fulfill that requirement?

As I've mentioned in other parts of this book, no. Shooting a firearm near others when it doesn't absolutely need to happen is not going to stop the threat. It's also the first shot in a presumably tense situation—a shot that could provoke others to shoot back.

CONCEALED CARRY LAWS

The previous sections segue nicely into concealed carry laws. These laws govern how a person in public may carry an obscured firearm secured to his or her body (aka being "strapped").

This is good information to know when outfitting a character, especially private detectives, with a concealed handgun.

With the addition of Illinois in July 2013, all fifty states—but not the District of Columbia—offer some form of a concealed carry policy, and each state outlines different requirements for legally carrying a concealed firearm in public.

Here are the three basic types of approved concealed carry, starting with the least restrictive.

- **CONSTITUTIONAL CARRY:** No concealed carry permit is required for anyone legally able to possess a firearm.
- **SHALL ISSUE:** If a person living in the state meets certain requirements, a permit will be issued.
- **MAY ISSUE:** If a person living in the state meets the requirements, a permit still might not be issued for a variety of reasons.

As of this writing, the states and territories fall into each category this way. These can change, so use this information as a starting point in your research.

- **CONSTITUTIONAL CARRY:** Alaska, Arizona, Arkansas, Kansas, Vermont, Wyoming
- **SHALL ISSUE:** Alabama, Colorado, Florida, Georgia, Idaho, Illinois, Indiana, Iowa, Kentucky, Louisiana, Maine, Michigan, Minnesota, Mississippi, Missouri, Montana, Nebraska, Nevada, New Hampshire, New Mexico, North Carolina, North Dakota, Ohio, Oklahoma, Oregon, Pennsylvania, Rhode Island, South Carolina, South Dakota, Tennessee, Texas, Utah, Virginia, Washington, West Virginia, Wisconsin
- **MAY ISSUE:** California, Connecticut, Delaware, Guam, Hawaii, Maryland, Massachusetts, New Jersey, New York, Puerto Rico, Virgin Islands
- **DOES NOT ISSUE CONCEALED CARRY PERMITS (NO CONCEALED CARRY ALLOWED):** American Samoa, District of Columbia, North Mariana Islands

As of this writing, there isn't a federal concealed carry law, but something does come close: Many states offer reciprocity agreements. That means they'll honor concealed carry permits issued in other states. These agreements change frequently. When writing about a character with a concealed carry permit traveling out of state, check the most current reciprocity agreement in the statutes. The website Handgunlaw.us is a good place to get started, especially the interactive reciprocity map at www.handgunlaw.us/LicMaps/ccwmap.php.

If a person is caught carrying a concealed firearm without a permit, the penalty could be a fine or jail time.

OPEN CARRY LAWS

Open carry is basically the opposite of concealed carry. Instead of keeping the firearm hidden, it's out in the open in full view. These laws apply to all firearms, not just handguns.

As with concealed carry laws, states determine how open carry is regulated. Legally speaking, it's generally easier for a character to openly carry a firearm than a concealed one.

Here's the catch: Even if open carry is allowed, that doesn't mean the character won't look out of place. Many real-world news stories chronicle arrests of open carriers on the grounds of disorderly conduct. The stories usually involve someone spotting a guy with a gun in a public area and calling the police.

The rule of thumb: If people aren't conditioned to seeing others walk around with guns in the public setting you are presenting (such as hunting areas, rural districts, farms, shooting ranges, etc.), then it's not a good idea to stick a character openly carrying a firearm in it—even if it's legal.

MATCHING A FIREARM TO A CHARACTER

It's important to match a character to an appropriate firearm. Assigning something disproportionate to the character could turn off readers. Once the firearm is selected, accurate depictions become a lot easier to write.

Here's the step-by-step way to do it. Some writers start with the gun, but I think it's better to start with the character.

1. DETERMINE THE ROLE OF THE CHARACTER

What does the character do in the story? Is he or she a law enforcement officer? A spy? A lowlife at a bar? A bad guy knocking off a gas station?

The role will determine the context of everything else. Start there. For example, you wouldn't give an M16, a machine gun available exclusively to the U.S. military, to a Girl Scout on a squirrel hunt.

2. IDENTIFY THE PHYSICAL ATTRIBUTES OF THE CHARACTER

If a character can't wield the firearm in the first place, there's little chance he will use it. That's why it's important to identify the physical attributes of the character.

There are infinite variables, but here are the three biggies.

Hand size is an important part of matching a character to a firearm. A hand too small for a firearm, as in this example, will have trouble pulling the trigger. (Photo courtesy of *Gun Digest.*)

1. How large are the character's hands? Can they easily grip the firearm?
2. What is the age of the character?
3. Is the character feeble or fit?

Maynard Soloman, for example, is somewhere north of eighty years old, is out of shape from all that RV driving and gas station food, has arthritis in every joint in his body, can't stand for longer than five minutes at a time, can't feel anything below the belt, can't hear out of his left ear, and suffers from terrible vision.

"But other than that, I'm perfectly capable of shooting a gun," Maynard says. "I don't even need the earplugs. Can't hear anything anyway."

Consider all of these things when assessing your character's ability to handle a firearm.

3. ASSIGN A FIREARM TYPE

From Grandma to the Green Berets, you can find a firearm to suit anyone. In this step, break down the firearm types into rifles, shotguns, pistols, and revolvers. Apply all you know about a character's attributes, role, age, and location before selecting a general firearm type.

For example, police officers are likely fit enough to carry even the larger rifles and shotguns, but due to their occupation, they will most likely carry a semi-automatic pistol as their weapon of choice.

An assassin might have a sniper rifle, complete with a suppressor. If the target will be up close, he or she may opt for the kind of sidearm that hides in a holster on the body, so think smaller, slimmer pistols.

Maynard is feeble and has smaller hands, so a simple compact revolver might be up his alley. Then again, he might keep a shotgun handy in his RV for emergencies.

4. CHOOSE A CALIBER

It's tempting to outfit a character with the biggest, baddest firearm possible. That little devil on your shoulder is Hollywood whispering into your writerly subconscious. As the Ten Golden Tips for Writing Weapons pointed out, Tinsel Town usually gets guns wrong.

Hits are all that matter in a gunfight, real or fictional. So when assigning a firearm or caliber to your characters, match it with respect to their physical attributes.

Physically small or frail characters will do best with lighter calibers (i.e., those with less firepower).

Medium-build characters might choose those lighter calibers or the midpower ones. In exceptional cases, high-powered calibers could also be assigned.

Large or strong characters can use anything. As the writer, you may want to take advantage of their brawny characteristics to assign a high-powered caliber.

As far as the specific calibers go, use this cheat sheet arranged from smallest to largest. Many calibers and cartridge configurations are out there, but the following information offers a solid base to work from when writing.

- **PISTOL AND REVOLVER CALIBERS, LEAST TO MOST POWERFUL:** .22, .25, .32, .38, 9mm, .40, 10mm, .357, .45, .44, .50
- **RIFLE CALIBERS, LEAST TO MOST POWERFUL:** .17, .22, .223, .243, .270, .300, .308, .30-06, 7mm, .338, .50
- **SHOTGUN GAUGES, LEAST TO MOST POWERFUL:** .410 (this is actually written as a caliber, not a gauge), 20, 16 (uncommon), 12, 10 (uncommon)

5. SELECT THE ACTUAL FIREARM

With the type and caliber selected, browse the firearm suggestions in this guide for possibilities. If you are still unsure, research other resources that might help you.

Do a little digging into a firearm's specifications, history, year of introduction, and background, including any applicable laws. Is it likely the character would have access to that particular model?

6. GET THE SPECS

Finally, make a note of the firearm's finer details. What kind of action does it use? How many rounds can it hold?

PUTTING THE STEPS TOGETHER

Going through the steps above will yield the right gun—or at least point you away from an unrealistic option. Here are my examples.

NAME: Maynard Soloman, gal-damn detective

1. **CHARACTER'S ROLE:** exceptionally arrogant and equally ignorant private investigator living in a dilapidated RV
2. **PHYSICAL ATTRIBUTES:** frail octogenarian of medium build—except for his large gut
3. **FIREARM TYPE:** revolver
4. **REVOLVER CALIBER:** Maynard is in rough shape, so the light firepower of a .22 seems like a good match.

5. **THE GUN:** A search of .22 revolvers drew my attention to the Charter Arms Target Pathfinder. Maynard is no Annie Oakley, and the description says this is a gun for novice shooters.

6. **THE SPECS:** This revolver weighs 20 ounces and holds six rounds. That's good to know, because Maynard is an awful shot. And he's just been hired to track down prescription painkillers reported as "stolen."

NAME: Bill Robber

1. **CHARACTER'S ROLE:** Bill runs a cartel that smuggles illegal pogs into the United States. Pogs ceased being popular in the 1990s, but Bill isn't the brightest bulb. Due to his paranoia, Bill needs to be ready to crank out a lot of ammunition in a short amount of time.

2. **PHYSICAL ATTRIBUTES:** Bill is average on all physical fronts, although his brainpower is limited.

3. **FIREARM TYPE:** submachine gun

4. **SUBMACHINE GUN CALIBER:** Bill says he could handle a .44.

5. **THE GUN:** Some research reveals that the .44 isn't a caliber commonly offered in submachine guns. The 9mm is popular, so let's switch things up and go with that. The Heckler & Koch UMP is offered in 9mm, so Bill will use that one.

6. **THE SPECS:** The fully automatic Heckler & Koch UMP packs thirty rounds of 9mm ammunition. Those rounds will go quickly, so Bill will need to do a lot of reloading.

NAME: Penny Flyswatter

1. **CHARACTER'S ROLE:** Penny is a SWAT team officer about to storm an illegal pog-smuggling operation.

2. **PHYSICAL ATTRIBUTES:** Penny is in top physical condition and has extensive firearms training. No firearm will be a problem for her.

3. **FIREARM TYPE:** If Penny has to storm a house and shoot, it'll be in close quarters. Shotguns are devastating at that range. She'll use one of those.

4. **SHOTGUN GAUGE:** A 12-gauge packs a nice punch, so let's go with that.

5. **THE GUN:** A check of firearms listings shows that the Benelli M4 Tactical looks promising. However, it was introduced in 2006, and Penny's story is set in 2005. So the Benelli M2 Tactical, a similar model introduced in 2005, makes a better fit.

6. **THE SPECS:** The Benelli M2 holds five rounds. That's not a lot, but it'll do for the story. Based on research, SWAT officers often use extended magazines for their shotguns, allowing additional rounds to be held inside the firearm. That can be

written in, if necessary, but shouldn't become an issue unless more than five rounds are specifically fired in the story.

REMEMBER THE ESCAPE ROUTE

If a character's firearm simply can't be determined, write around the weapon. Go generic.

Instead of assigning that six-shooter Charter Arms Target Pathfinder to Maynard, he might just use a generic "revolver" instead. It's not as fun to go generic, but it's passable. The depictions need to be equally generic and consistent. It's best to back up even mundane depictions with research.

HOW TO KILL A CHARACTER WITH A FIREARM

Here's the down-and-dirty version of this section: Shoot the character in the head or heart, then kick back and call it a day.

For anything beyond a quick and convenient kill, answer these questions in order.

1. HOW FAR AWAY IS THE CHARACTER?

First, determine the range of the character being shot. There's no need to break out the yardstick; ranges can be broken down into general categories. There are a few ways to do this, but I like the approach thirty-year law enforcement veteran Scott Wagner takes in his book *Gun Digest Book of Survival Guns*. The designations here are inspired by that work and the following quoted material from the book.

- **EXTREME RANGE:** about 300 to 2,000 yards. "While our modern military snipers are getting kills out to 2,000 yards [6,000 feet] or so, this is performance reserved for a few highly trained and exceptional individuals with very specialized rifles," Wagner writes.
- **LONG RANGE:** 300 yards maximum. "For the average shooter or law enforcement officer, 'long range' is anything beyond 100 yards," according to Wagner.
- **MID-RANGE:** Wagner says, "Anything from 100 yards down to about 25 yards."
- **CLOSE RANGE:** This category includes anything 25 yards down to "eye-gouging distance," according to Wagner.

2. IS THE FIREARM USED BY THE SHOOTER EFFECTIVE AT THAT RANGE?

With range determined, next figure out if the firearm is effective at that distance. Writers are free to use longer-range firearms for shorter distances but not vice versa.

- **EXTREME-RANGE FIREARMS:** rifles specifically designed for extreme distances (.338 and .50 calibers)

- **LONG-RANGE FIREARMS:** intermediate to large caliber rifles (.243, .270, .30, .30-06, .30-30, .300, .308, 7mm)
- **MID-RANGE FIREARMS:** small to intermediate caliber rifles (.17, .22, .22-250, .223, .243, .270); shotguns firing slugs (out to 100 yards); shotguns firing BBs (out to 50 yards); submachine guns; machine guns
- **CLOSE-RANGE FIREARMS:** pistols, revolvers, shotguns, submachine guns

3. COULD A SHOT HIT THE TARGET IN A VITAL AREA?

If a character is in range of the shooter's firearm, the next element to assess is the possibility of a lethal shot.

There are many variables to this equation, but a hit in one or more of these areas will most likely result in death:

- head
- face
- neck
- chest (heart, lung)
- upper back (lung)
- lower middle back (kidneys)
- upper thigh (femoral artery)

Areas that would most likely inflict severe damage, but perhaps not death, include:

- spine
- inner arm (brachial artery)
- abdomen (the "guts")
- groin
- ribs (splinters of bone penetrating heart or lungs)

Areas that would wreck someone's day but may not be considered a mortal wound:

- face (without piercing brain or neck)
- hands
- wrists
- knees
- feet
- ankles
- outer arms

Again, these are rules of thumb. Variables can change a lethal hit into a mere injury or vice versa.

4. HOW LIKELY IS THE SHOOTER TO HIT THE CHARACTER?

If all the conditions are met up to this point, it's time to assess whether a hit is likely at all. Factors that can cause a miss include the following:

- The shooter and/or the target character are in motion.
- The shooter lacks firearms experience.
- An obstacle comes between the shooter and the character.
- The shooter is firing in a confusing or chaotic setting.
- The shooter is firing in low-light settings.
- The shooter is injured or impaired.
- The firearm misfires or jams.

If none of those factors apply, or are negated by some other variable, chances are good that a well-placed shot with a firearm will kill a character.

A QUICK NOTE ABOUT MOVING TARGETS

A shooter must "lead" a target that's in motion. That means firing ahead of the moving target. The faster the target, the more lead must be granted. This can vary from a few feet to several yards.

This is tricky to do and requires some shooting experience. Characters inexperienced with firearms would have a tough time hitting a moving target at any range.

EXAMPLE SCENARIOS

Would a kill with a firearm be likely in the following scenarios?

Scenario 1: The Getaway Car

> Barreling down the crowded freeway, gal-damn detective Maynard Soloman steered his RV parallel to Bill Robber's convertible. He rolled down the window and aimed a revolver at Bill's head only a few feet away.
> "Eat lead, ya mug," Maynard said and pulled the trigger.

Would Maynard have made a kill shot? Maybe.

Bill was in range of Maynard's revolver, but both of them were in motion. This makes landing a kill difficult. It's hard enough to be accurate with a handgun standing still. However, there's enough wiggle room for creative license to plant the kill shot successfully (or not). Bullets travel faster than cars.

Scenario 2: The Eagle's Nest

Maynard climbed up the tall bell tower of the church, shotgun in hand. With a pair of binoculars, he spotted Bill Robber on the far side of a long parking lot several blocks away. Maynard lined up the shotgun's sights and pulled the trigger, sending BBs rushing toward Bill.

Is this a kill shot? No.

Bill is a long way from Maynard. That range sounds better suited for a sniper rifle, not a shotgun.

Scenario 3: The Midnight Intruder

Maynard woke to the sound of someone kicking down the side door of his RV. In the light of the full moon, he could see the glow of Bill Robber standing in the filthy kitchenette.

Maynard quickly popped a magazine into his bedside pistol and took aim at Bill's chest. His trembling finger found the trigger just as Bill stepped into the bedroom.

Did Maynard get Bill this time? Probably.

Maynard's pistol is the right choice for an up-close-and-personal encounter. But that "trembling finger" and the nighttime conditions might have resulted in a miss.

In this case, it's up to the author to determine how the scene plays out.

A QUICK NOTE ABOUT DEATH

As mentioned in other sections of this guide, not everyone shot in the vitals dies immediately. Just as chickens with their heads lopped off still run around (that's not a myth, by the way; I helped butcher chickens as a kid), humans can stay in motion for a short time after a lethal hit.

In The Midnight Intruder scenario, this could mean Maynard makes a lethal shot but still winds up with injuries if Bill can cover the short distance between them before he dies.

[PART TWO]
KNIVES

KNIFE SAFETY

Like firearms, knives have their own safety guidelines for proper use. Characters familiar with knives would understand these basic principles:

- Knives are a little like guns in that they shouldn't be directed at people and things that shouldn't be cut. So when using a knife, cut away from your body—or anyone else's body for that matter—because if the knife suddenly jerks forward, you don't want it to cause an injury.
- Running with scissors is a bad idea, and the same goes for knives. Dramatic foot chases involving knives are just begging for an accident. Stick those knives back in their sheaths.
- Avoid using the knife for utility purposes inside your own "Triangle of Death." Picture the triangular space between your inner thighs and groin when your legs are spread apart—that's the Triangle of Death. A cut to these areas could cause severe blood loss or death in a matter of minutes. This concern is most common when sitting hunched over and using the knife to cut rope, whittle, etc.
- A dull knife is more dangerous than a sharp one. Duller blades slip easier when attempting to cut through something. And a knife that slips is going to cut something you didn't intend to cut—never a good thing.
- Not every knife that folds works the same way. It's a good idea to find out exactly how it works before fumbling around with one. That's how people lose fingers.
- If a knife falls, don't try to catch it. Let it hit the ground. The same goes for a knife in flight—unless you're Jack Burton. On that note, *Big Trouble in Little China* is required viewing for learning how *not* to depict knives and firearms. Kurt Russell's character commits almost every sin this guide tries to dispel, although that may have been intentional.
- Passing a knife with an exposed blade (such as a butcher knife or an open folding knife) to someone else is always tricky. Should you hand it over handle first or blade first? Handle first is the best method, but that doesn't mean you should grip the blade and risk an injury. Turn the knife over so the spine (the thin, unsharpened edge on top of the blade) rests between your thumb and index finger, then grip the handle. Extend the handle to the other person to pass off the knife. Of course, throwing the knife to the other person is another option, but it's not polite.

In many cases in fiction, these guidelines will have to be broken, but it's still a good idea to keep them in mind.

KNIVES 101

Unlike firearms, it's easier to get away with writing knives generically. Just writing "knife" and describing its function can be enough in thrillers and crime fiction. However, in reality knives can be just as nuanced as guns. There's a reason so many kinds of knives exist. Different designs perform better for certain tasks. A firm understanding of these differences will add a stroke of realism to your stories.

And don't forget about striking characters with specialized knobs or studs on the pommel (the bottom of the knife's handle). These studs are sometimes called "skull crushers" for a good reason.

SWITCHBLADES

Note: Be sure to read about assisted opening knives later in this section before writing a switchblade into a story.

When most people think of a switchblade, they imagine the long, thin profile of an Italian stiletto. That doesn't necessarily mean the knife comes from Italy. It's just the name of a style of switchblade, made by various manufacturers since the early 1900s. The Italian stiletto is the knife depicted most often in thrillers and crime fiction.

For the purposes of this guide, assume all switchblades refer to Italian stilettos. There are, however, many styles of switchblades in the real world.

Switchblades are the *"assault weapons"* of the blade world. Because *switchblade* is used to both label a large category of restricted knives and to describe a particular mechanical design, it can lead to some confusion about what a switchblade actually is. Here's the federal definition:

- A switchblade opens a blade concealed inside the handle of the knife.
- The concealed blade is *biased to come out of the handle* (that's an important distinction). In other words, the blade wants to come out of the handle. Springs are usually used to create the force for this bias.
- A *button or switch on the handle of the knife* is pressed to make the blade come out of the handle. The blade can come out the front or side of the handle. Moving the blade back inside the handle recharges the force in the springs.

If a knife doesn't meet those criteria, it's not a switchblade, regardless of how it's labeled. Read more in the section on knife laws.

Fiction's love affair with switchblades is left over from a cultural paranoia of the mid-twentieth century that permeated fiction and film. To understand why, rewind to the 1950s. Movies like *Rebel Without a Cause* and *The Wild One* highlighted the use of switchblades by "problem youth" and biker gangs.

Whether there actually was a problem with these groups wielding knives is up for debate. As *BLADE Magazine* editor Steve Shackleford told me in an interview, movies sensationalized the use of switchblades by gangs, and then moral-crusading politicians looking to make a name for themselves latched onto these movies. They identified switchblade restrictions as a way to crack down on gangs. A movie-watching public responded enthusiastically.

Joe Kertzman, *BLADE* magazine managing editor, said that larger social issues were also at play. "Politicians capitalized on the fears of white suburbanites about violent inner-city gangs. Because of joblessness and poverty in the inner city at the time, most of these gangs consisted of minority groups."

Popular culture reinforced these fears with its depiction of gangs using switchblades, a notable theme and major plot point in the Reginald Rose jury room drama *Twelve Angry Men*, later remade into an Academy Award-nominated film in 1957.

Kertzman stressed that growing urban poverty, not switchblades, fueled the violence committed by these gangs. Still, switchblade restrictions were seen as a way to calm fears in the white electorate.

These factors led to the passage of the 1958 Federal Switchblade Act. Combined with similar state laws that followed, the Act limited the switchblade industry to a handful of states and municipalities that permit the knives. You can find more information on the subject in the section on knife laws.

None of this means writers can't play up switchblades in their stories. However, there's nothing exceptionally deadly about them compared to other knife types. Fixed blade knives will always open faster than switchblades because they're never closed. Folding knives are just as concealable. Assisted opening knives offer identical one-handed use.

It's important to note that most switchblades still in circulation are antiques. If a present-day character buys a switchblade, it's probably as old or older than he or she is. The new switchblades are custom jobs manufactured in the states that allow them. A character with dubious intentions could probably obtain one no matter the setting.

New, high-quality switchblades are still manufactured for law enforcement and military (and available to civilians in switchblade-friendly states). When writing in these modern switchblades, call them *automatic knives*. Write them as such to stand out from the herd, although *switchblade* is still appropriate.

Automatic knives are the modern equivalent of switchblades. They're designed for heavy-duty purposes and are therefore not Italian stilettos. They stab, cut, and slice using the latest materials and technology. Automatics are ideal fighting knives for thrillers and crime fiction and share many of the characteristics outlined in the section on assisted openers. Automatic knives can open from the side, like the traditional switchblade, or from the front. When they open and close from the front, they are called "out the front" (OTF) knives.

Advantages

- The stigma of crime surrounding switchblades makes their mere presence intimidating. In fiction, a well-timed *pop-click* sound from a switchblade opening means it's time to get down to business.
- They're easy to conceal and transport.
- A switchblade can be opened and operated with only one hand. It may require two hands to close it, though.
- A switchblade's design makes it ideal for stabbing, when the force is concentrated on the tip of the blade.

Disadvantages

- Switchblades are red flags for criminal activity. Characters who don't want to stand out probably wouldn't carry one.
- Switchblades are not as tough as they look. They lack a long tang, which is an extension of the blade that runs inside the handle to offset pressure during use. Thus, they can't handle as much pressure as other knives. Think of switchblades like drill bits. If a lot of force is concentrated anywhere but the tip, there's a chance the blade could snap off of the knife.
- Like most folding knives, switchblades use a lock, which is a mechanism that holds the blade open. It's located at the joint of the blade and handle. The older a lock is, the more likely it will unintentionally release the blade. This is especially true if pressure is put on the blade anywhere but at the tip. A failing lock could close the blade back onto the hand of the person using it. Because a lot of antique switchblades are in circulation, a character might consider this when heading to a fight.
- Switchblades are not the most reliable. Springs wear out and can be difficult to replace. Old switchblades have old springs, and their blades don't always open completely. The character using it would have to manually open the blade the rest of the way. That's precious time wasted during a fight.

- Because of their age, those ubiquitous antique switchblades don't usually come with pocket clips. A pocket clip is a metal clamp on the handle of the knife. It hooks onto the top of a pocket. This makes the knife easier to carry and to draw from the pocket. Since they lack pocket clips, switchblades spend a lot of time at the bottom of pockets. That means lint, dirt, and other grime can gum things up and affect how fast the blade opens. It also means a character would have to dig around in her pocket to access the knife—not ideal if she's about to enter a fight.
- Italian stilettos are not exactly ergonomic. No matter the character, it's unlikely he will have a rock-solid grip on one. That's not good if the character is in a fight.
- Switchblades and their parts are harder to obtain than other knives. This has to do with their legal restrictions.
- For scenarios involving stealth, the *pop-click* of a switchblade opening could give away a character's position.
- Compared to other knife types, switchblades have a steeper learning curve. They're better for characters who have experience with knives.
- Even the fastest switchblade cannot be ready for a fight as fast as a fixed blade knife can. Fixed blade knives, covered in another section, don't contain moving parts.
- The market for switchblades is ripe for scams. This is another hurdle a character seeking a switchblade must overcome. Sellers may charge a buyer a premium for a switchblade when what they're actually selling is a perfectly legal assisted opening knife. Those are covered in the next section.

Inaccurate Example

"Is it my imagination, or is someone hiding behind that trash can?" Maynard Soloman said to himself. He stared at the can a few feet away and listened.

Crouched behind the large receptacle, Bill Robber popped open his switchblade and waited for Maynard to continue walking.

"I must be hearing things again," Maynard said and turned away. "Either that or I'm talking out loud instead of thinking in my head. Gotta stop doing that."

Bill sprang into action as soon as Maynard started walking. He slit the detective's throat from behind and watched him die on the sidewalk. To cover his tracks, Bill cut up Maynard's body and dumped the pieces into the trash can.

"Colonel Sanders himself couldn't put a better bucket of meat together," Bill said as he slipped away.

Accurate Example

"Is it my imagination, or is someone hiding behind that trash can?" Maynard Solo-man said to himself. He stared at the can a few feet away and listened.

Crouched behind the large receptacle, Bill Robber gripped his fixed blade hunting knife and waited for Maynard to continue walking.

"I must be hearing things again," Maynard said and turned away. "Either that or I'm talking out loud instead of thinking in my head. Gotta stop doing that."

Bill sprang into action as soon as Maynard started walking. He slit the detective's throat from behind and watched him die on the sidewalk. To add insult to injury, Bill cut up Maynard's body and dumped the pieces into the trash can.

"Colonel Sanders himself couldn't put a better bucket of meat together," Bill said as he slipped away.

What Went Wrong?

Switchblades are deceiving when it comes to stealth. On the one hand, they can easily slip into a pocket. On the other, they make a distinctive noise when opened. Bill must've forgotten that in the inaccurate example. He opened the switchblade while Maynard was staring at the trash can. The sound should've given him away.

After he killed Maynard, Bill needed more than a switchblade to dismember Maynard's body. Switchblades aren't cut out for hard use. They're better for stabbing or light slicing (slitting Maynard's throat was an ideal application, by the way, that was on target in the inaccurate version). The ruggedness of a fixed blade knife is the better call. Switching to that type of knife also kept Bill quieter behind the trash can. No moving parts means no noise.

Remember to keep track of blood loss and to consider how it plays into the story. Maynard's injured throat would've spilled a ton of blood onto the sidewalk. Why would Bill bother hiding the body in the trash can at that point? This is remedied in the accurate version as a way to further insult Maynard's demise.

Left uncorrected, though, is how messy Bill must be after exiting the scene. He's going to be bloody, both from slitting Maynard's throat and working with the detective's body. This is a blind spot in many stories featuring knife violence. Does a bloody Bill impact the plot later? Would his condition raise suspicions with other characters?

One final note: This scene could've worked with the switchblade. Bill could've had the switchblade open in the first place, slit Maynard's throat, and ran away. Either way, keep the action consistent with the knife type.

ASSISTED OPENING KNIVES

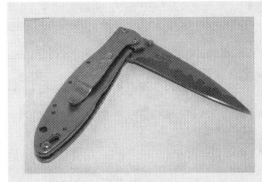

The Kershaw Leek is one of my favorite assisted opening knives. Instead of a switchblade, write an assisted opener instead. As this image shows, the blade doesn't open automatically. It must be swung open manually more than halfway before an assisting mechanism takes over. That all happens very fast. For practical writing purposes, it functions like a switchblade, but the writer looks more knowledgeable. (Author's photo.)

Popular assisted opening knives: Benchmade Barrage, Columbia River Knife & Tool M4, Gerber F.A.S.T., Kershaw Leek, SOG Aegis

Not familiar with assisted opening knives? Here's a tip. Replace the word *switchblade* with *assisted opening knife* or *assisted opener* in a story. The two types function so similarly that they're identical for the practical purposes of writing. The difference is assisted openers are popular and switchblades are not (due to legal restrictions), although that's not obvious to someone outside knife enthusiasm.

An assisted opening knife functions almost exactly like a switchblade. To the eye, it might appear they're identical, since each opens with that classic *pop-click*. However, there are two important differences.

First, when the blade is inside the handle of an assisted opener, it's *biased to stay inside the handle*. Only after opening the blade manually about halfway does a mechanism "assist" it the rest of the way.

Second, there is *no button or switch on the handle* that is pressed to open the knife. Instead the operator moves a piece of a blade itself, usually a stud, disc, hole, or notch. This swings the blade out from the handle until it becomes biased to open. At that point, springs or torsion bars "assist" the opening of the blade. Most assisted openers open from the side of the handle, not the front.

That's different from the federal definition of a switchblade. Those knives use blades always biased to open, and they feature a release button or switch on the handle. Because of these two key differences, assisted opening knives are legal in most of the United States. That's made this type of knife incredibly popular since it was introduced in the mid-1990s.

Characters in settings prior to 1996 would not have encountered an assisted opening knife. As a matter of fact, the best, earliest year to assign a character an assisted opener is 1998.

Because of their one-handed operation and legal status, assisted opening knives are popular with consumers. A person is much more likely to possess an assisted opening knife than a switchblade or automatic knife.

Advantages

- Assisted openers offer all the advantages of a switchblade, plus some big leaps forward in technology, with none of the legal drawbacks.
- They're easy to conceal and transport.
- Because of their legality, assisted openers are easier to purchase and more ubiquitous than switchblades.
- One-handed operation makes assisted openers easy and quick to use. Blades open as fast or faster than switchblades. Advances in design and technology make closing the blade with one hand possible.
- For characters looking to intimidate, assisted opening knives benefit from the stigma of switchblades. The *pop-click* of an assisted opener sounds and looks just like a switchblade.
- The mechanism that holds the assisted opener's blade open, called a *lock*, is more reliable than the locks on switchblades. Some even become more secure as they age. Since they're legal, manufacturers can pursue better lock design and technology. This means the blade isn't as likely to close unintentionally onto the character's hand. It can still happen, though.
- Unlike switchblades, most assisted openers come with a pocket clip. This makes them easier to pull from a pocket than switchblades, which don't usually have clips. Clips also cut down on lint and grime from the pocket gumming things up, making assisted openers even more reliable.
- Most assisted opening blades are designed to take pressure on the tip as well as along the edge. They're suitable for stabbing, cutting, and slicing. These capabilities put them a step ahead of the classic Italian stiletto, which is better suited to stabbing and light slicing propositions.

Disadvantages

- Like switchblades, assisted opening knives lack a long tang. which means the blades are susceptible to snapping off. However, the better locks and better overall design of assisted openers make this less likely to happen.

- The locks sometimes fail (allowing the blade to close on the hand of the operator), so characters who need to perform intense cutting tasks would be better off using a fixed blade knife.
- The fastest assisted opening knife will never be faster than a fixed blade knife. A fixed blade knife doesn't need to unfold.
- Springs and torsion bars wear out over time, weakening the "assisted" component of these knives. Unlike switchblades, though, manufacturers have made it easier to access and replace these parts.
- For scenarios involving stealth, the *pop-click* that an assisted knife makes when opening could give the character away.

Inaccurate Example

"You musta got that nice tan when you went to the Cayman Islands to make that special bank deposit," said Maynard Soloman to Bill Robber. The tanned Bill sat tied to a chair in the detective's RV. "Or is that just the bullshit leaking through your skin?"

"I don't know what you're talking about. I never went to the Caymans, and I'm not full of BS," Bill said as he struggled against the restraints. "I've been here in New York City the entire time."

"Fine, let's talk about a different trip then," Maynard said. He reached into his pocket and pulled out an Italian stiletto. "Ever been to Italy? I just bought this brand-new switchblade from the shop down the street. I could bring Italy to you. Into you."

"Okay, I admit it. I went to the Caymans," Bill said. "I'll give you all the account numbers you need."

Accurate Example

"You musta got that nice tan when you went to the Cayman Islands to make that special bank deposit," said Maynard Soloman to Bill Robber. The tanned Bill sat tied to a chair in the detective's RV. "Or is that just the bullshit leaking through your skin?"

"I don't know what you're talking about. I never went to the Caymans, and I'm not full of BS," Bill said as he struggled against the restraints. "I've been here in New York City the entire time."

"Fine, let's talk about a different trip then," Maynard said. He reached into his pocket and pulled out an Italian stiletto. "Ever been to Italy? I just bought this brand-new switchblade from the shop down the street. I could bring Italy to you. Into you."

Bill blinked twice at the tip of the Italian stiletto, then once more for good measure.

"Uh, Maynard, normally when people threaten me, they do it with a knife," Bill said. "That's a woman's high-heeled shoe."

Maynard raised an unruly eyebrow and checked the stiletto in his hand. He rearranged the bags around his eyes and looked again.

"Those gal-damn punks pulled a fast one on me again," Maynard said and pitched the shoe at the wall. "This is the last time I try to buy a knife off the street at midnight. These eyes just aren't what they used to be."

Bill leaned his head back and laughed, popping the veins in his neck.

"Funny joke, isn't it, Bill? Laugh away, chuckle-face," Maynard said. He produced the new assisted opening knife he'd actually bought at the shop and opened it with a pop-click. "It'll make it easier to slit your throat."

"Okay, I admit it. I went to the Caymans," Bill said. "I'll give you all the account numbers you need."

What Went Wrong?

Here's a tip about big cities: They have the strictest knife restrictions. That can mean more legwork for writers setting a knife scene in a metropolis.

The Big Apple is exceptional in many ways, especially when it comes to knife laws. A little research reveals that New York City doesn't allow sale or possession of Italian stiletto switchblades, with some convoluted exceptions. Maynard wouldn't be able to buy one at a law-abiding "shop down the street," as he does in the inaccurate version. In fact, the assisted opener in the corrected version may not even be available, but I gave Maynard the benefit of the doubt. With his assisted opener in hand, he's free to intimidate Bill.

That intimidation proves effective when the assisted opening knife plays off the stigma of a switchblade's iconic *pop-click* sound. Bill folds and decides to tell Maynard about the money.

See how that worked? Assisted openers are the shortcut around switchblade laws. They offer all the benefits of switchblades with none of the legal hassle.

BUTTERFLY KNIVES

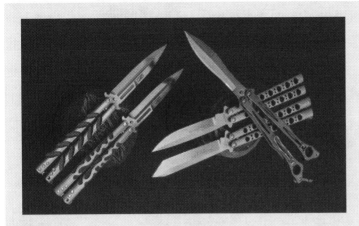

Butterfly knives are great for characters with a streak for intimidation. They offer more sizzle than steak in the world of knives. (Photo courtesy of *BLADE*.)

Popular butterfly knives: Benchmade 42 Bali-Song, Bear and Son Butterfly Knife, Bradley Kimura, Microtech Metalmark, Spyderco SpyderFly

A butterfly knife contains a blade positioned inside two handle halves. The handles are hinged into the blade. In the closed position, the handles conceal the blade. Swinging open one of the handle halves 360 degrees until it meets the other handle half exposes the blade. The two handles can attach to each other for a secure grip.

When you see a hoodlum in an action movie twirling a knife around in a flash of swirling metal just before a fight, he's probably using a butterfly knife—and probably slicing his hand to pieces, unless he's an experienced user.

Butterfly knives are also called balisong knives, or balisongs. It's sometimes written as Bali-Song, which is a registered trademark of the Benchmade company. But *butterfly knife* is probably the safest choice when choosing a term to use.

Butterfly knives can be opened with one hand, but it takes some practice because they don't have any automatic mechanisms. Beginners would likely use two hands. The operator manually controls all three moving parts (two handles and the blade).

Experienced users can open the blade quickly. Novices will still take their time. In other words, how fast the blade deploys doesn't depend on a button, as it does for a switchblade. It's dependent on user experience.

Advantages

- There is a definite cool factor to butterfly knives. Experienced butterfly knife users can execute impressive tricks with them. Working the swinging handles is an art form unto itself. Take a look at videos of butterfly knife pros on YouTube—it's pretty impressive to see them in action.
- Unlike other knives with folding or moving blades, butterfly knives aren't as prone to gumming up with lint and gunk because their design is looser.
- Like switchblades, butterfly knives are ideal for intimidation and, therefore, for less savory characters. Law enforcement and military characters wouldn't likely carry one, though, since they have access to modern automatic knives.
- Butterfly knives are concealable and portable. They are perfect for stealthy characters.
- In the hands of an experienced user, butterfly knives can quickly deploy their blades with one hand.
- Unlike switchblades, which are designed specifically for stabbing, butterfly knives can handle light cutting, slicing, *and* stabbing.
- The butterfly knife is the only type of knife that has two separate handles. This adds an extra measure of durability.

Disadvantages

- Butterfly knives are for looks. There's a reason butterfly knife demos are so popular on YouTube. They look cool, but they're not practical. Characters who need to actually use the knife will probably opt for anything but a butterfly. Show-offs are a different story.
- Many municipalities and states have restrictions regarding butterfly knives. Like switch-blades, they've been targeted because of a perception that they're used for violent and criminal activities. They're still easier to come by than switchblades, though. Check regulations against a character's setting.
- In restricted areas, butterfly knives are red flags for suspicious activity. Characters wanting to keep on the down low won't walk around with one.
- Overall, butterfly knives are difficult to operate. If a character hasn't put in the practice, there's a good chance she could injure herself. Novices will need two hands to open this knife because it could do as much damage to the operator as it could a target.
- Handles aren't designed for ergonomics. In most cases, they're straight and flat. A character could easily lose his grip in an intense situation.
- Two handles means more weight than other types of knives.
- Since they lack a long tang, butterfly knives aren't as tough as fixed blade knives. They aren't the best choice for hardcore cutting jobs.

The Writer's Guide to Weapons

- The handles can be latched together while the blade is open, but that doesn't mean they're secure. The latch can slip open during operation and turn the handles loose. Likewise the latch can come undone while the knife is in the closed position.
- The fastest butterfly knife is still slower than a fixed blade knife. That's because fixed blade knives never need to be unfolded before use.

Inaccurate Example

"How'd you know where to find me?" said Bill Robber from his computer desk in the motel room.

"I checked your status on social media, ya coffin-varnished crowbaiter," said Maynard Soloman.

"Yeah, but you should see the hashtag retweets I get," Bill said.

"You'll have plenty of time to tweet when you're a gal-damn jailbird, hashtag shit-for-brains. Let's go," Maynard said and put a hand on the revolver holstered to his hip.

"Hashtag come and get it," Bill said. He stood up and produced a butterfly knife, showing off his expertise with a few complicated twirls before taking a run at Maynard.

Maynard quickly drew his revolver and planted two well-placed shots into his assailant, dropping Bill to the floor.

Accurate Example

"How'd you know where to find me?" said Bill Robber from his computer desk in the motel room.

"I checked your status on social media, ya coffin-varnished crowbaiter," said Maynard Soloman.

"Yeah, but you should see the hashtag retweets I get," Bill said.

"You'll have plenty of time to tweet when you're a gal-damn jailbird, hashtag shit-for-brains. Let's go," Maynard said and put a hand on the revolver holstered to his hip.

"Hashtag come and get it," Bill said. He produced a butterfly knife and took a run at Maynard.

Maynard tried to draw his revolver, but after a brief struggle succumbed to Bill's vicious knife attack. Bill limped away from the room, knife in hand, his leg and hands bleeding from the melee.

What Went Wrong

Did this one throw you off a little? At first, it would seem Maynard's lethal revolver shots made sense. After all, a gun beats a knife, right?

That's not always the case. See the Tueller Drill from the Myths section of this guide in Part Three. A character with a knife at distances of 21 feet or less can overcome a gun-toting individual before that person draws the handgun and fires. Maynard and Bill are in a motel room. It's reasonable to assume they're within 21 feet of each other. Therefore, Bill is able to get to Maynard and kill him before the detective can draw his revolver.

As for the butterfly knife, it's tempting to write in a few tricks for the sake of intimidation. But Bill's tricks waste precious time that could allow Maynard a shot. It's always better to err on the side of practicality with knives, so the tricks don't appear in the corrected version.

Now, I mentioned earlier that butterfly knives are for show. That's true, but they're still knives, and they can still injure other characters. Just consider how they perform during the action. Butterfly knives don't offer much for ergonomics. Bill's grip likely slipped during the life-and-death struggle with Maynard, leading to self-inflicted injuries. While these injuries are common to any intense knife action, they're even more likely to occur when a butterfly is involved. That's why Bill's leg and hands bleed as he leaves the room. Creative license might say otherwise, especially if Bill held a far superior physical advantage over Maynard, but you should consider self-inflicted injuries the default position.

Also, even if Maynard did manage to shoot Bill, keep in mind people don't always succumb right away. Adrenaline might keep Bill alive long enough to stick the knife in Maynard.

One other thing. Although @MaynardSoloman is a real Twitter handle anyone reading this can tweet to, talking in hashtags is #obnoxious.

FIXED BLADE KNIVES

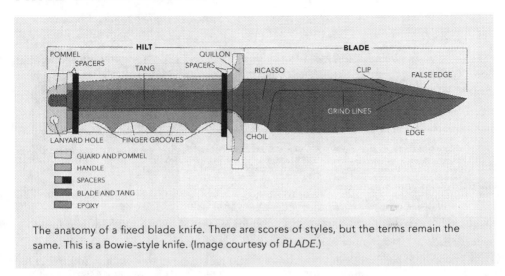

The anatomy of a fixed blade knife. There are scores of styles, but the terms remain the same. This is a Bowie-style knife. (Image courtesy of *BLADE*.)

Popular fixed blade knives: A.G. Russell Sting, Benchmade Nimravus, Bowie knives (a style manufactured by many companies and individuals since at least the early 1800s), Kukri (a boomerang blade style made by many companies), Fairbairn–Sykes fighting knife, Applegate-Fairbairn fighting knife, KA-BAR USMC knife, machetes

Fixed blade knives sport blades that do not move. They are in a fixed position, attached to a handle or handle material. This is a broad category that includes many styles, from smaller knives with 3-inch blades to machetes with blades a foot long or longer.

Fixed blades are the toughest, most durable knives around. They can do it all: stab, slice, cut, chop, hack, slash, rib-split, meat-gnarl, shoulder-shovel, and any other colorful knife verb. This is because most fixed blade knives have a greater measure of tang. The tang may run down half the length of the handle or the full length (that knife would be said to have a full tang). Some tangs perform double duty, acting as the handle itself.

Because the blades don't fold into the handle, fixed blade knives are usually transported in a sheath. The sheath may attach to a belt, or loop into a lanyard to be worn around the neck.

Fixed blades come in a variety of sizes and styles to match their purposes. This makes for some confusion with generic and branded names. Some knives are known by their brand name, such as *Buck knife*. Buck is a company that makes fixed blades, folding knives, and more. The generic term would be *hunting knife*. A *buck knife* also describes any generic hunting knife.

The same goes for *KA-BAR*. This term is sometimes used in place of a fixed blade, military-style knife. However, KA-BAR is a brand. If you are not using that specific brand of knife, use *tactical knife* instead, which refers to rugged knives designed for defense or combat.

Things are a little different with a Bowie knife, a term which can be used generically. Even though it's capitalized, *Bowie* refers to a person—that'd be Jim Bowie—and not a company. Bowie took part in the infamous Sandbar Fight of 1827, a Louisiana brawl so brutal it cemented the style of his knife to the Bowie name.

A Bowie knife is defined as a fixed blade knife sporting a large blade with a concave curve toward the tip. It looks as if part of the spine (the unsharpened edge at the top of the blade) has been carved out. Bowie knives are great choices for characters set in the early 1800s through the present day. There's some evidence that the style even may have been around since the late 1700s.

Adding yet another layer of confusion, a *boot knife* doesn't necessarily refer to a knife that slips into footwear. This is a generic term for a short, slender knife. It might fit into a boot sheath, but it might not.

Remember to pair fixed blade knives with sheaths. As the examples later in this section show, sheaths are important considerations whenever figuring in a fixed blade knife.

Kitchen, butcher, and steak knives are also types of fixed blades, as are machetes. They are covered in depth in their own sections.

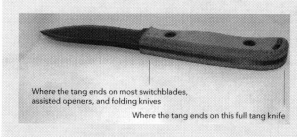

Where the tang ends on most switchblades, assisted openers, and folding knives

Where the tang ends on this full tang knife

Full-tang knives can take more of a beating. Switchblades have a small tang or lack one entirely, which makes them more likely to fail. They're just not intended for hard use. Better to write them for intimidation purposes. (Author's photo.)

Advantages

- Of any knife, fixed blades are the toughest. They can take a beating without fail. It all goes back to that tang. Fixed blades are the least likely to snap off. They're ideal for a character going into a fight or for intense knife work, such as butchering or prying.
- Unlike a switchblade or an assisted opener, a fixed blade knife is ready for use as is and will always be faster. No tabs to flip or buttons to press and no blade to unfold.

- No moving parts means no worrying about pocket grime affecting how fast the knife opens. Sheaths keep blades clean and protected.
- In stealth situations, characters wouldn't have to worry about giving away their positions when drawing the blade. There isn't a *pop-click* sound, as with switchblades and assisted opening knives. There may be some noise created by drawing a fixed blade from a sheath. Sheaths come in a variety of materials. Some are noisier than others, given they sometimes entail buttons and straps.
- Fixed blades come in a variety of styles, making them ideal for thriller and crime-fiction characters. There are knives for fighting, camping, hunting, clearing, skinning, gutting, pruning, and, of course, fruit sampling.
- Fixed blades are the least restricted of all the knives. A character would be able to find one just about anywhere. If they're restricted, it's usually because of blade length. Check real-world regulations against the setting. For example, a 6-inch blade might be illegal, but a 3-inch model would be okay.
- Handles tend to be more ergonomic than other knives, since they're not used for concealing the blade. Designs focus on materials and shapes that offer a secure grip. A character is less likely to lose hold of a fixed blade compared to other knives.
- Fixed blade knives can be operated with one hand.

Disadvantages

- Fixed blades lack the cool factor of switchblades and assisted opening knives. When they're glamorized in movies, they're usually big blades. Think of the one used in the Rambo movies. However, large knives may not be practical depending on the situation. Compared to smaller knives, they are harder to conceal, weigh more, and may be difficult to maneuver in a fight or surprise attack.
- Sheaths are bulky and are dead giveaways for characters trying to conceal fixed blades. Sheaths worn around the neck and tucked under the shirt have become popular in recent years. Still, a character would have to wear a lanyard. This is the number one reason to go with a different kind of knife, such as a folding or assisted opening knife.

Inaccurate Example

Sitting in his RV, Maynard Soloman recalled the instructions from his mystery client earlier in the day: Sneak into the hospital's VIP ward and cut a lock of hair from the patient in room 27. And just to be a jerk, steal a box of tissues to add a few thousand bucks to the patient's bill.

Maynard pulled out the new assisted opening knife he'd purchased for the job. Using a ceramic rod, he worked the knife's edge to a razor sharpness. Then he dropped the knife into his pocket, exited the RV, and headed across the parking lot to the hospital.

Accurate Example

Sitting in his RV, Maynard Soloman recalled the instructions from his mystery client earlier in the day: Sneak into the hospital's VIP ward and cut a lock of hair from the patient in room 27. And just to be a jerk, steal a box of tissues to add a few thousand bucks to the patient's bill.

Maynard examined the small dagger he'd brought along for the job. He fixed a sheath to his belt and slipped the knife inside, being sure to pull down his shirt to conceal it. He exited the RV and headed across the parking lot to the hospital.

What Went Wrong?

This one is tricky, since it involves anticipating what happens next in the hospital.

An assisted opening knife is going to make some noise when the blade is deployed. If silence is a must, which it might be given the VIP ward setting, this isn't the right choice. A fixed blade knife, like the dagger (be sure to research local laws, since daggers are sometimes restricted), would add the necessary stealth to the equation. Maynard tucked the dagger's sheath underneath his shirt. For those reasons, the fixed blade is the better choice.

Or is it? Accessing the sheath under Maynard's shirt and drawing the knife could still make noise—maybe even more than the assisted opener would. It all depends on what happens inside the hospital.

Although I gave Maynard the fixed blade knife, it was a judgment call, one that's tough to define. But it does drive home the point about anticipation. Will the knife selection work for scenes beyond the current one?

Still, there is one solid correction in the accurate example: Writers may use knife sharpening to build drama. As the section on sharpening shows, sometimes this makes sense and sometimes it doesn't. There's usually no reason to sharpen a brand-new knife. They come sharpened and ready to use right out of the box.

FOLDING KNIVES AND POCKETKNIVES

Popular folding and pocketknives: Buck 110, Benchmade Griptilian, Columbia River Knife & Tool Ripple, Spyderco Delica, Spyderco Endura

Pocketknives are sometimes called *folding knives*. Either term is correct for writing fiction. They refer to the same thing: knives with one or more blades that are manually moved in and out of the handle. There are no mechanisms to assist with the opening or closing of the knife.

There are a number of ways to open a pocketknife. The most common nowadays are a fingernail notch, thumb stud, or tab that flips the blade open (these are sometimes called *flippers*). Pocketknives in the early twentieth century used a number of innovative methods, such as metal rings.

Pocketknives and folding knives don't have to be small. They come in a variety of sizes. Some use a lock; others don't.

Like other knives, folders fall victim to the "Kleenex effect"—no matter the brand, people call all folders the same thing. The terms *Buck knife* and *buck knife* are sometimes used to mean any folding hunting knife. The iconic Buck 110, one of the most popular folding knives of all time, is the origin of these terms. Use *Buck knife* when referring to the 110 or a knife made by the Buck company, and *buck knife* when using the term generically for any hunting knife.

Pocketknives enjoy a rosy place not only in the history of American culture but also across the planet. They're easy to buy and usually legal to possess. Pop them into a story without worry.

Advantages

- These knives are easy to conceal and transport.
- Their simple designs make them great choices for characters unfamiliar with knives.
- Characters would have no problem buying a folding knife or pocketknife. What few restrictions exist address blade length.
- Some pocketknives come with multiple blades, a feature that increases versatility and reliability. If one blade goes dull, you can use another.
- These knives come in a variety of styles and designs to fit any number of needs. Some of the aforementioned flipper designs can open as fast as assisted openers.
- Most modern pocketknives come with pocket clips. This reduces the collection of lint and grime on the knife, which can affect how fast the blade opens. Clips also make the knives more accessible.

Disadvantages

- In general, folders and pocketknives lack the cool factor that fiction likes to employ. When selecting a knife to help flesh out a character (figuratively speaking, of course), folders will probably match an occupation, a hobby, or a task rather than establish the kind of street cred that assisted openers, switchblades, automatics, and butterfly knives can offer.
- Most folders and pocketknives must be opened with two hands. If they can be opened with one hand, doing so requires extra attention. This fact could slow down a character in a fight, reveal the character's concealed position, or prevent the knife's use entirely depending on the scene.
- Locks range from secure advanced designs to nothing at all. That means the blade can close on a character's hand during hard use. Consider how much of a beating the knife will take. It might help to identify a particular model to determine whether it uses a modern locking mechanism.

Inaccurate Example

Although it felt good to see him in dire straights, Maynard Soloman didn't want Bill Robber to die in an overturned car. Maynard couldn't collect the bounty on Bill's head if the fugitive was dead.

Maynard took the Buck knife out of his pocket, unfolded the blade, and aimed the tip at the driver's side window. The glass shattered, but the opening wasn't large enough to pull Bill out. Maynard pried at the mangled driver's side door with the knife until it opened. Breathing hard, Maynard managed to tug Bill's unconscious body away from the car.

"Thank goodness you're so gal-damn stupid, Bill," Maynard said. "If you'd worn a seat belt, your sorry carcass would still be in there."

Accurate Example

Although it felt good to see him in dire straights, Maynard Soloman didn't want Bill Robber to die in an overturned car. Maynard couldn't collect the bounty on Bill's head if the fugitive was dead.

Maynard unsheathed a Bowie knife and aimed the glass-breaking stud on its pommel at the driver's side window. The glass shattered, but the opening wasn't large enough to pull Bill out. Maynard pried at the mangled driver's side door with the knife until it opened. Breathing hard, Maynard managed to tug Bill's unconscious body away from the car.

"Thank goodness you're so gal-damn stupid, Bill," Maynard said. "If you'd worn a seat belt, your sorry carcass would still be in there."

What Went Wrong?

The inaccurate example actually gets an important detail right. Remember: The term *Buck knife* indicates either a knife made by the Buck company (which makes folding and fixed blade hunting knives) or the Buck 110, an iconic pocketknife. Both are consistent with Maynard removing the knife from his pocket and unfolding a blade.

Things went awry when Maynard used the knife to rescue Bill. First, stabbing a window with the tip of a knife probably won't shatter the glass. If it does, it'll likely come at the expense of the tip or the operator's fingers—vehicle windows are hard and slippery. Second, a folding knife isn't the best pick for prying open mangled car doors. Because the folding knife lacks a tang, the blade will likely break off.

Both concerns are eliminated when Maynard uses a Bowie, a type of fixed blade knife. As explained in the section on fixed blade knives, a Bowie knife—even when capitalized—is a generic term for a certain style, not brand, of knife. That allows some wiggle room for Maynard to have a convenient glass-breaker stud on the Bowie's pommel (the bottom of the knife handle). Toss in the assumption that the Bowie knife is built for hard use, and Maynard can successfully pry open the car door.

As for that seat-belt reference, I just wanted Maynard to get in a zinger. Had Bill been wearing a seat belt, Maynard would've used his knife to cut it in both examples. Keep in mind that there are knives with seat-belt cutters built into them. That's explained in the section on survival knives.

KITCHEN, BUTCHER, AND STEAK KNIVES

Butcher knives have a long history in the horror genre. Ever wonder why slasher villains carry them in their hands like ice cream cones everywhere they go? It's because butcher knives don't usually come with sheaths. Their lack of portability might be a concern for characters on the move. (Photo courtesy of Chuck Ward for *BLADE*.)

Popular brands: Al Mar, Calphalon, Ginsu, J.A. Henckels, Shun

These are the knives people around the world use every day. They are the most commonly owned of any knife, and therefore available to all characters. Their ubiquity means they can pop up in almost any scene. However, there are still a few considerations to make before writing them into your book.

This category of knives is generically called *cutlery*. It's still accurate to use *butcher knife* when being specific. It's redundant to write *kitchen cutlery* or *steak cutlery*. Use *kitchen knife* or *steak knife* instead.

A *Ginsu knife* is sometimes used generically, but it's more appropriate when referring specifically to the Ginsu brand. Go with *chef's knife*, *butcher knife*, or another generic term instead.

Kitchen, butcher, and steak knives are fixed blades 99 percent of the time, but they don't all sport tangs. Tangs make a big difference with how much of a beating a knife can take. The cheaper the knife, the less likely it has much of a tang. Higher-quality knives will probably include a lengthy, or full, tang.

From my experience reading fiction, knives from the kitchen are often thrown at target characters. While any aerial knife can be dangerous, there are reasons knife throwing rarely works. Remember that old circus trick where the magician throws butcher knives at a spinning wheel? Those weren't the same knives most people have in their kitchens—they were throwing knives. Throwing knives focus their weight (center of gravity) in the middle. This helps them spin without veering off course.

A meat cleaver is an example of a knife that's not suited for throwing, although fiction uses them quite a bit for that purpose. These knives focus almost all of their weight on a formidable blade to help with chopping jobs. Factor in that they lack a tip, and meat cleavers aren't ideal choices for throwing.

One characteristic of these knives that's often overlooked is blade flexibility. Cutlery is usually more flexible than other types of knives. They're manufactured that way for durability given their frequent use (a knife that can bend instead of break will last longer). This trait can be good or bad depending on the scene you're writing, but it's worth considering. The knives in your kitchen right now aren't the same ones found in the sheaths of first responders and military personnel for a reason.

Advantages

- It's virtually a guarantee these knives are in every home in the world. A character would certainly have access to them. They're perfect for characters in a pinch.
- These are the easiest knives to buy. Who doesn't need a steak knife?
- Because they are so common, kitchen knives don't draw suspicion when presented in everyday situations. Is the steak knife on the kitchen counter going to be used for eating dinner or something nefarious? No one will know until it's too late.
- Kitchen, butcher, and steak knives are ready for use as is. There's no learning curve and no blade to open. They will always be faster than switchblades or assisted openers.
- In stealth situations, characters needn't worry about revealing their positions due to the sound of the blade opening.
- Kitchen, butcher, and steak knives are designed for cutting power. If a character needs to butcher someone or something, these knives will maximize each cut.
- In fiction, there's something especially sinister about using such a mundane knife for murder and mayhem.

Disadvantages

- Portability is the number one disadvantage to kitchen, butcher, and steak knives. These knives rarely have accompanying sheaths, since it's unusual for them to leave the kitchen. If they do go anywhere, it's usually in a box. They're best for scenes around the home, unless a character feels like walking around holding a knife for everyone to see.
- Cutlery found outside its normal environment can raise suspicions. A meat cleaver with blood on it means something different when discovered in the garage instead of, say, the kitchen.
- Kitchen, butcher, and steak knives are not designed for fighting. That doesn't mean they can't be used for violent tasks. It does mean that they come with disadvantages in combat. For example, a meat cleaver is only effective when chopping or hacking. It's no good for stabbing since it doesn't have a tip. Steak knives may seem a good choice, but they usually have flexible blades. It's possible the blade could become bent in a fight. And a chef's knife looks menacing, but its delicate edge is intended for precise slicing and dicing. The edge might dull up during the intense knife work fiction can demand.

- These knives tend to be on the larger side. The larger the knife, the harder it is to control in a struggle and the greater the chance the character using it will hurt himself.

Inaccurate Example

"Back in the day, the priest told us we'd go blind if we didn't stop it with all the selfies," said Maynard Soloman as he snapped a photo of himself with Bill Robber's unconscious body on the floor. "Nowadays, it's a different story. I like to tweet the lowlifes I catch."

Except Bill, ever the fraudster, wasn't unconscious at all. From the floor of Maynard's RV, he waited for the right moment, then jumped to his feet. Bill bolted to the RV's kitchenette and grabbed a long Ginsu knife from the kitchen cutlery.

Before Maynard could react, Bill hurled the knife into the detective's chest. Without pausing, Maynard snapped off the blade lodged in his sternum and chucked it back at Bill. The Ginsu knife clipped Bill's jugular as it twirled past. A cascade of obscenities cluttered the night air as each realized they wouldn't live to watch the other die.

Accurate Example

"Back in the day, the priest told us we'd go blind if we didn't stop it with all the selfies," said Maynard Soloman as he snapped a photo of himself with Bill Robber's unconscious body on the floor. "Nowadays, it's a different story. I like to tweet the lowlifes I catch."

Except Bill, ever the fraudster, wasn't unconscious at all. From the floor of Maynard's RV, he waited for the right moment, then jumped to his feet. Bill bolted to the RV's kitchenette and grabbed a long chef's knife from a drawer.

Before Maynard could react, Bill hurled the knife at the detective's chest. The blade's handle connected with a thump before the knife fell to the floor.

"Speaking of church, now would be a good time to go back to pretending to be asleep," Maynard said as he unholstered his revolver.

What Went Wrong?

The term *Ginsu knife* often stands in for a generic butcher knife or chef's knife. I don't think the term warrants the "Kleenex Effect," though. Ginsu is a company that makes cutlery. Go with the generic term instead. Also, using *kitchen cutlery* is redundant. Swap in some other generic term, or eliminate it outright.

Throwing a knife is tough to do, even with the right conditions and the proper blade. Chances are good that Bill's toss wouldn't connect with Maynard's chest.

Creative license might say otherwise and work in a hit anyway. In that case, Maynard probably wouldn't snap off the blade. Remember that cutlery is designed for flexibility. He could bend it until it breaks, but that's not much comfort when the knife is plugged into his sternum. In fact, it could make the injury worse. Snapping or bending is more dramatic, but the better route, had that knife made a hit in the first place, might be for Maynard to simply pull the blade out.

That scenario works only if Maynard is physically able to do it. Prior examples have pointed out that this particular character has stubby arms and a wide chest. Is he capable enough, while injured, to pull out a long chef's knife? Physical traits are worth considering every time a character picks up a knife or firearm.

SURVIVAL KNIVES AND MULTI-TOOLS

Popular multi-tools: Swiss army knife (a generic type, not a specific model), any number of Gerber models, any number of Leatherman models, CRKT Guppie

A survival knife is defined less by its physical characteristics and more by how it's used. Sometimes it's just a fixed or folding knife. Other times it's a knife combined with tools.

As survival instructor Creek Stewart writes in his book *Build the Perfect Bug Out Bag*, a survival knife should be able to assist with at least a few of the following:

- cutting
- hunting
- dressing game
- building shelters
- digging
- defending oneself
- splitting or chopping wood (when done with a knife, this is called *batoning*)
- making fire
- carving
- signaling for help
- building shelter
- preparing food

A number of tools might be built into a survival knife to help make it even more ubiquitous, including a flashlight, a screwdriver, a USB drive, a fire striker, a seat belt cutter (a notch in the handle with a sharpened edge inside), a glass breaker (a stud on the bottom of the handle for breaking windows), eating utensils, and signal whistles. But once all those tools start to overshadow the blade, it's no longer a survival knife. It's a multi-tool.

The classic multi-tool is the Swiss army knife, which has been around since the 1880s. The term *Swiss army knife* is generic, and it's appropriate to write it that way. In the knife world and in catalogs, it's sometimes abbreviated as SAK.

Only two knife companies can lay claim to the Swiss army knife in any official sense: Victorinox and Wenger. Still, the best bet is to write *Swiss army knife* generically and have it contain the tools needed for the scene.

The other commonly used, generic multi-tool is the *Leatherman*. Whereas the Swiss army knife resembles a typical pocketknife (but often with the trademark red color), a Leatherman is more like a pair of pliers. The Leatherman Tool Group introduced the first one in 1983, billed as the Leatherman Pocket Survival Tool. It exploded in popularity and spawned countless imitators, resulting in the generic term *Leatherman*. Although there are scores of varieties and manufacturers (most notably Gerber), it's still appropriate to use *Leatherman* generically when referencing such a multi-tool. Just don't lowercase the *L*.

Advantages

- Dedicated survival knives—those without any tools attached—are built with hard use in mind. Fixed blade survival knife designs take full advantage of tangs, modern metals, handle materials, and ergonomics to take a dump truck's worth of hell. They are the true do-it-all knives, the ones to have handy in survival situations and fight scenes. Folding survival knives are made with the same mentality, but they're not as durable since they lack the tang of fixed blades.
- Survival knives with tools attached can work wonders in your fictional scenes. The best tools are those without electronic or moving parts that are integral to the knife itself. Glass breakers, seat-belt cutters, and wrenches are among the tools that work well in reality. Any character, especially first responders and criminals, can take advantage of these features.
- Multi-tools' primary advantage is found right in their name. They're like portable toolboxes. For characters requiring versatility, they're a great pick.

Disadvantages

- Not every tool attached to a survival knife works out in reality. Fire strikers are notorious for failing to light anything in the field. Built-in flashlights drastically cut down on the knife's durability. Have the character use separate, dedicated items instead.

- Has anyone actually used the toothpick in a Swiss army knife? Multi-tools suffer from diminishing returns, trading practicality for variety. For small, low-impact tasks, they're great. But a dedicated tool on its own will almost always do a better job than the one in a multi-tool.
- Multi-tools aren't suited for combat. Avoid writing them into fight scenes if at all possible.

Inaccurate Example

For the third time that week, Maynard Soloman locked his keys inside his beloved RV. To further complicate the situation, he'd just spotted his arch nemesis, Bill Robber, fresh out of jail and steaming toward him like a freight train on fire from across the parking lot.

Maynard reached into his pocket and pulled out his trusty Swiss army knife. He unfolded a long, thin blade and picked the lock on the driver's side door in a snap.

"What in the dank hell?" Maynard said after he secured himself inside the RV. His fingers fell on a metallic bulge near his trouser luggage. "Aw, horsefeathers, the keys were in my pocket the whole time."

Accurate Example

For the third time that week, Maynard Soloman locked his keys inside his beloved RV. Fortunately, the RV already had three wheels in the grave. Busting a window wouldn't ruin the quaint aesthetics.

Maynard reached into his pocket and pulled out his trusty folding knife, the one that would make MacGyver proud. He made a short, sharp jab at one of the windows with the glass breaker on the bottom of the knife's handle.

The window shattered, allowing Maynard access to unlock the door. He didn't act fast enough, though. Bill caught up with Maynard just in time and grabbed a sleeve through the shattered window.

Maynard reached over and clocked Bill with the glass breaker. It took a few hard blows to make Bill feel anything through his thick skull, but he finally relented and let Maynard go.

Safe inside the RV, Maynard flicked on the flashlight attached to the knife's handle in an attempt to find the keys. But the intense blows to Bill's skull had knocked the light out of commission.

"What in the dank hell?" Maynard said when his fingers fell on a metallic bulge near his trouser luggage. "Aw, horsefeathers, the keys were in my pocket the whole time."

What Went Wrong?

Here's an instance where switching up the knife led to more problems to address.

Let's kick it off with the lock picking, something that pops up in fiction. Swiss army knives can offer many tools, but it'd take a real expert to figure out how to pick a lock with one. Maynard needs to act quickly, so picking the RV door in a few seconds falls a bit beyond the suspension of disbelief.

Where does this trope come from then? Its genesis can probably be traced to opening standard doors, like those in a home, with a knife. Slipping a knife between the lock and the door frame and giving the knife a twist will usually "pop the lock," allowing access.

Those simple locks are a whole other kettle of fish compared to car doors and secured entries. Those cases call for specialized tools for accessing the locks themselves. Even if such tools are present on a Swiss army knife, it's going to take some time and talent.

A better choice for Maynard is that "trusty folding knife," the one that would make Mac-Gyver proud. Although it's not stated explicitly, it's a survival knife given its glass breaker and built-in flashlight. That's the nice thing about survival knives—they can match a writer's imagination and needs. In this case, Maynard used the glass breaker to shatter the window and hit Bill in the head.

As for the flashlight, it became damaged in the struggle with Bill and wouldn't turn on, which highlights the trade-off of survival knives. The knives themselves are cut out for hard use. The extra features built into the knives often aren't. Parts may come loose, fall off, or fail to work. That was the case with the flashlight.

However, that struggle would never have happened had Maynard not broken the window in the first place. In fact, switching to the survival knife only complicated things for this scene.

So was the extra hassle worth it? The answer depends on the writer. This is a time creative license might've simplified things by having the doors on Maynard's decrepit RV unlock with the Swiss army knife. Or maybe Maynard's an experienced lock picker.

That's a judgment call every writer will have to make eventually when it comes to knives and firearms. Do you apply creative license to keep the story moving or play it closer to reality? As a reader, I appreciate the extra time a writer takes to get those things right, but you may think differently.

MACHETES

Popular brands of machetes: SOG, United Cutlery, Ontario Knife Company, Gerber

When does a standard fixed blade knife become a machete? It's mostly a length thing. Machete blades are long—up to a foot or more—and are designed for hacking. They're the limb takers of fiction.

Machetes are common tropes in horror, war, and survival fiction, though slightly less so in crime and mystery stories, unless your character is particularly vicious. Machetes come in many designs, not just the prototypical jungle-clearing hacker.

One for writers to consider for limb work—trees and otherwise—is the *kukri* (a.k.a. *khukuri, khukri,* and about a dozen other spellings). This knife's blade looks like a boomerang from hell, with an edge running along the inside of the curve. The kukri traces its roots back to Nepal, where people used it for centuries for fieldwork and combat. It's since found use in modern militaries around the world. The secret is the design: The boomerang shape focuses most of its weight toward the front, making it a highly efficient chopper. Not that a run-of-the-mill machete won't cut it, but writers looking for an exceptionally devastating way to take off a character's head or limb should consider the kukri.

Because of their size, all machetes need sheaths. Be it a proper sheath or a rolled up newspaper, consider how the machete is transported when writing about it. Because of their bulk, many machetes come with a lanyard for looping around the wrist. This keeps them from flying out of the operator's hand.

Some machetes come with sawlike teeth built into them, usually on the spine, or top, of the blade. In that case, the model is referred to as a *sawtooth* or *sawback* machete. As the name suggests, these teeth are useful for sawing materials, although a proper saw works better for tasks like this. A character with a wicked streak could put that feature to creative use.

Advantages

- Machetes are a favorite of fiction, and for good reason. A blow from a machete is absolutely devastating. They're the perfect choice for inflicting brutal injuries on other characters.
- Because of their obvious cutting power, machetes are ideal for intimidation. A character with a machete makes a statement without uttering a word.
- Machetes offer a great deal of utility outside of combat, too. They can tackle almost any large cutting job, from clearing brush to splitting wood. Their versatility earns them a high ranking on the list of survival tools.

- Like all fixed blade knives, machetes offer plenty of durability. A machete isn't likely to break. Feel free to hack, chop, and slash away.
- A razor-sharp machete isn't necessary and actually performs poorly. Machetes are designed for blunt force. A supersharp edge isn't going to stand up to this hard use. Think of machetes as you would axes. Staying relatively sharp is important but not to the high degree of a standard fixed blade knife. For this reason, sharpening a machete for intimidation might be unnecessary.

Disadvantages

- The best thing about machetes—their size—is also the worst. Compared to other knives, machetes are clunky to operate. All that weight swinging around must be controlled without unintentionally injuring the operator or someone else. It takes practice to use them effectively. An inexperienced character, or one that's not physically strong, would find it difficult to use a machete. If you're having trouble picturing it, imagine your character using an ax: There's a windup, a swing, contact, and follow-through. It's all about controlling that heavy blade.
- Portability is an issue with machetes. They're bulky and tough to conceal. Characters requiring stealth may want to choose something else.
- Because machetes aren't supposed to be razor sharp, they're not as useful for detailed cutting tasks. Big, blunt cutting jobs are best.
- Running with machetes, just like scissors, is incredibly dangerous. Fiction seems to forget that, but it's also an easy area to suspend disbelief. Sheathe the damn thing.

Inaccurate Example

They say alcohol and machetes don't mix, but Maynard Soloman put his mind to proving them wrong. After the bar closed, he paid a visit to Bill Robber, an ex-con on parole and living in a van down by the river.

Maynard stripped down to his underwear, crawled on top of the van after a few failed attempts, and hacked at the roof with the machete until he could see a startled Bill inside.

"What the hell are you doing?" Bill said as he sprinted outside the van.

"Just doing a welfare check, that's all," Maynard said.

"Are you drunk?" Bill said.

"Nope, I'm sober as a judge," Maynard said. He shaved a few whiskers from his chin to prove his point.

Accurate Example

They say alcohol and machetes don't mix, but Maynard Soloman put his mind to proving them wrong. After the bar closed, he paid a visit to Bill Robber, an ex-con currently on parole and living in a van down by the river.

Maynard stripped down to his underwear, crawled on top of the van after a few failed attempts, and hacked at the roof with the machete.

"What the hell are you doing?" Bill said as he sprinted outside the van.

"Just doing a welfare check, that's all," Maynard said.

"Are you drunk?" Bill said.

"Nope, I'm sober as a judge," Maynard said as blood trickled down his bare chest and legs.

What Went Wrong?

Let's first address the most obvious question: Could a machete hack through the roof of a van? Actually, this is possible, given machetes are perfect for brutal hacking tasks. It depends on the quality of the machete and the condition of the roof. I toned this down in the corrected version because I didn't think Bill would wait until Maynard installed a new sunroof to exit the van.

Now for the shaving bit. The Internet is full of knife companies showing their machetes hacking down trees and shaving hair or paper only seconds later. The point is to demonstrate the resiliency of the blade edges. It's a little misleading, since the tree and hair are cut at different spots along the machete's edge.

That said, a machete can certainly shave hair, but it's really not set up for precise cutting tasks in the first place. These weapons are built for hacking. Even a machete that has not been sharpened will be effective for cutting trees, brush, and, yes, other characters. But the blade's edge probably won't shave hair after hard use.

And that hard use is sure to send debris flying, something to keep in mind whenever machetes are used. A bare-chested Maynard would become injured after hacking on that roof, as in the corrected version. He may also have struck himself with the machete, since it would be hard to control, even when sober. Keep that in mind whenever a character uses one of these blades.

Finally, where is the sheath in this scene? Or is there one? Whenever you're writing about a fixed blade knife, always consider how (or if) the character is carrying the sheath. If the machete is loose in Maynard's hand, he may have injured himself while drunkenly climbing the van.

THROWING KNIVES

Popular brands of throwing knives: SOG, United Cutlery, Hibben, Cold Steel

It's possible for any knife or edged object to be thrown and to hit a target, but it takes skill and a knife that's specifically designed for throwing to do it reliably. For this reason, *throwing knives* are considered a separate type altogether and carry their own considerations for a story.

Throwing knives come in a variety of sizes, from finger length to as long as a forearm. Many throwing knives work because their weight is focused near the center. The blade and handle are often tapered. This encourages the knife to spin, which keeps it from veering off course. This variety of throwing knife is most difficult to master.

Other throwing knives are designed so that their weight is focused at the handle or blade instead, and sometimes both. They're somewhat easier to throw.

No-spin throwing knives are designed to do exactly that—they don't spin. The weight is distributed more or less evenly across the knife. Because of this design, some resemble spikes instead of knives, and when that is the case, they're called *throwing spikes*. They're a popular choice with those new to throwing knives.

It might surprise some to know that most throwing knives don't have sharpened edges. The only part that needs to stick into a target is the tip. A sharpened edge wouldn't serve much of a purpose other than to cut the thrower. That's why hurling knives that aren't designed for throwing is such a bad idea, especially when the thrower is inexperienced. The edge could catch the thrower's hand or other body part.

Knives and spikes don't have a monopoly on aerial edges. Axes, hatchets, and tomahawks are also good choices, so long as they focus weight on the blade. They're easier to throw successfully than knives, but it still takes practice and physical acumen to properly use them.

Advantages

- Nothing screams stealth like an attack with a throwing knife. This weapon offers an attack that won't make the noise of a firearm. This makes them ideal for ambushes by assassins and other covert characters.
- Throwing knives can quickly establish a character's weapon know-how. Because they require a lot of practice to master, and due to their relatively low popularity, a character handy with throwing knives likely possesses advanced weapons skills.
- Throwing knives can serve as a last-ditch weapon in a fight. Any number of smaller throwing knives can be secured to a character.
- A hit from a throwing knife can be devastating. The kinetic energy focused on the tip upon impact means the blade will likely penetrate well beyond a mere flesh wound.

Disadvantages

- Throwing knives, and even axes or hatchets, require a lot of practice to master. Characters wouldn't be able to pick up the skill in an afternoon. A concerted effort must be made in order to learn the skill and develop muscle memory.
- Throwing knives, as well as axes and hatchets, lack range. They're usually good to about 20 feet at most, depending on the thrower. Accuracy is greatly reduced beyond that distance.
- Here's something those trick knife throwers at circuses and magic shows won't tell their audiences: They become really good at throwing to a specific range but are terrible at other distances. This is because of the muscle memory required to throw accurately. Move them out of their comfort zone, and the accuracy of their throws suffers. Although an exceptionally skilled character in fiction might do well at any range, keep this point in mind.
- Body positioning has to be perfect for an accurate throw. This means being able to stand up with enough room for an overhead toss. Fiction likes to feature characters hurling knives in contorted positions for dramatic effect. Accuracy would certainly suffer in those cases. The slightest rotation of the wrist can throw a knife well off its target.
- For all of these reasons, much of knife throwing is just choreographed stunt work. It's cool to watch and imagine, but these trick throws need near-perfect conditions to work.

Inaccurate Example

"I'm interested to know your opinion," said Bill Robber to Maynard Soloman. He held his signature throwing knife up to the bound detective's throat. "Do you want me to slit your throat or your wrists?"

"There was a time when people cared about my two cents, but inflation took care of that," Maynard said. His flabby arms struggled against the extension cord tying him to the lamppost in Bill's backyard. "How about you cut me loose and we can chew the fat on it?"

"Since it'll stop your one-liners, I think I'll start with your throat," Bill said and opened Maynard's neck with the edge of the razor-sharp blade. "Now, if you'll excuse me, my bowling league meets in fifteen minutes."

Accurate Example

"I'm interested to know your opinion," said Bill Robber to Maynard Soloman. He held his signature fillet knife up to the bound detective's throat. "Do you want me to cut out your throat or your wrists?"

"There was a time when people cared about my two cents, but inflation took care of that," Maynard said. His flabby arms struggled against the extension cord tying him to the lamppost in Bill's backyard. "How about you cut me loose and we can chew the fat on it?"

"If it'll stop the one-liners, I think I'll start with your throat," Bill said and filleted Maynard's throat open. "Now, if you'll excuse me, my bowling league meets in fifteen minutes."

What Went Wrong?

The edges of throwing knives aren't sharpened, so Bill wouldn't slit Maynard's throat with one. He'd have to use the point instead.

Even so, a throwing knife wasn't the right fit in the first place. Just as other knife types aren't cut out for hurling across a scene, throwing knives aren't the sharpest choice outside of aerial attacks.

To switch things up, I gave Bill a fillet knife (a flexible fixed blade knife used for cleaning fish) instead.

STRAIGHT RAZORS

A straight razor refers to a shaving blade that folds into a handle. These are sometimes called *cutthroat razors*. Because of their centuries-spanning use (they've been around since about the 1600s), straight razors are appropriate for characters in just about any setting.

Straight razors are best used for the intimidation and mutilation of characters. They're not designed for fighting, since their manufacturers (hopefully) didn't have violence in mind for their products.

The thin edge on a straight razor is what drives that legendary sharpness. Cutting is all about the dispersal of force through the metal of the blade. The thinnest edges, like those on straight razors, concentrate the most force in the smallest area. Sharpening and stropping provide the thin edge with a row of microscopic teeth to bite into what's being cut (dull edges are roundish and lack those teeth). The teeth make it possible for a razor to cut things that would usually bend instead of break, like hair or whiskers.

Straight razors are often stropped against a piece of leather or other material before use. This freshens the edge in two ways: first, by cleaning off any debris, and second, by aligning the grains of the metal so that they stand up, providing that row of teeth.

Advantages

- Most straight razors are foldable, making them exceptionally concealable. They're perfect for stealthy characters.
- The TSA may not allow passengers to stow them inside carry-ons, but straight razors are mundane enough that they won't raise suspicion elsewhere. No one will think twice about the character with a straight razor in the bathroom.
- Straight razors are designed for finesse work. This means a character carving a cryptic message into a victim's backside will appreciate the penlike delicacy of a straight razor.
- They're tricky to shave with, but straight razors don't carry quite the same learning curve when it comes to mutilation. That supersharp edge makes it easy to claim an ear or throat.
- Compared to other knives, there's a special brutality about giving a nefarious character a straight razor.

Disadvantages

- The thin edge that makes razors so sharp is cursed to require constant refreshing. Because the edge is so thin, it doesn't take long for the grains in the metal to roll over. Stropping can straighten those grains back up.
- That thin edge also means hard use is out of the question. Mutilation, intimidation, and quick cutting are all appropriate, but straight razors are too flimsy and prone to failure for anything else.
- Straight razors lack a tip. This is great when a barber shaves near the throat in the real world. In fiction, it can be inconvenient. It means razors aren't cut out for stabbing.

Inaccurate Example

Maynard Soloman waited in his RV at the stakeout. The job was simple: Identify the door-to-door missionary collecting donations for a nonexistent school in Africa. All he had to do was wait for the knock.

Since the missionary had a higher power on his side, Maynard sharpened his old-fashioned straight razor to even the odds. He turned on an electric knife sharpener and let the spinning wheels grind the razor for a minute or so. That's when he heard the knock.

Maynard opened the door to a mustached man in a cheap suit and slicked back hair. The missionary launched into a rehearsed speech about the meaning of life.

"Yeah, yeah, this is all fascinating stuff. But I've found that the more someone says they have a purpose on this planet, the less they actually do. I call BS on you,"

Maynard said.

The missionary was about to respond, but his mustache dislodged from his lip and fluttered to the ground.

"Well, I'll be dipped. If it isn't Bill Robber, failing at another crummy disguise," Maynard said.

Bill turned to run, but not before Maynard could hurl the razor into his back.

Accurate Example

Maynard Soloman waited in his RV at the stakeout. The job was simple: Identify the door-to-door missionary collecting donations for a nonexistent school in Africa. All he had to do was wait for the knock.

Since the missionary had a higher power on his side, Maynard stropped his old-fashioned straight razor on a leather belt to even the odds. That's when he heard the knock.

The mustached missionary launched into a rehearsed speech about the divine plan to build the school as soon as Maynard opened the door.

"I've found the more someone says they have a purpose on this planet, the less they actually do. I call BS on your hokum," Maynard said.

The missionary was about to respond, but his mustache dislodged and fluttered to the ground.

"Well, I'll be dipped. If it isn't Bill Robber, failing at another crummy disguise," Maynard said.

Bill turned to run, but not before Maynard could slice a long wound down his back.

What Went Wrong?

I'll let you in on a little knife humor: What do you call a straight razor that's sharpened in an electric knife grinder? A stick. (Please, hold your applause. I'm here all night, ladies and gentlemen.)

Electric knife sharpeners (basically two abrasive wheels that spin inside a small tabletop machine) are great for removing metal to form a new edge. The problem is that straight razors, because they're so thin, don't have a lot of metal to remove in the first place. An electric knife sharpener will eventually "eat" the razor. Even before that happens, it'll ruin the razor by warping it with heat and by replacing the edge with another angle not cut out for shaving. That's why when razors do require sharpening, the job is done manually to control angle and temperature.

Stropping (lightly running the edge of the blade over a durable but soft material) is always a good idea for a razor. This straightens grains of metal that have rolled over, causing the edge to dull. That's why barbers strop their straight razors before a shave instead of going to a sharpener. Anything more than a quick refresh of the finely tuned edge is overkill. Maynard uses a typical leather belt for his stropping, although alternatives such as newsprint and cloth work, too.

As discussed in other sections, hurling anything that isn't a throwing knife isn't usually effective. That goes double for straight razors—they lack a tip. A quick slice, as in the accurate example, is the better route.

KNIFE SHARPENING AND SHEATHS

Knife sharpening is an art form unto itself. It involves metallurgy, geometry, muscle memory, and an understanding of abrasives to get it right.

For fiction, knife sharpening doesn't usually involve those things. Instead, it's employed as a means of intimidation. There's nothing wrong with that from an accuracy standpoint—characters can sharpen knives all they want—but here are a few basics to understand what's actually happening.

SHARPENING IS A PROCESS

Sharpening a knife is kind of like sanding wood. A person would start with the coarsest-grit sandpaper and end with the finest.

The same goes for knives. Coarse materials, such as diamond-infused abrasives, remove metal until the outline of an edge is formed. Finer abrasives shape the edge. Strops, such as leather or cloth, hone the edge so the grains of metal stand up to form "teeth." Each one of those steps is important in the sharpening process. Some passages in fiction go wrong simply by doing them out of order.

When characters sharpen knives for intimidation, it makes the most sense for them to hone the blade on a strop or exceptionally fine abrasive. Doing so refreshes the edge and prepares it for mayhem. However, sometimes in fiction, the character will use a coarse abrasive, such as a commercial knife sharpener or even a rock, just before slicing and dicing. All those drastic measures do is remove a perfectly good edge (unless the knife was unusably dull in the first place). The idea isn't to replace an edge; it's to maximize how well that edge performs. That's what honing—such as stropping the blade on a piece of leather—does best.

If that's confusing, think back to sanding wood. Let's say guests are coming over in three minutes, and the wooden dining room table needs to look its best. Does it make sense to run coarse-grit sandpaper over the table right before they arrive? Or would it be better to hone out tiny slivers in the wood with a cloth?

The Crash Course in Knife Sharpening

Learning how to sharpen knives opens up an entirely new understanding of these seemingly simple objects.

For a crash course to try at home, get a permanent marker, a nonserrated knife, and a basic commercial sharpener (manual is best, not electric). Draw a line with the marker along either side of the blade's edge. Now run a few strokes of the blade along the sharpener.

It'll be easy to spot where the metal is coming off the edge, because the ink will be gone. The goal is to remove all of the ink, indicating the knife is sharp. Repeat the process from coarse grits on down.

Does this matter to writing a story? It might not, but it does offer a better understanding of knives and sharpening.

SHEATH MATERIALS: STEEL AIN'T IT

The sheath for this Spyderco Enuff Leaf sports lanyard holes for wearing around the neck. Its profile could also slip into a character's footwear or other apparel. (Photo courtesy of *BLADE*.)

Unless a character literally possesses balls of steel, transporting a nonfolding knife also means carrying a sheath. That can be a pain to think about when writing, but it's even more so for the character if a sheath isn't present.

Sheaths can be made from just about anything. The only requirement is that the material used is softer than the blade. If it's not, the sheath will dull the blade.

Wood, cloth, and leather have been popular sheath materials throughout history. Modern synthetic materials dominate sheaths today. Plastics, such as Kydex, are inexpensive, durable, and lightweight. Composite materials like Micarta blend cloth with synthetics, used for both sheaths and knife handles.

Where Sheaths Are Worn

The classic sheath worn on the belt, either vertically or horizontally, is a go-to choice. If need be, here are some other styles.

Inside-the-waistband (IWB) sheaths are a take on the traditional belt sheath. Like their handgun counterparts, the sheath slips between the pants and the leg or tucked shirt. This offers better concealment, especially when paired with a jacket or long shirt. Characters new to knives probably wouldn't feel comfortable using an IWB sheath, though.

Neck sheaths are one of the most underappreciated in fiction. This is a sheath attached to a lanyard for wearing around the neck. It sounds dangerous on paper, but it's actually one of the safest carries in reality—so long as the blade fits snugly in the sheath. Neck sheaths allow a knife to be carried under a shirt or jacket. Drawing is as easy as pulling down on the handle. It's perfect for stealthy characters using small- to medium-sized knives. Keep in mind the lanyard will be exposed, though.

Larger knives will work with neck sheaths, but they might not be practical for a character. Go with a shoulder sheath instead. This type of sheath sports a harness that secures to the shoulder. The sheath itself is at chest level with the knife handle pointed down for an easy draw.

Shoulder sheaths aren't appropriate for machetes, though. If wearing the machete on the belt isn't an option, go for the back sheath. This type goes by many names, but they all function the same way. The sheath is designed to secure behind a shoulder blade. The machete is drawn up and away from the body from behind.

Boot sheaths are designed to slip inside footwear. Short and slender boot knives are ideal for use with these types of sheaths. Fiction likes a good boot knife, but the sheaths make walking or running awkward. The longer the knife, the more it will restrict a character's movement.

Sheaths for the arms, legs, and chest are often used in tandem with MOLLE (modular lightweight load-carrying equipment) gear. MOLLE gear, a recent development, consists of a customizable harness used by military and law enforcement organizations for carrying tactical items, including sheaths. MOLLE systems are also available to civilians.

Where Sheaths Shouldn't Be Worn

Characters with a lot of knife know-how might want to avoid placing a sheath on a belt behind the back. Drawing the knife from this position won't be a problem. But what about putting it back? One miss in this blind spot and the character could pierce a kidney.

Sheaths for Folding Knives

Although they have their own sheaths built-in by design, folding knives can have exterior sheaths, too. These pouches are secured with Velcro, snaps, or other fasteners. Folding knives might also be outfitted with pocket clips.

That Special Sheath Sound

When drawing a knife (or sword), some stories will toss in a dramatic, metallic *shink* sound. That's entirely the invention of fiction. In reality, the sound is much different.

First off, where is the noise of drawing the knife originating? It's coming from the metal blade rubbing against the inside of the sheath, right? If the sheath is made from wood, cloth, leather, or synthetics, the sound produced wouldn't be *shink*-y at all. It'd be more like someone unfurling a canvas or drawing a pair of scissors from a pocket.

In order to get that *shink* sound, the sheath would need to be made of metal. Listen closely to the next *shink* that pops up in a movie or TV show. It sounds a bit like two pieces of metal grinding together. That kind of metal-on-metal action is great for a monster truck rally but not for blade durability. The edge would become dull in no time. That's a problem, and it's why metal sheaths aren't used for practical knives. (Ceremonial ones are another story.)

The point is that sheaths aren't noisy. Avoid writing them like they're party favors on New Year's Eve.

Sheaths: The Original Bag of Tricks

Sheaths aren't only for knives. People throughout history have doubled up on them, and the modern age is no exception. Feel free to write spare ammo, flashlights, a handgun, lighters, tools, and any other small item into knife sheaths.

One popular model from the past few years is the CRKT 2-Shot Skinner. Designed by Russ Kommer, it holds a proper fixed blade knife plus two shotgun shells. Why? Well, why not?

Fiction often forgets about sheaths as a source for emergency items. Don't overlook them. They can be the perfect remedy for a character—or a writer—stuck in a rut.

IMPROVISED AND CUSTOM KNIVES

Writers have four routes for characters in need of improvised knives: shivs, disguised, ballistic, and custom. No matter the style, keep this in mind: If a character can make a point or edge, he or she can make an improvised knife.

SHIVS AND SHANKS: KNIVES THAT WOULD MAKE MACGYVER PROUD (OR NOT)

Knives put together from pieces of otherwise mundane materials are called *shivs* or *shanks*, although they could go by any number of names.

In his memoir, crime writer Les Edgerton, who speaks from personal prison experience, advises not using the term *shiv*. To his eye, the word makes a writer look phony. He prefers *shank*.

Shiv may well be passé with some writers, but it still gets the point across. Just pick a term and stick with it. This section will use *shiv* for the sake of consistency (sorry, Les).

No matter the materials used, the principles for building a shiv are the same:

- Create a point or an edge.
- Add a handle or design a way to hold the point or edge.
- Take a cheap shot at an opponent.

It's that point that counts. Unlike a traditional knife, shivs don't necessarily need edges, although those help. This simplicity is what makes shivs so versatile.

How that point or edge is created requires imagination. Here are a few ideas to get the brain percolating, sorted by material.

- **CERAMICS AND PORCELAIN:** A shard of ceramic material or porcelain can make an ideal shiv. Getting a toilet to break is another story.
- **CIGARETTE FILTERS:** The cotton inside cigarette filters is actually a synthetic material. Remove it from the paper wrapper and apply a flame. It can be melted and formed into a point. How effective this is may depend on the writer's tolerance of creative license.

- **CLOTHING:** Unless a garment is made from 100 percent natural fibers, it probably contains enough synthetic material to melt. Melt the garment into a mold to form it into a point.
- **GLASS:** A shard of glass, even a small one, makes for the perfect shiv. Handles could be fashioned from a strip of cloth, a melted piece of plastic, or other materials.
- **METAL:** Softer, flexible metals work best for shivs, such as the kind used in silverware, beer cans, or crappy furniture, such as a folding chair. To make a point, you can file, cut, bend, or melt the metal.
- **PAPER:** Roll up some paper, then fold it to create a point. This is surprisingly effective with newsprint but can work with other paper products as well. Every fold and layer of paper will make the point stronger.
- **PLASTIC:** Melt down the plastic material, then mold it into a point or insert pointed objects into it and use the plastic part as a handle. This is the basis of the classic prison shiv: the melted toothbrush with a razor stuck in it.
- **ROCK, CONCRETE, AND BRICK:** Bust off a shard. Voila, you have a point. The rock, concrete, or brick would probably work well on its own as a handle.
- **WOOD:** Channel your inner Boy Scout and whittle a point. This can be done without a knife given enough time. Just like metals, harder woods can bludgeon and shape softer woods. Of course, wood is also the perfect handle.
- **TOOLS, WRITING INSTRUMENTS, AND OTHER SMALL, POINTY THINGS:** If it has a point, it can be a shiv.

Chances are good that nonincarcerated writers have shiv-making material within arm's length at any moment. That's actually a pretty disturbing thought, but it's true. If it can be melted, molded, cut, folded, shaved, filed, smashed, ripped, or elbow-dropped into a point, it can be made into a shiv.

Because of their hobo aesthetics, remember that shivs lack durability and ergonomics (i.e., they're not easy to hold firmly). They're for scenes involving surprise attacks. In all likelihood, they'll fall apart after the first use. Characters might use them to damage the most vulnerable areas, such as the eyes or face, for this reason.

DISGUISED KNIVES: PROBABLY ILLEGAL, DEFINITELY DRAMATIC

The Cardsharp is about the size of a credit card and folds into a knife. It can't pay for dinner, but it can cut the steak. (Photo courtesy of *BLADE*.)

Knives disguised as mundane objects come in handy in fiction. If it matters to the plot, check local and state laws about the legality of these items, since they are usually restricted.

Here's a list of the most common disguised knives available commercially:

- ammunition shells (just don't load them into a gun)
- belts
- canes
- coins
- combs and brushes
- credit cards (the cards fold into a knife; check out the Cardsharp for an example)
- lipstick
- pendants on necklaces
- pens
- rings
- umbrellas

The law limits the field of commercial products, but characters with time and ingenuity could come up with other ways to disguise knives.

These items bring a definite cool factor to a story. For practical purposes, that's about as far as they go outside of slicing an apple. Yes, they can be used for combat. But like shivs, they lack ergonomics. They'll probably wind up on the ground during a struggle.

Unlike shivs, the surprise of disguised knives isn't in the attack—it's the fact they even appeared at all. Characters might use disguised knives for intimidation rather than for fighting. It's up to the writer.

BALLISTIC KNIVES: JUST ONE TRIP TO THE HARDWARE STORE AWAY

A ballistic knife is usually homemade from parts available at most hardware stores. There are many styles, but typical construction involves a cylinder, a spring, a knife or other edged projectile, and some sort of release. The spring is compressed and released to launch the projectile. These knives are often restricted, so research state and local laws against the setting if it will matter to the story.

Characters could throw a ballistic knife together with the right tools and some time. Ballistic knives are best for a surprise attack, when throwing a knife is either not possible or beyond a character's abilities.

It's my opinion that ballistic knives make a bad substitute for the real thing—a firearm or a regular knife—unless circumstances are dire. The spring must be reset with each shot, which means reloading is a chore. There's not much to speak of for accuracy, so unless the target character is a few feet away, it will probably miss the mark,. That means the target character could pick up the knife and retaliate.

CUSTOM KNIVES: TURNING TRASH INTO TALONS

One of the most popular custom knife-making books on the market is *Wayne Goddard's $50 Knife Shop*. In it, Goddard describes how to use $50 worth of common tools to make a knife. Metal is heated, shaped, cooled, and sharpened, or just cut into a knife. It's not as easy as one, two, three, but it's doable. The result is a fixed blade knife ready for hard use (or opening mail, depending on the results).

It's not like Goddard holds some secret to that process. Humans have been making knives for eons. Lost in the modern world is how relatively easy—and cheap—it can be to do so. A character with mechanical know-how and the right tools could make a rudimentary knife in a day or so.

MUST-KNOW KNIFE LAWS

A PRIMER ON HOW KNIVES ARE PURCHASED

As with firearms, it's important to understand a bit about the way knives are purchased and possessed in the United States. This may impact characters or the plot.

Knife laws can be a hodgepodge mess, sometimes varying widely at the state, county, and city levels. Possessing a certain knife can become a crime during a ten-minute drive down the street. Restrictions usually center on type (such as switchblades), blade length, and whether the knife can be opened with one hand (in the case of folding knives).

With no single set of regulations to follow, the responsibility to comply with knife laws falls mostly to the buyer. Take this notice on the Buck Knives website as an example:

> Due to the complex and changing nature of knife laws, it is your responsibility, not Buck Knives', to investigate and comply with international, federal, state, and local laws relating to the purchase, possession, use, transport, and resale of knives. Consult applicable laws if you are in doubt. By placing an order, you represent that the product(s) will be used in a lawful manner and you are of legal age. Absolutely no sales to minors. You agree to hold Buck Knives harmless from failure to comply with these terms and conditions of sale.

That's the attitude most online knife sellers take. In-person sellers are a little more discerning, since the transaction takes place face-to-face.

These things actually matter quite a bit when writing fiction. For stories set after the advent of the Internet, consider it possible for characters to obtain just about any knife, whether its possession is legal or not. What the character does depends more on his moral compass than the laws.

If the setting is prior to the Internet, or the character can't get online, research local laws to see what's legal. Law-bending characters might still buy an illegal knife under the table.

Law enforcement and the military will always be exceptions. Consider those characters able to obtain any knife.

SWITCHBLADE LAWS

Each state applies switchblade laws in a different way, but all use the federal 1958 Switchblade Act as a template. The Act can be read in its entirety at tinyurl.com/switchblade-law.

Two knife traits define a switchblade under the Act.

1. Inside the handle, the knife contains a concealed blade that is *biased to open*. That means it would exit the handle unless held in place by another mechanical element. The blade wants to open. That's an important distinction that warrants further discussion.
2. The blade opens automatically when a button or switch *on the handle* of the knife is pressed. Blades that use gravity or inertia to open are also considered, but the button or switch on the handle is what matters most.

These knives cannot be traded through interstate commerce. Under Section 1242 of the Act, "whoever knowingly introduces, or manufactures for introduction, into interstate commerce, or transports or distributes in interstate commerce, any switchblade knife, shall be fined not more than $2,000 or imprisoned not more than five years, or both."

Military and law enforcement organizations are exempt from these penalties. A person with one arm may also possess a switchblade under the Act, so long as the blade is less than 3 inches long. However, even beyond these exemptions, switchblades are not completely illegal in the United States. That's because the Act regulates only interstate commerce. Each state is left to determine how to deal with switchblade commerce that exists within its borders.

Most state laws still prohibit switchblades through some variation of the Act. Others offer private ownership yet prohibit sales, while some have removed all restrictions. Laws are so nuanced from state to state that it is almost impossible to sum them up here. If the legality of a switchblade is important to a story, take the time to research specific state and local laws.

Of course, a character outside the law could get ahold of a switchblade no matter the location.

SWITCHBLADES ARE SO TWENTIETH CENTURY: MEET THE ASSISTED OPENING KNIFE

Assisted opening knives, such as this Kershaw 1985ST RJI, look like regular folders. But inside is a mechanism that "assists" the blade once it's halfway open. (Photo courtesy of *BLADE*.)

Interstate commerce isn't the area the Switchblade Act plays with the heaviest hand. That honor is reserved for the importation of knives. In 2009, an importation conflict led to the most significant change in knife laws (and stories featuring knives) in decades.

Most major U.S. knife companies outsource the manufacturing of their knives overseas. When ships with foreign-made knives hit U.S. ports, their cargo is regulated by federal law and enforced by U.S. Customs and Border Protection (CBP). The CBP doesn't care what state laws say. As a federal agency, it's there to enforce the 1958 Switchblade Act.

Things became messy when assisted opening knives hit the market in the mid-1990s and surged in popularity in the 2000s. Assisted openers, explained in detail in the Knives 101 section of this book, are almost identical to switchblades. However, their blades are *biased to stay shut in the handle* and they *do not contain a switch or button on the handle that opens the knife*. Those two key differences set them apart from switchblades, although to the eye they appear to function like switchblades.

Regardless, the CBP seized shipments of assisted openers at the U.S. border in the 2000s, citing the 1958 Switchblade Act. This created a huge amount of legal confusion. Assisted opening knives didn't exist yet in 1958, when the Act was written; yet the CBP used it to confiscate imports. U.S. knife companies wound up paying hefty sums to retrieve their impounded knife shipments.

As a result, the knife industry, in conjunction with advocacy groups and enthusiasts, pressed Congress to exempt assisted openers from the 1958 Switchblade Act. Soon after one of the largest organized knife lobbying efforts in U.S. history, President Barack Obama signed an amendment to the Act in October 2009.

From that point on, assisted opening knives wouldn't be considered illegal switchblades so long as:

- the blade is biased to stay closed inside the handle.
- the blade doesn't open with a button or switch on the handle.

Just remember, a state or local law may view assisted openers differently (though most are tolerant of them). The exemption only applies to the federal Switchblade Act.

WRITERS AREN'T LAWYERS, SO WHY DO THESE KNIFE LAWS MATTER?

This legal background actually impacts fiction writing in a number of ways.

- Although they may look like switchblades when used, assisted opening knives are not switchblades. There is an important legal difference between the two, so you can't call them switchblades in your writing.
- Assisted opening knives have been available to characters across the country from the mid-1990s through today. It's a better bet that a character would be using an assisted opener versus a switchblade.
- Military and law enforcement characters are able to carry new switchblades, but they call them *automatic knives* when used in recent settings.
- The switchblade market for civilians is limited. Most models are expensive custom jobs or antiques. Keep that in mind when assigning a character a switchblade instead of an assisted opener. Should the character be carrying an old switchblade? Does she have access to or an interest in newer, custom switchblades?
- Actual switchblades are best for use in stories set prior to the mid-1990s.
- If a character really needs a restricted switchblade, chances are good he would be able to obtain one from a dubious source.

Finally, my rule of thumb is to give characters living in the mid-1990s onward assisted opening knives instead of switchblades. If *assisted opening knives* is too clunky, go with *assisted opener* or just *assisted* after the first reference.

OTHER HIGH-REGULATION KNIVES

Switchblades aren't the only knives with exceptional restrictions. Butterfly knives, knives disguised as mundane objects (canes, belts, etc.), concealed carry knives, dirks, daggers, knives with lengthy blades, and even folding knives may be subject to special attention from lawmakers.

These knives aren't addressed at the federal level, though. They're left to state and local jurisdictions. If a private investigator in your book needs to lawfully carry a concealed knife, for example, you should do a quick check of the city or state laws.

POCKET CLIPS

Starting in the 1980s, many knives were sold with pocket clips, which allowed users to hook them into a pocket for easier carrying, sort of like a pen.

But pocket clips can also tip off others that the character has a knife. When dealing with law enforcement, this may initiate something called a "Terry Stop." That means a police officer conducts a limited search of a person's clothing on the suspicion that he or she has a weapon. This is sometimes called a *frisk*.

For this reason, a character who's experienced with knives might not use a pocket clip if stealth is a must. It's just a matter of slipping the knife into the pocket instead of clipping it.

IS THERE A PERFECTLY LEGAL CARRYING KNIFE?

When writing this guide, I made every attempt to identify a universally legal, go-to knife for characters to carry around in fiction, but to no avail. Outside of nail clippers and plastic picnic cutlery, no one in the knife industry will make the claim that a certain blade is legal absolutely everywhere in the United States.

That doesn't mean there aren't rules of thumb based in real-world experience. Mike Haskew came up with a couple of pointers in the Winter 2013 issue of *Living Ready* magazine. Knives that are generally legal in most locations should:

- be a maximum blade length of $2\frac{1}{2}$ inches.
- look like something Grandpa would've used.

These pointers are no guarantee, but a small, classic-looking pocketknife is the best bet for a universally legal carrying knife. If a story demands legality, go with that.

THE PERFECTLY ACCEPTABLE RESPONSE

A solid set of rules exists for how characters should respond to law enforcement officers when knives are involved (if they want to stay out of trouble, that is). Haskew wrote his suggestions for real people who carry a knife and have a run-in with police.

- When asked why the knife is being carried, the response is always, "Because it's a tool."
- Never refer to the knife as a weapon.
- Never say the knife is being carried for self-defense.
- Never argue with officers about the knife.
- Do not consent to a search without a warrant, but do not resist physically.
- If arrested, say nothing other than to ask for an attorney.

Protagonists and antagonists in fiction will likely act in more dramatic ways, but at least you now have a good base from which to work.

KNIVES AND SELF-DEFENSE

The law is not on the side of those who use knives violently, even for self-defense.

The most generous legal interpretation of self-defense in the entire United States permits violence only until the threat is stopped. One shot, one stab, one punch, one kick over that line, and it's no longer considered self-defense.

With knives, the only self-defense application clearly within the bounds of law is to inflict an injury that allows a retreat that would not otherwise be possible. Even if you use a knife to prevent great bodily harm, things can get gray in a hurry.

That's due to the nature of knife violence itself. The successful use of a knife (in a fighting situation) requires the person with the knife to hold a physical advantage over another. This leads to some murky legal territory, since self-defense laws are grounded in disparity of force (i.e., the one using the weapon is outmatched by a threat).

Stabbing someone to death for thirty seconds requires thirty seconds of holding a physical advantage over another. No disparity of force exists if the one with the knife can spend that time stabbing the other person to death—even if the one being stabbed was originally the "bad guy" in the situation. A jury might see such an incident as murder instead of self-defense.

Let's drag Maynard's sore bones out of his decrepit RV for an example.

Maynard Soloman, gal-damn detective, is standing in line at a goat burger stand. Bill Robber, hungry from a recent jog evading his baby mamas, budges in front of Maynard.

The two get in an argument, and Bill pulls out a gun. Maynard, fearing for his life, takes out a knife and stabs Bill in the hand. Bill drops the gun. Maynard picks up the gun and continues to stab Bill in the hand and arm before both stagger away from the scene. Both Maynard and Bill survive.

Did Maynard break the law?

Depending on the setting, Maynard likely wound up on the wrong side of the law.

The threat to Maynard's life was gone when he picked up Bill's gun. He shouldn't have stabbed Bill past that point, even if the budging bastard deserved it.

This is why the frenzied knife violence in thrillers and crime fiction doesn't often reflect legal realities. Characters might think they're acting in self-defense when they cut one hundred holes in the devil incarnate. But a prosecutor may not let that slide.

As suggested in the Must-Know Firearm Laws section, keep this nugget in mind: Stop the threat. That's the point of self-defense.

A BRIEF WORD ABOUT CONCEALED CARRY OF KNIVES

Just like firearms, knives are subject to concealed carry laws. These vary by state and local municipality. Research the laws of a particular setting to be certain. In general, states with relaxed firearms laws take the same attitude toward knives.

MATCHING A KNIFE
TO A CHARACTER

When assigning a knife to a character, writers enjoy much more wiggle room compared to fire-arms. It's more important to get the knife type right than it is to reference a specific model.

Therefore, this section will focus on matching a character to a knife type, not to a specific knife. Writers can stop the search at the end of the step-by-step instruction, or they can use the result they come to as a launching pad to investigate specific models. I like any excuse to go to a sporting goods stores, but that's just me.

Remember, it's perfectly acceptable to use the generic term *knife* if it saves time and trouble. But when a knife matters a good deal to writing a character, follow these steps for the best match.

1. WHAT IS THE ROLE OF THE CHARACTER?

What part does the character play in the story? A police officer on patrol? A cranky private in-vestigator living in a rattrap RV? Identical twins selling goat burgers outside a flea market? This identification is the first step in assigning a knife.

2. HOW WILL THE KNIFE BE USED?

What cutting tasks are on deck for the knife? From opening mail to gutting a thief, this is impor-tant to know ahead of time.

The most common knife tasks in thrillers and crime fiction are:

- attacking
- dismemberment
- intimidation/effect
- mundane cutting jobs
- outdoor work (utilitarian tasks involving wood, rope, chores, etc.)
- self-defense

Choose one or more, then go to the next step.

3. HOW HARD WILL THE KNIFE BE USED?

Knives can only take so much before they fail. Physically large cutting jobs require more rugged knives (think of hacking through a dense jungle or a side of beef). Delicate cutting jobs are reserved for a similar type of knife suited for gentler use (such as digging out a bullet from a wound).

With that in mind, how hard will the knife be used?

- very hard (anything that exerts a great amount of pressure on the blade)
- somewhat hard (a workout akin to cutting up a chicken)
- not hard (levels of pressure similar to opening mail or shaving)

4. HOW MUCH DOES STEALTH MATTER?

A steak knife doesn't offer much in the way of stealth; it's hard to conceal. On the other hand, a folding knife slips easily into the pocket. This can be crucial to a pivotal plot point.

How much stealth is required for the character?

- a lot
- some
- none

5. HOW SKILLED IS THE CHARACTER?

Knife skills matter, and slicing cheese doesn't make a person an expert. I've witnessed all sorts of people catch a cut from their own blades—including those very familiar with knives.

Setting the skill level for a character matters. Is this someone with a lot of knife know-how? Or is a plastic picnic knife the only thing she has ever picked up? Choose from the following skill levels:

- beginner
- intermediate
- expert

6. CHOOSE THE KNIFE TYPE

Select the knife type that most closely matches the previous choices. These are categorized by their best fit based on real-world applications. Of course, creative license can provide some wiggle room. I included axes and straight razors for reference, although those aren't technically knives.

Ax/Hatchet

- **APPROPRIATE TASKS:** attacking, dismemberment, intimidation, outdoor work
- **INTENSITY OF USE:** very hard
- **STEALTH OFFERED:** none
- **SKILL LEVEL REQUIRED:** intermediate

Butcher Knife

- **APPROPRIATE TASKS:** attacking, dismemberment, intimidation, mundane cutting jobs, self-defense
- **INTENSITY OF USE:** somewhat hard to very hard
- **STEALTH OFFERED:** none
- **SKILL LEVEL REQUIRED:** beginner

Butterfly Knife

- **APPROPRIATE TASKS:** attacking, intimidation, self-defense
- **INTENSITY OF USE:** not hard
- **STEALTH OFFERED:** a lot
- **SKILL LEVEL REQUIRED:** expert

Fixed Blade Knife

- **APPROPRIATE TASKS:** attacking, dismemberment, intimidation, mundane cutting jobs, outdoor work, self-defense
- **INTENSITY OF USE:** very hard
- **STEALTH OFFERED:** some
- **SKILL LEVEL REQUIRED:** beginner

Folding Knife/Pocketknife

- **APPROPRIATE TASKS:** attacking, intimidation, mundane cutting jobs, outdoor work, self-defense
- **INTENSITY OF USE:** somewhat hard
- **STEALTH OFFERED:** a lot
- **SKILL LEVEL REQUIRED:** intermediate

Kitchen Knife (Excluding Butcher Knives)

- **APPROPRIATE TASKS:** mundane cutting jobs, self-defense
- **INTENSITY OF USE:** somewhat hard
- **STEALTH OFFERED:** none
- **SKILL LEVEL REQUIRED:** beginner

Machete

- **APPROPRIATE TASKS:** attacking, dismemberment, intimidation, mundane cutting jobs, outdoor work, self-defense
- **INTENSITY OF USE:** very hard
- **STEALTH OFFERED:** none
- **SKILL LEVEL REQUIRED:** expert

Straight Razor

- **APPROPRIATE TASKS:** intimidation, mundane cutting jobs
- **INTENSITY OF USE:** not hard
- **STEALTH OFFERED:** a lot (they're usually foldable)
- **SKILL LEVEL REQUIRED:** beginner (for cutting other characters, not for shaving—that takes practice)

Switchblade/Automatic/Assisted Opening Knife

- **APPROPRIATE TASKS:** attacking, intimidation, mundane cutting jobs, outdoor work, self-defense
- **INTENSITY OF USE:** somewhat hard
- **STEALTH OFFERED:** a lot
- **SKILL LEVEL REQUIRED:** expert

SPECIAL NOTE: Prior to the mid-1990s, assisted opening knives didn't exist, so you must assign a switchblade for earlier occurring settings. Modern switchblades would be called *automatic knives*. See the section on knife laws in this book.

Throwing Knife

- **APPROPRIATE TASKS:** attacking
- **INTENSITY OF USE:** not hard
- **STEALTH OFFERED:** none
- **SKILL LEVEL REQUIRED:** expert

EHAMPLE SCENARIOS

Example Scene 1: Garage Sale from Hell

The scene calls for a knife fight. Maynard Soloman is browsing a crowded garage sale. The cheap gumshoe can't resist a bargain on golf pants.

Also at the garage sale is Bill Robber. He's not there for the deals, though. He's seeking revenge on Maynard for cracking the case that put him in prison for ten years. Bill's plan is to quickly stab Maynard in the chest at the crowded garage sale, then use the confusion to make a clean getaway.

What would be the best knife for Bill to use? With the character's role in the scene identified, the knife requirements break down like this:

- **TASK:** attacking
- **INTENSITY OF USE:** not hard (the scene calls for a quick stab)
- **STEALTH REQUIRED:** a lot (it's a crowded garage sale and Bill wants to be sneaky)
- **KNIFE SKILL LEVEL:** intermediate

Using that information, Bill's options are a butterfly knife, a folding knife/pocketknife, and a switchblade/automatic/assisted opening knife. I'll give Bill the butterfly knife, since they're hard to use. I hope he cuts himself. Jerk.

A fixed blade knife kept in a concealed sheath almost made the cut. It might've worked, but the scene required too much stealth for Bill to risk it.

Example Scene 2: Outsourcing Crime

For this scene, Bill Robber realizes he could save time and money for his criminal activity by outsourcing the work. He hires an expert criminal named Mary Johnson to bust up—literally—a sidewalk vegetable stand in an urban area. Bill wants the stand's owners to pay a protection fee for the privilege of selling sweet corn and tomatoes. He tells Mary to dismantle the stand in the cover of night.

What knives should Mary carry on her visit to the vegetable stand?

- **TASK:** mundane cutting jobs
- **HOW HARD THE KNIFE WILL BE USED:** very hard
- **STEALTH REQUIRED:** some (this is an urban vegetable stand)
- **KNIFE SKILL LEVEL:** expert

Mary's knife options are limited to a fixed blade knife. An ax or hatchet is a close second, but neither of those can be concealed as they're carried down the street. Of course, chopping up a vegetable stand in an urban area is a pretty obvious thing to begin with, but Bill isn't the best criminal. As an expert, Mary would still be selective about the kind of knife she uses. It'll come in handy when she turns on Bill after he "forgets" to pay her.

Example Scene 3: On Patrol

The final example scene isn't as action oriented as the others. This time, police officer Penny Flyswatter wants a knife to have on her person for when she patrols criminal hot spots, such as garage sales and sidewalk vegetable stands.

What's the best option for Penny?

- **TASKS:** mundane cutting jobs, self-defense
- **HOW HARD THE KNIFE WILL BE USED:** somewhat hard
- **STEALTH REQUIRED:** some (it would benefit Penny to have a concealable knife)
- **KNIFE SKILL LEVEL:** expert

The field is wide open for Penny. Her choices include a fixed blade knife (with a well-placed sheath; see the section on sheaths in this book), a folding knife/pocketknife, and a switchblade/automatic/assisted opening knife. If a fixed blade knife is assigned, a well-placed sheath would also have to be written into the story. Those are covered in another section.

Because Penny is in law enforcement, I'll give her the automatic knife. She can use it without restriction.

TAKE IT ONE STEP FURTHER

Once an appropriate knife type is assigned to a character, you may decide that you are finished. But if you want a more in-depth depiction, you can take it one step further.

With the knife type in mind, choose a specific model using the listings in the Hit List section of this guide. A visit to a sporting goods store or online knife shop will also outline your options.

When choosing a knife model, take note of the weight, blade length, overall length, style, and history. Do those specs jive with the scene and character? Remember: Bigger isn't always better. A manageable knife that suits the character is the best bet.

As noted at the beginning of this section, the knife type matters more than the specific model. In this way, knives differ from firearms. However, the world of knives is rich with variety and innovation. Dive as deeply as you like.

HOW TO KILL A CHARACTER WITH A KNIFE

DISSECTING KNIFE VIOLENCE: THE THREE PURPOSES

Knife fights are a brutal business in both fiction and reality. The personal nature of the violence almost requires a reversion to primitive instincts. Maybe that's why stories of attacks with edged weapons have been around since storytelling itself.

However, *knife fight* might not be the best term to describe the situation. *Fight involving knives* may be the better way to put it. Unlike firearms, knives don't define the fight. Knives are accessories to a scene. They're in the picture, but they aren't the frame.

That's because a prolonged fight involving only knives is unlikely in the real world. As an online editor for *BLADE*, I attended several knife-fighting demonstrations at various events. These choreographed martial arts demonstrations involved two combatants, each with a knife. While these performances were certainly interesting and required great talent to master, they had more in common with dancing than they did with fighting.

Sure, a character can break out some gratuitous mall ninja knife moves that would make the ghost of Bruce Lee proud. But for violent knife depictions grounded in reality, there really are only three practical applications:

1. attacking another character using the element of surprise
2. a last resort for self-defense
3. mutilating or intimidating another character who cannot fight back

Pick up a newspaper and flip to the crime section. The majority of knife violence, unfortunately, will fall into those three categories. Note the circumstances that led to the violence, then work backward to determine how the type of knife influenced the outcome. It's surprising how well this can inform a scene, though it's a bit morbid.

Fiction isn't journalism, but recognizing the nature of this violence is key to understanding the knives themselves. Some knives are better than others for carrying out brutal tasks.

THINK QUICK, KNIVES ARE FAST FIGHTERS

When writing a fight, think of knives as racecars careening through a scene at 200 mph. They're fast. In the time line of the story, they should cross their finish line faster than a football captain on prom night. There are four reasons for this.

First, as stated in the section on knife laws, using a knife in a violent encounter—even if it's for self-defense—treads some gray legal grounds. If a character intends to stay on the right side of Johnny Law, a prolonged knifing just isn't going to look good in the courts of law or public opinion.

Second, a struggle involving a knife dramatically increases the risk of a self-inflicted injury. Blades don't come with an off switch. They cut anything they touch. The shorter the encounter, the better the odds that the character with the knife will make it out unscathed.

Creative license can influence those odds. Michael Myers managed to murder scores of victims in the *Halloween* movies without accidentally cutting himself. Thrillers and crime fiction are certainly allowed to take the same liberties. But in the real world, people have difficulty slicing bagels without injuring themselves. My father chopped all but a shred of a finger off while butchering a chicken. And unlike a character in fiction, the headless, plucked chicken wasn't fighting back.

Third, there's going to blood. For some reason, thrillers and crime fiction overlook this fact all the time—it's as if blood disappears into the ether after a cut. The character using the knife is going to get messy. Maybe that matters to the story, maybe it doesn't. But the blood has to go somewhere.

Fourth, even if none of the three other points matter, knife fights are physically taxing. Get out of that chair and run in place for a solid minute. It's exhausting, right? Now imagine doing that with a knife while another person tries to kill you.

Granted, characters might be in better shape than the average writer (not you, though; I mean those other writers). It's still worthwhile to have a perspective on the physical toll anything beyond a quick knife encounter will take.

KNOW THE THREE WAYS TO INJURE

There are essentially three ways to inflict injury using a knife.

1. **STABBING:** The knife is thrust into a target.
2. **SLASHING AND CUTTING:** The knife is in motion as a laceration is made along the edge of the blade.
3. **CHOPPING AND HACKING:** The knife's edge is pushed deeper into a target.

These definitions might seem obvious, but things get fuzzy when knives are part of the action in a scene. Is the particular knife suited to stabbing, slashing, chopping, or some combination of the three? Keep it consistent.

A kitchen cleaver is ideal for hacking a hunk of meat off a character, but it's not designed for stabbing. It's a metal square. There's no tip.

A generic folding knife might take care of stabbing plus slashing, but not chopping or hacking.

A straight razor will slash an ear clean off. It might be up for limited stabbing action, but straight razors lack a tip. Chopping or hacking is off-limits, since straight razors are on the flimsy end of the knife spectrum.

The idea is to keep injury routes consistent with the knife design.

A less-common way to injure with a knife is by sawing, which for the purposes of this guide is considered a type of hacking. Striking a character with an unsharpened component of the knife, such as the bottom of the handle (pommel), is another way to inflict harm.

KNIFE COMBAT ESSENTIALS

Four essential scenes make up the bulk of knife violence in fiction. These are similar to the three purposes outlined previously but focus more on the *what* than the *why*.

- grappling
- mutilation
- self-defense
- surprise attack

In all situations, remember the 21-foot rule of thumb. As determined by the Tueller Drill (a law enforcement drill), an attacker with a knife 21 feet or less away can inflict a lethal injury before the defender can draw, aim, and fire a gun. This may help to explain news reports of police officers shooting people with edged or blunt weapons to death. Consider the 21-foot rule when writing fiction, too. It applies to both the attacker and the defender.

Grappling

Intense struggles involving knives are so profoundly brutal in the intimacy of their violence that they leave little wiggle room between life and death. In the same way no one can be a little bit pregnant, a knife fight is an all-in proposition, a commitment to seeing through to the death of an opponent who is only an eyelash's distance away.

These struggles make for great fiction for that reason, but many depictions leave out one critical element: The character with the knife is probably going to get cut—maybe even worse than the one under attack. For whatever reason, fiction awards injuries only when they're convenient. That's fine, but I'd make the case that everyone in the struggle is going to get cut at some point.

Regardless, I suggest six routes to take as characters grapple with knives:

1. One character gains a physical advantage and uses the knife to injure the other.
2. The character without the knife gains a physical advantage and/or control of the knife, then injures the other.
3. The character without the knife manages to escape.

4. The character with the knife manages to escape.

5. Both characters succumb to injuries.

6. Both characters come to the conclusion that knife fights are crazy. They shake hands and get lunch.

Okay, that last one is unrealistic. A little humor never hurts.

The meat of the scene will be how these ends are achieved. How is the physical advantage obtained? Does the knife change hands? Toss in some dramatic descriptions, and it's a knife fight.

Just remember that during that struggle, the blade will change its orientation many times, and the edge will lacerate whatever it touches.

Also keep in mind the injuries inflicted on the periphery of the violence. Decisive cuts, slashes, and chops are worth words. So are the fingers sliced off as the defender shields his face, the arms gouged as the character slouches into the fetal position, and the cuts made in hesitation before plunging the blade deeper.

Mutilation

When the character with the knife has total dominance or control over the other, it's no longer a fight. It's mutilation.

Serial killers in fiction are most often involved with this category of knife violence. So are torturers of immobilized characters.

This is still a type of combat; it's just one-sided. The only sage advice for writing this scenario is to make sure the type of knife you choose is up for the task.

Self-Defense

As explained in the section about knife laws, self-defense is a difficult proposition when it comes to knives. At best, the knife will be used to inflict an injury that allows a hasty escape when no other means are possible. Hanging around to inflict further injuries when retreat is possible won't look good in court, given the disparity of force would tip in the defender's favor.

That doesn't mean self-defense knife scenes have to be tame. Even a quick knife jab can be forged in fear.

Surprise Attack

Depending on the scenario, a surprise attack is arguably the best way to off a character while using a knife. It removes much of the risk of the attacker becoming injured with her blade during the encounter. For the writer, it can also be a lot of fun to set up.

There are a few classic surprise knife attacks that form the template for the technique.

One of the most widely used in fiction is the quick cut to the throat from behind. This is effective for obvious reasons, but there's a caveat. It may take two hands: one to pull the head back to expose the throat and one to work the knife. Remember that the attacking character likely cannot see the victim's throat. If the victim is looking downward, the knife might catch the chin instead of the throat.

Another standard is the hidden assailant cutting the Achilles tendon at ground level. Writers often put the attacker under a vehicle to catch someone walking nearby.

The aerial knife attack is also common. The classic aerial attack usually involves a concealed character tossing a knife or other edged object into the chest of a target victim. In scenes such as these, remember that, like bullets, these blades are not freight trains. They don't hurl the victim backward upon impact. They make contact, that's it. The victim might stagger, sure, but the knife wouldn't launch him 30 feet. The impact from such a hit also wouldn't stop a running victim in his tracks. In my opinion, the aerial attack is overused without merit in stories, but, hey, it's fiction. (See the discussion of throwing knives in the Knives 101 section for more.)

One surprise attack comes from old military manuals: The kidney stab is perfect for scenes requiring stealth. The attacking character sneaks up from behind, places a hand over the mouth, stabs the kidneys in the lower back, and holds the victim silently in place. The victim dies quietly from blood loss.

No matter how the surprise attack is written, consider what happens immediately after the cut. Human beings, like any other creature, have a will to survive. Drawing their blood doesn't turn them into helpless mannequins. That blood doesn't magically evaporate, either. Ask yourself: Is there a struggle following the attack? Does the attacker get soaked in blood, and does that affect the story? Does the victim make noises during and after the attack? Consider the variables.

WHERE TO USE A KNIFE ON A CHARACTER: KILL-'EM-QUICK HOT SPOTS

When having a character inflict a knife injury, consider some vulnerable hot spots that will put enough blood on the floor to render the victim unconscious or dead in minutes. I won't go too deeply into the anatomical reasoning here, but you might want to consider consulting an anatomy textbook when slicing and dicing your characters to pieces, just so you know what is where.

An additional note: For maximum damage, have the character further twist or gouge these areas with the knife after making a puncture. This will open up the wound further and allow more blood to spill out.

Throat and Neck

These areas house the jugular veins and carotid arteries. Along with the carotid artery, there are three pairs of jugular veins: external, internal, and anterior. They all share a common intersection in the neck as they pump blood to and return blood from the head and the heart. A solid knife strike to the side and front of the neck and just under the jawline will likely sever one of these vital veins.

In fiction, a prominent misconception about jugular veins is that they spew blood. The high-pressure carotid artery, not the internal jugular veins, actually paints the ceiling with blood. When athletes and first responders feel for a pulse in the neck, they are feeling for the carotid artery. The internal jugular vein is right next to it. Although both are probably severed with the same cut, be sure to use the right term for which is spewing the blood—the carotid artery.

"Talk about a pain in the neck," Maynard Soloman, gal-damn detective, says.

On that note, also beware of terrible puns when writing these throat injuries.

Upper Inner Thigh

This is where you will find the femoral arteries, which deliver fresh blood into the legs before tucking behind the knees and branching off. A cut (or shot) to a character's inner thigh near the groin down to just above knees is going to paint the scene red. There's a reason the area from the inner thighs up to the groin is called the "Triangle of Death," as explained in the section on knife safety.

"Will my jorts stop a cut in the Triangle of Death?" Maynard asks.

Probably not, Maynard. The femoral arteries aren't protected by bone and travel dangerously close to the skin. Even a shallow cut can be lethal.

Upper Inner Arms

This is where you'll find the brachial arteries. The brachial arteries deliver fresh blood to the arms. They run along the inner arms skirting the bottom of the bicep. From about the armpit down to the elbow, a cut in the middle inner arm will result in significant bleeding.

Brachial arteries don't get a lot of attention in fiction, probably because they're hard to reach. Writing one into a scene might set the author apart from all those who rely on passé jugular cuts, since it requires some extra imagination.

Kidneys

These beans are the low-hanging fruit of potential knife injuries. A pile of veins and arteries near the kidneys will bawl blood when cut.

The kidneys are located in the lower back on either side of the spine. A character does not need to know much about the exact location. A stab to the lower back will likely suffice.

Genitals

A character playing exceptionally dirty might go for the genitals. Does this area need much explaining? It's a knife to the genitals. That about sums it up.

WHERE TO USE A KNIFE ON A CHARACTER: CHALLENGING AREAS

Bone is the last defense against a knife attack, and it's a surprisingly effective one. It can deflect or stop anything from a bullet to a blade, depending on conditions. That's bad news for characters wielding a knife as some of the most lethal arteries and veins are protected by bone. A skilled or lucky character can inflict a mortal wound in these areas, but it's harder to accomplish.

Heart

Penetrating the heart or its many arteries and veins with a knife is a death sentence, but only if the blade can find its way past the ribs and breastbone.

Thrillers and crime fiction often depict stab wounds to the heart as if the character were mutilating a boneless turkey breast. The ribs and breastbone (sternum) are there for a reason, and they'll take one hell of a beating before they yield. That presents a problem for writers. Here are three suggestions for getting around it.

1. The character makes a blow with the knife powerful enough to break through the hard plate of the breastbone and/or the ribs to puncture the heart. This requires a physically able character.
2. The character slips the knife "between the ribs" and into the heart. This maneuver would still take some skill or luck. Thankfully for those in the real world, the ribs don't offer gaping spaces for easy access to insides. Neither does the breastbone.
3. If the knife punctures the flesh underneath the breastbone and then pushes up behind it into the heart, the problem is solved. But such a move is just brutal, and it would require a character with some serious strength (and anger issues).

The point is this: The human body is designed to protect the heart at all costs. It takes some doing to reach it with a knife.

Brain

A knife to the brain isn't always fatal, but it may as well be in fiction. Like the heart, the brain is protected by bone, and the skull is one of the toughest bones in the body. Still there are three access points to consider that don't involve the skull.

The first is through the ear canal and into the brain. This would require an exceptionally powerful stab and a longer knife. But it's possible.

Another is through the eyes. This vulnerable area is always a top choice for bringing down a physically dominating character. In addition to being the fleshy doormen to the brain, the eyes can also become blinded with a horizontal cut to the forehead. Of course, a knife to the eye would have a more lasting effect.

The third is up through the nose. It's an overlooked area. Remember those ice pick lobotomies from back in the day?

"I had one as a kid," says Maynard Soloman, gal-damn detective. "Although the ice pick got stuck up there for a few days, the procedure did help me stop lighting fires."

Yes, Maynard, you did, and those quack doctors reached your brain through your nose. A blade up a nostril could take that concept to the next level.

Subclavian Arteries and Veins

These arteries and veins are hard-to-reach sweet spots tucked beneath the clavicle (collarbone). A cut to the subclavians takes extra effort, but it's worth it. Because of the subclavians' awkward positions under the collarbone, the character has zero chance of applying a tourniquet to stop the bleeding.

WHERE TO USE A KNIFE ON A CHARACTER: PAINFUL, BUT NOT ALWAYS DEADLY

Knife wounds can inflict tortuous pain and injury without imposing an immediate death sentence. Shallow stabs and cuts to the legs, arms, sides, and other "meaty" areas can be painful but not necessarily mortal. Here are some specific and particularly painful places to plant a knife without necessarily causing mortal wounds.

"The Guts"

A knife to a character's abdominal area can cause a serious injury, but it's no guarantee of death. It may take time for things to turn south in a major way. Or it might not. This gray area allows for plenty of creative license. But there are a number of organs and arteries (the abdominal aorta, for one) in the guts that, if severed, can ruin someone's day, year, or life.

"And if the knife doesn't work, just have them hit up a cheap buffet. That'll ruin their guts in no time," Maynard says.

Spine

A cut to the spine will render the character immobile. Death is no guarantee, but the inability to move can definitely increase the chances of it.

Tendons

Snipping a tendon anywhere on the body will result in complications. The classic spot to hit in thrillers and crime fiction is the Achilles tendon, located just behind the heel. Cutting it will render the character unable to stand or walk on that foot. Cut both tendons and the character isn't going anywhere. This is one trope from books and film that is actually based in reality.

"Does that mean I should stop wearing black socks and sandals?" Maynard says.

If you're concerned about a slice to the Achilles tendon, it's best to wear thick work boots. Be sure to consider a character's footwear when writing such an attack. Is the Achilles easily accessible or not? High heels, for example, offer little protection.

Infection

True, this isn't a "location," but any wound, even a superficial one, can become infected and thus painful and deadly if untreated. Speed the process up with a dirty knife or seal the wound with filth and you've got a surefire infection on the way. This can lead to drama long after the knife fight is over.

Bleeding Out

Again, not a location, but a serious threat. Any deep cut has the potential to kill, not just the ones located in the various sweet spots. As with infection, it just takes patience and creativity to kill a character this way. And a small cut lengthwise along any artery or vein (even a small one) can cause a flood of blood.

HOW TO DISMEMBER A CHARACTER

Thankfully I have zero real-world experience with the violent dismemberment of a deceased human being. Perhaps unsurprisingly, resources for this topic were hard to locate for this guide (outside of a few death metal bands with questionable medical credentials).

However, chopping up a body isn't all that uncommon in fiction, especially for plots that feature serials killers and organized crime. Here are a few pointers for those stories.

One of the most infamous scenes from the movie *Scarface* involves a drug dealer using a chainsaw to dismember another character in a bathroom. Chainsaws come up quite a bit for dismemberment scenes, but I get the feeling they make cleanup more difficult. A character trying to cover her tracks might opt for knives instead to better direct the carnage.

Also, using a chainsaw indoors is suspicious and could draw unwanted attention, not to mention exhaust fumes. "Unless using chainsaws indoors is a common thing for that setting, of course," Maynard says. "I always use one for carving turkeys in the RV."

Uh, yeah, of course.

Do the tools fit the task? Characters would need heavy-duty knives, usually fixed blades, to complete this gruesome work. If none are available, it's time to get creative.

Does the character fit the task? Dismemberment is physically demanding. Is the character up for the job? Maynard, for example, is frail and has a bad back. He's no Buffalo Bill or Deputy Lou Ford.

Writers are free to conduct research firsthand and write me from prison about the results, but I'm not suggesting they do.

A QUICK WORD ABOUT FORENSICS

The use of forensic science in fiction is a topic that deserves its own separate guide—it's actually a subject that could fill several volumes—but there are some important points to mention here.

In his article *Forensic Autopsy of Sharp Force Injuries* for Medscape.com, Dr. Joseph A. Prahlow, a forensic pathologist at the South Bend Medical Foundation, busts three myths about *CSI*-ing knife injuries Hollywood style.

First, he says, "Forensic pathologists are usually unable to determine the direction of infliction of an incised wound." The shape of a wound doesn't necessarily indicate whether it was made right to left, left to right, up-down, etc. The exception is when flesh alongside the wound points to a particular route.

Second, forensic pathologists can't tell if the attacker was right-handed or left-handed based on the injury, or whether the attacker was in front of or behind the victim. For example, an injury might appear the same with a right-handed attacker standing in front as a left-hander from behind.

Finally, a knife injury has little to say about the blade characteristics. Wound depth, width, and length could all be smaller, equal to, or larger than the blade's dimensions.

So just because your favorite movie includes one of these forensic scenes, it doesn't mean the information gleaned therein is true or accurate.

[PART THREE]
MUST-KNOW
WEAPONS INFO

TOP WEAPONS MYTHS

In this section you'll find common myths and misconceptions found in thrillers, mysteries, and crime fiction. These tropes are easy to trip over, so avoiding them will really juice that writer cred.

1. *CLIP* AND *MAGAZINE* MEAN THE SAME THING.

They don't. And when most writers use *clip*, they really mean *magazine*. Colloquially that may not make a big difference with readers, but, technically speaking, they're not synonymous. Confusing the two is also a major indication that the writer isn't familiar with firearms. In the vast majority of cases, *magazine* or *mag* is accurate.

A *magazine* holds cartridges in reserve inside the firearm, where they wait to be loaded for firing. Some magazines are built into the firearms themselves. Others are detachable.

A *clip* holds cartridges together for insertion into a magazine. Taking the extra step to put the cartridges into the clip can be necessary depending on the firearm's design. However, most firearms don't require a clip outside of a few older models.

Let's say you select a firearm for a story and you can see that it uses a detachable container housing ammunition but aren't sure if *magazine* or *clip* is the right term. Here's an easy rule of thumb for telling the difference: If most of the cartridges are exposed, it's a clip. If most of the cartridges are concealed, it's a magazine.

Again, *magazine* or *mag* are the safe bets in almost all instances. And remember, revolvers don't load with clips or magazines (moon clips are an exception, explained in the section on handgun ammunition).

If this seems like splitting hairs, it's not. This is a *major* gripe from the gun crowd—and therefore with many of your potential readers. It's also an easy fix with a tremendous return on investment.

2. *BULLET* IS THE SAME AS *SHELL, ROUND,* OR *CARTRIDGE.*

This is another set of terms sometimes used interchangeably. Like *clip* and *magazine*, they are *not* the same things.

A bullet is a component of a cartridge (a.k.a. a *shell* or *round*). It's the metal projectile seated at the top of the cartridge.

The cartridge (shell or round) is the whole thing, which includes the bullet, powder, primer, casing, and other components. When Maynard investigates a crime scene, he spots empty casings on the ground, not empty bullets.

These are empty casings, not empty bullets. Bullets are what fly through the air. (Photo courtesy of *Gun Digest*.)

3. PUMPING A SHOTGUN HEIGHTENS THE DRAMATIC EFFECT.

False. This usually happens when one character intimidates another with a shotgun during a tense situation. It actually makes no sense. Having a character pump a shotgun to punctuate the drama has less to do with looking tough and more to do with being stupid.

A pump-action shotgun loads a shell with a single pump. That same pump simultaneously ejects the previously loaded shell, whether it's been fired or not. An extra pump for dramatic effect after the shotgun is loaded is just dumping unfired ammunition onto the ground.

A dramatic shotgun pump is called for only if the firearm is not loaded. However, why stick a character into a tense situation with an unloaded shotgun in the first place?

Instead of Maynard pumping the shotgun to show he means business, he might drop a corny catchphrase instead.

"I'd ask him if he brought oyster crackers, because his face is about to be soup. And then when he asks what oyster crackers are, I'd shoot him in the gal-damn face," Maynard says.

Maynard's quip still isn't as groan inducing as the shotgun pump trope.

4. THE SAME GOES FOR COCKING THE HAMMER ON A HANDGUN FOR DRAMATIC EFFECT.

This trope is usually used when one character intimidates another with a handgun. It's unnecessary for the same reason as dramatic shotgun pumping. Why aim a gun at someone if it's not ready to fire?

Let's start with the basics. There are two kinds of handguns: revolvers and pistols. A revolver has a rotating cylinder of multiple chambers where cartridges are inserted (think Dirty Harry's .44 Magnum or a cowboy's trusty Colt). Pistols use only a single, stationary chamber where cartridges are fed in and out (think James Bond's iconic Walther or a police officer's Glock).

These revolvers and pistols can be further broken down into single-actions and double-actions. Each type addresses the hammer—the metal tab that must be pulled back (cocked) in order to ready the firearm to shoot.

With a single-action revolver, the shooter must manually cock the hammer before each shot. It's a little different with a double-action revolver. The shooter can either cock the hammer or not before pulling the trigger to shoot.

Pistols are another story. Most modern single-action pistols have hammers that must be cocked before firing. However, the hammer is cocked automatically as the firearm is loaded or fired.

With double-action pistols, cocking the hammer is not necessary prior to pulling the trigger. Now let's see if dramatic hammer cocking makes sense with each type.

- **SINGLE-ACTION REVOLVERS:** This type of handgun makes the best case, but dramatic cocking is still unnecessary. A single-action revolver's hammer *must* be cocked before firing. If the point is intimidation, however, don't wait to get the gun ready. Have the character cock it before meeting the opposition.
- **DOUBLE-ACTION REVOLVERS:** A shooter can simply pull the trigger to make this type of handgun fire, so consider additional cocking excessive. A revolver ready to fire is intimidating on its own. Don't add a needless step in the process.
- **SINGLE-ACTION PISTOLS:** Most modern single-action pistols cock automatically as the first round is loaded (explained in the section on handguns). So I'll pose the same question I posed for single-action revolvers: Why on earth would a character entering a taut situation wield a pistol and not be ready to fire? No need for dramatic cocking.
- **DOUBLE-ACTION PISTOLS:** This is an easy one. The character doesn't need to cock anything. Just pull the trigger and shoot. Dramatic cocking is totally unnecessary.

Writers experienced with firearms will think of exceptions to these rules, and they're free to do so. However, here's my rule of thumb: Ditch all dramatic cocking.

There are good reasons for eliminating dramatic cocking that go beyond the technical. A character pausing to unnecessarily cock the hammer is shifting attention away from the surroundings. That split second might be the perfect opportunity for someone else to attack. Also, a writer might lose count of the number of times a handgun is cocked. I've read more than a few stories where a single handgun was cocked multiple times without ever firing. The character kept cocking that hammer over and over.

If all of this went over your head, there's an easy fix: Don't write about characters cocking handguns as a way to accent the drama or highlight a point.

5. MOST RIFLES AND ALL SHOTGUNS RELOAD WITH A PUMP.

For some reason in fiction, it's somewhat common for characters to pump any shotgun (and sometimes rifle) within reach. After all, the *click-clack* sound of a shooter pumping a sliding mechanism underneath the barrel is iconic. That's fine if the firearm uses a pump to load and reload ammunition. But not all do.

As a reader, I've come across many examples of this misnomer. Bolt-action rifle? Pumped for dramatic effect. Sawed-off, single-shot shotgun? Reloaded with a pump. Fully automatic tactical rifle? Pumped. Handguns? Okay, I haven't seen those pumped. Yet.

Know how your weapon works before pumping away at a terrible mistake.

6. IT'S OKAY TO LOOK DOWN THE BARREL TO SEE IF IT'S LOADED.

Nope. Unless a character has a death wish, there is never a reason to look down the barrel of a firearm. If Maynard needs to see if his firearm is loaded, he can crack open the action for a peek at the chamber (the spot inside the firearm where ammunition is seated just before firing).

"Of course, pulling the trigger works, too," Maynard says. "You'll know in a real hurry if the gun is loaded."

7. THE TERM *ASSAULT WEAPON* IS A HANDY CATCHALL TERM FOR ANY RIFLE WITH MILITARY-STYLE FEATURES.

Actually, *assault weapon* is what *irregardless* is to the editorial world. It gets a certain point across, but it's better substituted by another more accurate word.

Federal, state, and local regulations usually use the term *assault weapon* when labeling a category of restricted firearms. None of these regulations are consistent. What was considered an assault weapon in the 1930s is different from the definition in the 1990s. It's also not a term the firearms industry often uses to describe its products.

The solution is to use a term other than *assault weapon*. *Tactical rifle*, *tactical shotgun*, *machine gun*, *submachine gun*, *fully automatic rifle*, and even the ubergeneric *gun* all work better than the vague *assault weapon*. (You can find these terms in the glossary at the end of this book.) They are blanket terms that cover firearms with features suitable for combat or defense. The firearm industry uses these terms, too.

And now for the caveat.

There's yet another way around the term *assault weapon*—using *assault rifle*. The term receives a special mention because of how closely it mirrors the image that, I think, many writers have when using *assault weapon*.

Assault rifle is defined, as Patrick Sweeney writes in *The Gun Digest Book of the AK & SKS*, as "a shoulder-fired, select-fire weapon used by an individual soldier, firing a cartridge of intermediate rifle caliber, with a detachable high-capacity magazine." *Select-fire*, by the way, means it can switch between semi- and full-auto modes.

If a writer is looking for something along those lines, *assault rifle* may be an appropriate upgrade over *assault weapon*.

8. SEMI-AUTOMATIC AND FULLY AUTOMATIC ARE PRETTY MUCH THE SAME THING.

False. A semi-automatic firearm will shoot one time with each pull of the trigger. This is a key difference compared to fully automatic firearms, which can fire multiple times with a single pull of the trigger.

Confusing one for the other is a major trip-up area when writing, especially when citing "automatic" firearms without deciding on the type. Pick one and stick to it.

9. FULLY AUTOMATIC FIREARMS ARE JUST AS ACCURATE AS ANY OTHER WEAPON.

In truth, they lose accuracy in a hurry. Sorry, wannabe Rambos, but holding down the trigger on a fully automatic firearm kills accuracy, not bad guys.

Fully automatic firearms are most accurate when fired in short bursts. This keeps the shots grouped together rather than air balling all over the place.

The reason for this has everything to do with recoil—the manner in which a gun jerks back when firing a round. The impact of recoil becomes exponentially greater the longer the trigger is pulled because there's no recovery time between shots. The shooter is budged off target little by little with each shot. That can translate into big, Shaq-at-the-free-throw-line misses.

Guns mounted to vehicles or structures are a different story, since they transfer that recoil energy into solid materials.

10. FULLY AUTOMATIC FIREARMS WILL FIRE CONTINUOUSLY FOR MINUTES ON END.

Again, wannabe Rambos need to check their egos at the door. Hold down that trigger and don't blink as the thirty-, fifty-, or one hundred-round magazine empties in a matter of seconds, not minutes. That's approximately 1.3 Rambo grunts per magazine—not nearly enough time to cover for Sylvester Stallone's acting abilities.

A character needs to reload every few seconds to keep a continuous stream of lead in the air. Figure that into a scene with a lot of full-auto gunplay. While you're at it, determine how the character is lugging around all that ammunition.

"This is exactly why I fire my fully automatic rifle in short bursts whenever my creditors come to repossess the RV," Maynard says.

Right on, Maynard. That method is more accurate and conserves ammunition.

11. IT'S EASY TO MAKE A VEHICLE'S GAS TANK EXPLODE BY SHOOTING IT.

It's actually pretty difficult. Here are three reasons why.

First, gas tanks are often surrounded by metal and other durable parts. Just take a look underneath any car. Metal can be difficult to puncture with a projectile from a distance, even when that projectile comes out of a firearm.

Second, just because a projectile enters a container of gasoline at high speed doesn't mean an explosion is imminent. Liquid gasoline isn't flammable. Its fumes are what combust. Gas tanks are designed with that in mind, because no one wants the tank to catch fire.

Last, a spark needs to meet those fumes in the presence of oxygen. Gas tanks contain some air, but they're closed off from the outside environment. A big explosion requires a lot of oxygen, which won't be found inside the tank.

"Now wait a minute," Maynard says. "I rolled my RV a few cases back trying to get away from some gun-totin' hippies. They got out and opened fire. The next thing I know, the gal-damn RV is burning hot like a toupee in a toaster. You telling me the sun was in my eyes?"

You weren't seeing things, Maynard. Those hippies executed the best-case scenario for lighting up a vehicle with gunfire. They punctured the gas tank, let the fuel drain out, and fired again to produce a spark off the vehicle or pavement to ignite the fumes.

This trick is the best choice for writers. However, keep in mind the resulting blaze will be more in line with dumping gas on a campfire than it will be an ear-shattering explosion of the sort you see in the movies.

In 2012, I interviewed the organizer of Boomershoot for *Gun Digest*. This for-fun event offers shooters the chance to hit explosive targets. Not kiddie Fourth of July explosives. Huge, might-want-to-take-another-step-back explosives.

The organizer told me the target must be hit solidly in order for the explosives to catch, though powerful firearms (from a safe distance) are used. Not every hit yields an explosion, he said, even those that are right on target.

Unlike vehicles, these explosives are not shielded in metal, they don't require fumes and a spark to ignite, and they are designed to explode when shot by a firearm. Still, they don't light up easily.

While that may make it more challenging to write certain scenes, it should be reassuring the next time you drive a car.

12. A FIREARM'S RATE OF FIRE EQUALS HOW MANY SHOTS IT CAN MAKE IN ONE MINUTE.

What does it mean when the specs on a semi-automatic or fully automatic firearm state its rate of fire is, for example, 1,000 rounds per minute? That means a person could fire one thousand rounds with the gun in one minute, right?

Nope. *Rate of fire* is a mechanical measurement that gauges how quickly consecutive shots can exit the firearm. It's the equivalent of miles per hour in a car, except for guns.

In reality, a firearm shooting for a solid minute is probably going to fail, due to either overheating or a jam, so hitting that rate of fire isn't likely.

Also, a weapon with a high rate of fire isn't necessarily better than one with a low rate. It just means it doesn't need as much time—usually fractions of a second—between consecutive shots.

13. BIGGER KNIVES ARE ALWAYS BADDER.

Nope, not always. Big knives, such as machetes, play a prominent role in horror, war, adventure, thriller, and crime fiction. In the real world, they are heavy, bulky, difficult to conceal, and harder to control than smaller knives.

Smaller knives are, as a rule of thumb, easier for characters to use for fighting, transporting, concealing, and opening their mail.

"I don't know what you mean. I always greet the mailman with my machete," Maynard says.

There are surely exceptions to this rule. But in my experience, smaller knives are usually more practical for the rigors of reality. For instance, the experts in professional knife-fighting demonstrations at *BLADE* events use small knives, not large ones.

The fuller, or blood groove, on this blade looks like a long trench carved out of the metal. The term *blood groove* has more to do with balance and aesthetics than blood and guts. (Photo courtesy of SharpByCoop for *BLADE*.)

14. BLOOD GROOVES (ALSO CALLED FULLERS) ON A KNIFE ARE NAMED AFTER THE BODILY FLUID.

Despite what their name implies, these long indentations along a knife's blade aren't actually used for channeling blood from a wound. They don't make it easier to remove the blade from a body, either. Rather they reduce the weight of the blade. That's about it. Knife designers use blood grooves to achieve a certain balance or feel. Blood grooves are actually pretty boring.

15. DULL KNIVES ARE SAFER KNIVES.

Actually, the Boy Scouts had it right: Sharp equals safe; dull equals dangerous. Dull knives are not safer than sharp knives. The sharper the cutting edge, the more efficiently it distributes force into what is being cut. A dull blade will actually look roundish when viewed under a microscope. The roundness doesn't offer much friction to grip with, so it moves force away from the cutting edge, causing the knife to slip.

"I look roundish when *not* viewed under a microscope. So I know all about dull knives," Maynard says. "Here's a tip. Everyone makes a big deal about sharpening knives before torturing someone. I say use a knife as dull as an orange slice in the sun. That'll knock some socks off."

16. A GUN IS ALWAYS MORE DANGEROUS THAN A KNIFE.

Surprisingly, this is false in some situations. Knives are as lethal as firearms at distances of 21 feet or less. There's an old saying about never bringing a knife to a gun fight, but when a knife-wielding bad guy confronts Maynard 21 feet away, the gal-damn detective's revolver is not guaranteed a win.

Sgt. Dennis Tueller created the Tueller Drill in 1983 to develop handgun skills during a knife attack. It was determined that an attacker could be shot and killed with a holstered handgun at a range of *only* 21 feet or more. At closer than 21 feet, the knife attacker could reach the gunman before he was able to draw and shoot.

This 21-foot rule has garnered its share of controversy, given the infinite variables of defensive situations. But it's still a good rule of thumb for writing fiction. Maynard has about 1.5 seconds (per the Tueller Drill) to draw his handgun from the holster and shoot the knife-wielding bad guy who is 21 feet away.

Even then, you must consider that mortally wounded people don't die right away. So there's still time beyond that 1.5 seconds for the bad guy to plant a blade in Maynard's chest.

17. SWITCHBLADES ARE THE MOST DEADLY KIND OF KNIVES.

In truth, they aren't any deadlier than other knives. The reason switchblades are illegal has less to do with their lethal ability and more to do with the politics of the mid-twentieth century. That's covered earlier in this guide.

The Writer's Guide to Weapons

There's not much a less restricted type of knife can't do just as well, or better, than a switchblade. For example, newer, legal knives called *assisted openers* appear to function identically to a switchblade. However, because of their mechanical design, assisted openers are far less restricted. Also, the lethality of any knife depends on how it's used, not necessarily its design.

18. SUPPRESSORS (A.K.A. SILENCERS) RENDER A GUN COMPLETELY SILENT.

Writing a silencer into a scene can be a necessary plot device. For obvious reasons, Maynard requires stealth when he takes out the sleeping mob boss.

But so-called silencers aren't nearly as effective at muting firearms as fictional accounts would have you believe. They take some of the sting out of the resulting shot, but they don't render the controlled explosion of gunpowder silent. And they certainly don't all make the muted *joot* sound from the movies. (See the Suppressors, Silencers, Scopes, and Sights section in this book.)

19. SAWED-OFF SHOTGUNS ARE FAR MORE POWERFUL THAN THEIR FULL-BARREL COUNTERPARTS.

Ammunition determines firepower, not barrel length. Nothing about sawing off the barrel of any firearm makes it more powerful. The advantages of sawed-offs are detailed in the Shotguns 101 section of this guide.

20. THE "SMELL OF CORDITE" IS IN THE AIR.

Writers depicting the "smell of cordite" in the air after gunfire are forgetting the stuff isn't used in modern gunpowder. It's been obsolete for several decades.

Here's the rule of thumb: If a story is set from the late 1800s to just before World War II, go ahead and reference cordite. After World War II, call it gunpowder or propellant and leave it at that.

21. TILTING A HANDGUN TO THE SIDE TO LOOK COOL IS AN EFFECTIVE WAY TO SHOOT.

Just say no to tilted handguns. The cool factor wears off when the shooting starts. (Photo courtesy of *Gun Digest*.)

Actually, it's a great way to hit nothing. Any character familiar with handguns would not attempt to shoot in this way.

Maynard likes to look badass at bingo halls. He tilts his handgun to the side, gangsta style, when demanding a review of the numbers called. He'll look plenty mean until the shooting starts.

With their short barrels, handguns are difficult to shoot accurately in the first place. Tilting a gun reduces accuracy even further.

Shots fired this way tend to pull horizontally to the left or right. This is because recoil moves force along the bend of the shooter's wrist. That's not helpful when Maynard aims at a vertically oriented bingo number caller.

Bottom line: Tilting is for looks or intimidation only. Correct it when the shooting starts.

Of course, the same applies to tilted shotguns and rifles.

22. BEING SHOT BY A GUN IS LIKE GETTING HIT BY A TRAIN LOADED WITH CONCRETE AND CIRCUS ANIMALS.

Physics says otherwise. For example, a bad guy shoots Maynard with a shotgun at close range near a window. The force from the shot blows Maynard through the window, sending him down ten stories to his death.

But Maynard's actually okay, because physics wouldn't allow for that to happen.

"Actually, I'm bleeding pretty bad," Maynard says.

Yes, Maynard would still be shot, but the blast wouldn't send him through the window to fall to his death. Replace the shotgun with another type of firearm, or the window with another structure, and the song remains the same.

Consider Newton's third law of motion: Every action has an equal and opposite reaction. If the gunshot carried enough force to throw Maynard through a window, an equal amount of force would be exerted on the shooter. The shooter should be blown backward just as Maynard was thrown forward.

That just doesn't happen with firearms. It's a good thing, too, for shooters and windows everywhere.

Even if he's shot at from a close distance, Maynard isn't going far. He'll take the shot, stagger, and probably fall to the floor. The projectile(s) will either lodge inside his body or pass through him. Keep in mind that humans are mostly water. Shoot a bag of water and it doesn't fly across the room, but it may explode, rip open, or leak.

"That's what I'm doing right now," Maynard says. "Please get a towel; I'm dying over here."

23. REAL-WORLD GUNFIGHTS CAN DRAG ON AND ON.

In truth, they are usually over in a few seconds. The 3-3-3 Rule is commonly cited in the defensive firearms arena. It goes like this: Most gunfights in the real world last for three seconds, involve three rounds of ammunition, and take place at a distance of 3 yards.

Sounds kind of boring, huh? That's why the world needs fiction writers.

Although the 3-3-3 Rule isn't set in stone, it's a great formula for writing. Figure in one shot per gun-wielding character per second. The most famous gunfight in U.S. history, the Gunfight at the OK Corral, likely took place in thirty seconds and involved an equal number of shots fired.

How you write gunfights is up to you. If you're shooting for accuracy, keep the 3-3-3 Rule in mind. If your aim is to entertain readers with something longer and filled with gunfire, at least you have an understanding of this concept.

24. HANDGUNS GO *CLICK-CLICK-CLICK* WHEN THEY'RE EMPTY.

A typical trope in fiction is for a character—usually an antagonist—to become surprised by an empty handgun at an inconvenient moment. The character pulls the trigger repeatedly, but the firearm just goes *click-click-click*.

For semi-automatic pistols, that's just not mechanically possible. A single click *might* be audible depending on the model, but certainly not multiple clicks with each pull of the trigger. This is because the pistol must actually be shot to reset the firing pin, which is the source of the click.

With revolvers, it's obvious after the first click that the handgun is out of ammunition, so pulling the trigger again isn't warranted. Same goes with rifles and shotguns.

Rule of thumb: Keep the clicks to one at most.

25. CHARACTERS SHOULD SHOOT THE LOCKS OUT OF DOORS TO GAIN ENTRY.

Doing so is dangerous and a bad idea. After encountering a locked door, Maynard *might* be able to gain entry by shooting the lock out. Much depends on whether the part of the lock destroyed is also the part latching the door. More powerful firearms are more likely to be successful. Even then there's no guarantee something as simple as a standard padlock will break apart.

But the real issue is the risk of injury. Shooting a lock a few feet away (or any object up close) could create a spray of deadly shrapnel. Ouch. Better find the key instead.

HALF-MYTHS TO KEEP IN MIND

In the process of creating this list, several myths came up that fell into a gray area. Here's a quick rundown.

- It is possible for a loaded firearm to fire when dropped, but it's not likely. It'd be even more unusual (read: highly unlikely) for the dropped firearm to shoot more than once.
- Bullets can create sparks when ricocheting off metal, but the visual effect is not nearly as dramatic as what's depicted in fiction. Sparks would be brief and tiny. They wouldn't light up a room as the bullet bounces here and there.
- It's possible for people to die immediately from a single gunshot wound, such as one to the head, but it's not always the case. The old cowboy movies liked to depict people getting shot once and immediately dying, as if bullets were the Grim Reaper's sickle. Death can come that quickly, but remember that it's also possible for mortally wounded people to survive for a short time. Deer hunters have told stories of game being shot through the heart and running dozens of yards. Humans aren't so different.
- A successful shot through a glass window is possible, but it's challenging to accomplish with any accuracy. Consider that glass, along with any obstruction, will affect (or stop)

a bullet's trajectory. The thicker the glass, the more energy it will absorb from the bullet and the more likely it is to stop the projectile. Bullet-resistant glass is built in layers designed to flex and absorb more energy than nonresistant glass, but it can still fail. In either case, creative license allows you to choose if a shot successfully breaks through the glass. In reality, there are no guarantees one way or the other.

- Chances are better than not that Maynard will be okay if he jumps in a lake as bad guys shoot at him. A bullet entering water will be slowed down and could change trajectory. It's no guarantee of survival, though. Maynard still has to come up to breathe.
- Shooting a tire on a moving vehicle is difficult but not impossible. Maynard should aim for the sidewall, not the tread, for the best chance of penetrating the tire. The sidewall isn't as tough as the tread, and more of it is exposed. That means Maynard needs to drive his RV so it's parallel to the bad guy's car before trying to shoot out the tires.
- Firing shots at a car speeding away is more likely to cause collateral damage than anything else. Sure, a lucky shot could take out a tire or window. What about the shots that don't hit the vehicle? Would they connect with an innocent bystander instead? And would a wounded or dead driver actually be more of a hazard?
- Misfires can happen, but fiction—as a matter of convenience—exaggerates their frequency and their timing.

ONE FINAL POINT: IT'S NOT THE SIZE OF THE BOAT BUT THE MOTION OF THE OCEAN

Big firearms and the power they pack get all the attention in thrillers and crime fiction. Their lethality seems to be proportional to their size.

However, there are many more factors at play than just size. Shot placement is a big one. If Maynard pops a bad guy in the heart with a light rifle, he has a good chance of making a kill. Likewise a poorly placed shot with a larger rifle may leave "just a flesh wound."

Distance, angle, properties of the projectile, environmental conditions, shooter ability, and interfering materials are as important as firepower.

Bottom line: Any firearm can be lethal, but not every firearm is always lethal. Don't outfit characters with a "big gun" to suggest lethality. Make the characters skilled shooters instead.

THE HIT LIST

What follows is a go-to catalog of firearms and knives to use for writing. The aim is to make it easy for you to find a firearm or knife to use for a character or scene.

TOP FIREARMS AND KNIVES OF FILM AND FICTION

.38 Special Revolvers/Snubnoses

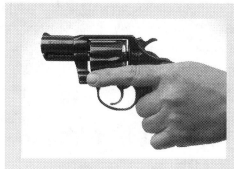

The Colt Detective Special embodies the classic "snubnose" revolver. Consider a character's hand size before assigning a snubbie or any handgun. As a rule of thumb, the size of the hands should roughly match the size of the gun. (Photo courtesy of *Gun Digest*.)

- **TYPE:** revolver
- **CAPACITY:** five or six
- various makes and models

It's hard to pin down exactly when the .38 Special revolver became forever linked to the hard-boiled PIs and dark-alley detectives of fiction. It may have started with Elliot Ness, the famous lawman of Prohibition, who carried a .38. Midcentury crime fiction, influenced by the gangster era of Prohibition, may have transplanted Ness' sidearm into its stories, placing the .38 in the hands of hard-drinking detectives as a sort of ironic twist. That's my theory anyway.

What isn't a theory is how often the .38 Special shows up in fiction. Although any revolver with a short barrel could be considered a "snubnose," the .38 is the most iconic. It's appropriate to write this revolver as a ".38" or ".38 Special," as both refer to roughly the same thing (caliber/ammunition).

Several companies make snubnose revolvers. Perhaps the most iconic is the aptly named Colt Detective Special. Introduced in 1926, it has a 2-inch barrel, holds six rounds, and is a double-action so the trigger can be pulled without the hammer being cocked first. It's still around today and available on the civilian market, where a private eye could pick one up.

While they are iconic, these guns are not without weaknesses. Remember that the shorter the barrel, the worse the accuracy. That snubnose barrel doesn't have much time to spin the bullet and straighten its trajectory. The most experienced characters could probably maintain accuracy out to 25 yards, but that's it.

Still, .38 Special ammunition is relatively easy to shoot, given its lower recoil compared to other calibers. Characters inexperienced with firearms could go with a .38 without breaking their wrists or worse.

Colt Model 1911

Not sure which pistol to assign a character? Write in a Model 1911 and call it a day. Chances are excellent the setting and circumstance will fit. (Photo courtesy of *Gun Digest*.)

- **TYPE:** semi-automatic pistol
- **CALIBER:** .45; the most traditional, but other calibers exist
- **CAPACITY:** varying; as low as six and as high as thirteen
- **YEAR INTRODUCED:** 1911
- single-action (hammer must be cocked manually before first shot)
- slide-action

Ladies and gentlemen, this is *the* handgun of film, fiction, war, law enforcement, and beyond. Originally manufactured by Colt in 1911, the Model 1911 is a platform that has deviated little from John Browning's original designs. Since then, nearly every firearms manufacturer has developed a take on the 1911.

Writers who are stuck about what kind of pistol to assign a character should go with the Model 1911. The classic Colt Model 1911 carries seven rounds of .45 caliber ammunition, although capacities and calibers vary.

Keep in mind that the 1911 is a single-action pistol (hammer must be cocked between each shot), but there's a twist. A character does not need to manually cock the hammer between each shot. The character would insert the magazine, then rack the slide (pulling back and releasing the sliding top of the gun) to chamber the first round. Racking the slide pushes the hammer back in the process. When the pistol is fired, the hammer moves forward and stays there for a brief moment until the force of the shot propels the slide backward, simultaneously cocking the hammer and chambering the next round.

All 1911s use safety mechanisms (multiple mechanisms, in fact) that must be thumbed off before firing. For writing, don't worry about which safety is switched off where. Just have the character "thumb the safety off" and leave it at that.

With that in mind, the 1911 is the perfect go-to choice for writing fiction.

Israeli Military Industries Desert Eagle

The Desert Eagle comes in many varieties, but the monster .50 caliber is most often used in fiction. (Photo courtesy of Shutterstock.)

- **TYPE:** semi-automatic pistol
- **CALIBERS:** .357, .41, .44, .50 (most iconic)
- **CAPACITIES:** nine (.357), eight (.41 and .44), seven (.50)
- **YEAR INTRODUCED:** 1982
- single-action (hammer must be cocked manually before first shot)
- slide-action

The Desert Eagle is the quintessential "hand cannon" in popular culture, permeating everything from books to movies to video games. Many variations exist, but it's the .50 caliber beast that's most often used.

This isn't a handgun for every character (or person). To say it packs a lot of recoil for a handgun is an understatement. Even experienced shooters in great physical shape can become injured operating the Desert Eagle.

This level of overkill may be appealing, or even necessary, to some writers' scenes. That's fine. Just don't assign it to a character who's not able to handle it.

Skilled characters able to plant a .50 caliber bullet into a target will find the imprint it leaves is absolutely devastating. There's no shrugging off a hit.

Although it's a single-action, the Desert Eagle does not require its hammer to be cocked before each shot. As with the 1911, the hammer is cocked as the slide cycles ammunition. The character would "rack the slide" to chamber the first round, then fire away.

Israeli Military Industries Uzi

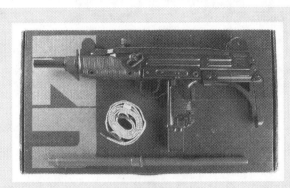

Fiction often puts Uzis in the hands of antagonists. Why? They're flashy, they pump out a lot of lead, and they look good paired with slicked-back hair and a moustache. But that's just one theory. (Photo courtesy of *Gun Digest*.)

- **TYPE:** fully automatic submachine gun
- **CALIBERS:** 9mm (most popular), .41, .45
- **CAPACITY:** twenty, twenty-five, thirty, thirty-two, fifty (9mm only)
- **YEAR INTRODUCED:** 1950
- uses a detachable magazine, not a clip

The term *Uzi* is sometimes written as a catchall for any modern-looking submachine gun, but it actually refers to a particular firearm. It's appropriate to write *Uzi* or *UZI*, although the first probably looks better in print.

Although the firearm's heyday was in decades past, it continues to be used by law enforcement and military organizations around the world. The Uzi's popularity means many variants exist, but go with the specs outlined here as a starting point.

The advantage of the Uzi is its fully automatic operation (multiple shots fire as long as the trigger is pulled) on a compact platform. It's generally considered more accurate than other similar models, although it's said to lack ergonomics. Characters would find the Uzi is best suited for close ranges and short bursts.

The bottom line: From 1950 onward, assigning any character in need of a compact submachine gun with an Uzi is a good call.

Smith & Wesson Model 29—The "Dirty Harry" Revolver

The Model 29 comes in several barrel lengths, which should give writers some leeway. This iconic .44 magnum revolver isn't the most powerful handgun in the world anymore, as Dirty Harry once claimed, but it can still make someone's day, punk. (Photo courtesy of *Gun Digest*.)

- **TYPE:** revolver
- **CALIBER:** .44 magnum
- **CAPACITY:** six
- **YEAR INTRODUCED:** 1956
- double-action (no need to cock the hammer first; just pull the trigger)

"I know what you're thinking. Did he fire six shots or only five? Well, to tell you the truth, in all this excitement I kind of lost track myself. But being this is a .44 magnum, the most powerful handgun in the world, and would blow your head clean off, you've got to ask yourself one question: 'Do I feel lucky?' Well, do you, punk?"

With those lines, Clint Eastwood as "Dirty Harry" Callahan made the Smith & Wesson Model 29 .44 magnum revolver famous around the world. Ever since the 1971 *Dirty Harry* movie, fiction across the board has included the .44 magnum. After all, as Harry says, it's "the most powerful handgun in the world." Or is it?

Actually, this time a movie got it right—in 1971. In this case, it was Hollywood that was feeling lucky. The .44 magnum maintained that title for a handful of years, until other factory ammunition caught up and surpassed it in the early 1980s.

Writers can have at it with the .44 mag for their stories. Call it by its proper name, the Smith & Wesson Model 29, for an added ring of authenticity. Just be sure the character using it can handle all that firepower. This isn't a firearm for first timers or those with weak arm strength.

Tommy Gun

A Thompson Model 1921, better known as the Tommy gun. (Photo courtesy of Paul Goodwin for *Gun Digest*.)

- **TYPE:** fully automatic submachine gun
- **CALIBER:** .45
- **CAPACITY:** twenty, thirty, fifty, one hundred
- **YEAR INTRODUCED:** 1921
- uses detachable magazines or ammunition drums

The iconic Tommy gun is the emblem of crime fiction. Does this need a lot of explaining? Didn't think so.

What writers need to know is that U.S. Brigadier General John Thompson pioneered the firearm during World War I. It took until 1921, however, for Auto-Ordnance to blow up the gun market with its production of the Model 1921 (gun names were so much simpler back then).

The Model 1921 grabbed the attention of police and military forces around the world. They wanted some tweaks for their purposes, and the Model 1923 was the result. However, that version didn't work out for some mechanical reasons.

The Model 1928, introduced in—incredibly enough—1928, got it right. That version and the Model 1921 both gained infamy during the Great Depression and Prohibition. They became so attached to rum-running gangsters that it prompted the passage of the National Firearms Act of 1934, the first significant federal regulation of fully automatic firearms.

Once World War II hit, the U.S. military formally adopted the Tommy gun in 1942, dubbing it the M1 Thompson. (Call it the M1 Thompson when used by U.S. forces in your writing). The war kicked off a ton of innovation that eventually rendered the Tommy obsolete in many respects. It gradually phased out of service after 1945. U.S. characters in the 1950s and 1960s might still use them, although their popularity was finished by the end of the

Vietnam War in the 1970s. International characters might continue to use them beyond the 1970s out of necessity.

For writers, just know that 1921 through the end of World War II in 1945 were prime years for the Tommy gun. Assign this classic to police, military, and criminal characters. Keep in mind, though, that the National Firearms Act restricted civilian purchases of Tommy guns. Average Joe characters would be able to order a Tommy gun out of a Sears catalog between 1921 and 1934, but after that they'd need federal and local permission to own one. See the section on firearm laws for more background on that.

Today new Tommy guns are semi-automatic reproductions for civilian markets. The fully automatics are collectibles and still subject to many restrictions.

Walther Model PPK

James Bond eventually switched to the Walther PPK in Ian Fleming's novels, but the Nazis used it first. Does that make it a bad handgun? Only if it's used by a Nazi. Walther handguns are marvels of firearm engineering, used by respectable organizations around the world. (Photo courtesy of *Gun Digest*.)

- **TYPE:** semi-automatic pistol
- **CALIBER:** .32
- **CAPACITY:** seven
- **YEAR INTRODUCED:** 1929
- double-action (no need to cock the hammer first; just pull the trigger)
- slide-action
- uses a detachable magazine

Author (and former special operative) Ian Fleming kicked off his James Bond novels by assigning the protagonist with a Beretta 418, a .25 caliber semi-automatic pistol small enough to conceal just about anywhere. Although Bond used many others, a British firearms expert pressed Fleming to upgrade 007's primary 418, feeling it wasn't powerful enough.

Fleming eventually came around to the replacement that would become synonymous with suave protagonists like Bond: the sleek .32 caliber Walther PPK.

Ironically the PPK already had a reputation with the Nazis. However, in World War II .32 ammunition (and its ammo twin in the metric system, the 7.65mm) proliferated around the world. That made perfect sense for a globe-trotting man of mystery like James Bond.

The Walther PPK is a mainstay of fiction and will likely remain so. That's great for writers, since the PPK wouldn't be out of place in the hands of characters around the world from 1929 through today. Note that the handgun also comes in .22, .25, and .380 caliber versions, although the .32 is most iconic.

Sawed-Off Shotgun

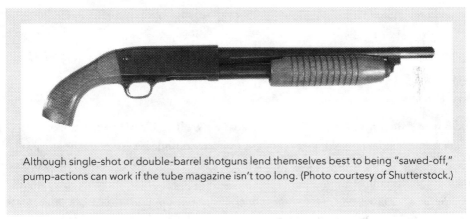

Although single-shot or double-barrel shotguns lend themselves best to being "sawed-off," pump-actions can work if the tube magazine isn't too long. (Photo courtesy of Shutterstock.)

- **GAUGE:** varies (see the Shotguns 101 section of this guide)
- most common with single-shot or double-barrel shotguns

In fiction, sawed-off shotguns are usually the domain of criminals, although any character could make use of one. It's been illegal to shorten the barrel of a shotgun to less than 18 inches since the National Firearms Act of 1934. Shotguns intentionally manufactured with barrels of less than 18 inches require special NFA permits.

As explained elsewhere in this guide, the only benefits to a shortened barrel are mobility, concealment, and a wider shot pattern at close ranges. Ammunition determines firepower, not barrel length.

Single-shot and double-barrel shotguns are the most common choice for sawed-offs, since they would be the simplest to cut down. Pump-action shotguns could be shortened, but there's more hardware getting in the way of those inches. The benefits wouldn't be as great.

Bowie Knife

Bowie knives come in many varieties, but all share a common style. The tip is lower than the handle, as if the spine of the blade has been clipped out. (Photo courtesy of Point-Seven Studios for *BLADE*.)

- **TYPE:** fixed blade
- **LENGTH:** varies

The Bowie knife (pronounced "boo-eee," not "bow-e") is one of the most popular fixed blades in all of fiction, and it's no wonder. It's been around since at least the early 1800s. The Bowie occupies a unique place in Americana, rooted in the hard-nosed ruggedness of the nineteenth century.

The Bowie knife isn't actually one model. It's a style popularized by Jim Bowie in the infamous Sandbar Fight of 1827. Conveniently for writers, that style is still around today. A Bowie knife is defined as a fixed blade knife sporting a large blade with a concave design toward the tip. It looks as if part of the spine (the unsharpened edge at the top of the blade) has been carved out.

The Bowie style may apply to any knife type, but the classic is the fixed blade. When referring to a non-fixed blade knife, such as a folder, specify the knife type. So a folding knife with a Bowie-style blade would be written as "folding Bowie knife." A "Bowie knife" references the fixed blade version of the knife.

Italian Stiletto Switchblades

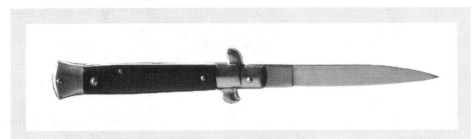

How a switchblade is legally defined can change with the era and location. However, the Italian stiletto style will always be associated with switchblades. (Photo courtesy of Shutterstock.)

- **TYPE:** switchblade
- **LENGTH:** varies

As mentioned elsewhere, the Italian stiletto switchblade dominates fiction. Is it appropriate for writing modern settings? Probably not, since so many better options, such as assisted openers, are available—and they're legal.

Antique and collectible switchblades are still in circulation where the law allows (if a state allows switchblades, and the commerce doesn't cross state lines, then it's legal). New switchblades are usually custom jobs and tough to find.

It's not inaccurate to include Italian stilettos in fiction. Writers will score more points using folders, fixed blades, or assisted opening knives (if the story is set after the mid-1990s) instead.

Jimmy Lile First Blood Knife—The "Rambo Knife"

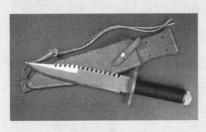

Sure, the famous "Rambo knife" looks flashy—it was made for a movie. From a practical standpoint, it's bulkier, heavier, and more cumbersome than a smaller low-key knife. If looks matter in a story, go with this classic. If usefulness is important, stick to more mundane fixed blade knives. (Photo courtesy of BLADE.)

- **TYPE:** fixed blade
- **LENGTH:** varies, but usually on the larger side
- **YEAR INTRODUCED:** 1982 (first in a movie, then imitated in the real world)

The screen adaptation of David Morrell's novel *First Blood* introduced a knife that would become as famous as John Rambo himself (although the original novel didn't feature such a knife). The original "Rambo knife," as it became known (it was formally called First Blood, just like the movie), was a custom job by knife maker Jimmy Lile.

As the movie grew in popularity, so did the knife. It spawned countless imitators, becoming so popular that *Rambo knife* became a catchall term for any big, stylish combat or survival fixed blade knife.

Here's the thing: Jimmy Lile designed the original knife for a *movie*. It needed to have a certain visual appeal. That's why it worked in Hollywood. Reality is another story.

Soldiers probably aren't eager to carry the Rambo knife into the field. It's just not practical. It's bulky, heavy, and not compatible with the efficient gear systems of most military organizations. Sure, a soldier *could* carry a Rambo knife—and writers are certainly free to use Rambo knives in their stories—but if one of the many modern, lightweight, durable, versatile knives available would work just as well, why not use one of those?

TOP SHOTGUNS

Benelli M4

The Benelli M4 semi-automatic shotgun comes in a variety of styles, but it primarily serves as a tactical firearm. Put it in the hands of a character ready to knock down some doors. (Photo courtesy of *Gun Digest*.)

- **TYPE:** semi-automatic shotgun
- **GAUGE:** 12
- **CAPACITY:** five (civilian), seven (military and law enforcement)
- **YEAR INTRODUCED:** 1999 (military); 2003 (civilian market)

In his book *Gun Digest Book of the Tactical Shotgun*, Scott Wagner writes that the M4 is "the Lincoln Continental of semi-automatic tactical shotguns." The U.S. Marines agreed and adopted it in 1999. (Call it the M1014 when the military uses it in your writing.)

For law enforcement and military characters, the M4 can be the go-to semi-auto shotgun model. It's recognized across the board as an excellent choice in the civilian market, too.

Because this is a semi-automatic, the character would only need to pull the trigger to fire. One trigger pull equals one shot fired—no need to pump anything to reload.

Browning Auto-5

The Browning Auto-5 is more popular with Joe Citizen than Johnny Law. That doesn't mean it can't show up in any number of scenarios, but it's best to avoid giving it to military or law enforcement characters. They'd likely have better tactical options available. (Author's photo.)

- **TYPE:** semi-automatic shotgun
- **GAUGES:** 12 or 16
- **CAPACITY:** five
- **YEAR INTRODUCED:** 1903

The Benelli M4 is a great choice for modern semi-autos, but what about years ago? The Browning Auto-5 is a top pick for scattergun-wielding characters from the turn of the twentieth century through today.

Granted the Auto-5 is a sporting shotgun at heart. It's popular with hunters, but it does find some use as a home defense gun. It's probably not ideal for tactical purposes unless it's been overhauled with custom parts. Military and law enforcement characters might opt for something else.

The Auto-5 changed hands throughout the years. At one point, Remington manufactured it. If you're unsure of the maker, just write it as the "Auto-5."

Remember that since this is a semi-automatic, there's no need for pumping action in between shots. The gun reloads itself.

Browning Superposed

The Browning Superposed is a terrific choice for a character's over-under or sawed-off shotgun. A gun enthusiast could talk all day about differences in over-unders, but writers can treat each model about the same. (Photo courtesy of *Gun Digest*.)

- **TYPE:** over-under shotgun
- **GAUGES:** 12, 20, 28, .410 (the .410 is actually referred to as a caliber)
- **CAPACITY:** two (one shell inserted into each barrel; no pumping)
- **YEAR INTRODUCED:** 1930
- a good candidate for a character's sawed-off shotgun

Over-under shotguns sport two barrels, one on top of the other. This classic setup is most often used for sport and hunting, but writers might choose to saw off the barrel for nefarious characters.

For writing purposes, there's not a ton of difference in over-unders. The Browning Superposed is a no-fail pick, having been made from 1930 to 1986. It also comes in every common gauge, including the .410 (which is technically a caliber), so there's plenty of versatility.

No matter how you write the Superposed (or other over-under) into a scene, don't show a character pumping it.

Ithaca Model 37

In the decades since its introduction, the versatile Ithaca Model 37 shotgun has adapted to fit changing needs. With a few tweaks, such as the custom stock and pistol grip shown, it can shift from a classic sporting shotgun to a more tactical feel. It's the perfect do-it-all shotgun. (Photo courtesy of *Gun Digest*.)

- **TYPE:** pump-action shotgun
- **GAUGES:** 12, 16, 20
- **CAPACITY:** five, eight (extended magazine version)
- **YEAR INTRODUCED:** 1937
- many variations throughout the years

The Model 37 is a shotgun for the ages. It's remained popular ever since it hit the market in 1937. Consider it the default choice for writing sporting or tactical shotguns. There's no need to overthink this pick.

When assigning the Model 37 to military and law enforcement characters after 1968, take advantage of the extended magazine for extra shots. This feature is also available to civilians, but it's not usually legal for hunting purposes.

The 12-gauge is the most popular version of the Model 37, and it offers the most firepower. It debuted in 1937. Two others followed: the 16-gauge in 1938 (discontinued in 1973) and the 20-gauge in 1939 (still available).

The Model 37 isn't the only pump shotgun looming large. The Mossberg Model 500, Remington Model 870, and Winchester Model 12 (introduced in 1912) are all worthy of mention. For the sake of space, the Model 37 is this guide's top pick for pumps.

Winchester Model 21

Side-by-side shotguns don't have to be boring. Characters could saw off the barrels, throw on a couple of bayonets (one on each side of the barrels), or affix a laser sight. (Photo courtesy of *Gun Digest*.)

- **TYPE:** side-by-side shotgun
- **GAUGES:** 12, 16, 20, 28 (rare), .410 (rare)
- **CAPACITY:** two (one shell inserted into each barrel; no pumping)
- **YEAR INTRODUCED:** 1931
- a good candidate for a character's sawed-off shotgun

A side-by-side shotgun isn't all that different from an over-under. The barrels are next to each other horizontally instead of vertically.

Writers have scores of side-by-sides to choose from. The Winchester Model 21 is a nice, practical choice. Saw the barrel off or have the character use it as is. There's nothing too special about this particular model. It's just a solid example of the form.

Although Winchester stopped making the Model 21 in 1991, it stayed in the side-by-side business. Write in the Model 21 if it fits the time frame. A generic "side-by-side shotgun," "Winchester double-barreled shotgun" or "double-barreled shotgun" will also do the job.

TOP HUNTING AND SPORTING RIFLES

Browning BAR (Browning Automatic Rifle)

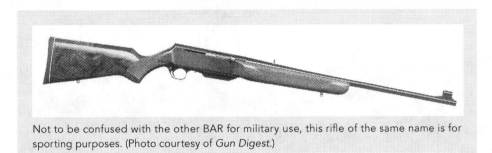

Not to be confused with the other BAR for military use, this rifle of the same name is for sporting purposes. (Photo courtesy of *Gun Digest*.)

- **TYPE:** semi-automatic rifle
- **CALIBERS:** .243, .25-06, .270, .300, .30-06, .308, .325, .338, 7mm
- **CAPACITY:** five (.243, .25-06, .270, .30-06, .308), four (.300, .325, .338, 7mm); use these capacities as a guideline since specific models can vary
- **YEAR INTRODUCED:** 1967
- uses a detachable magazine (not a clip)

Don't confuse this with the fully automatic Browning BAR used by the U.S. military from World War I through the Vietnam War years. Despite the identical name, the BAR here is a semi-automatic sporting rifle and looks nothing like the military version. One pull of the trigger equals one shot fired. It's immensely popular and successful, finding use primarily in the hunting arena. Writers should feel free to assign it to characters outside that spectrum, too.

Colt AR-15

Although it's been around for decades, Colt's AR-15, along with the many rifles emulating it, is a standard bearer for modern rifles today. Writers should feel free to customize it to their liking, as this is a firearm cut out for accessories. Just don't write an AR-15 as a fully automatic—it's a semi-automatic. One pull of the trigger equals one shot fired. (Photo courtesy of Colt.)

- **TYPE:** semi-automatic rifle
- **CALIBER:** .223
- **CAPACITIES:** ten, fifteen, twenty, thirty, fifty, others
- **YEAR INTRODUCED:** 1964
- uses a detachable magazine (not a clip)

Like the 1911 pistol, the Colt AR-15 represents both a stand-alone product and a platform emulated by other companies. Armalite produced the original AR-15 in 1958, which would later be adopted by the U.S. military as the fully automatic M16. That's where the *AR* comes from in *AR-15*. It stands for *Armalite*, not *assault rifle*.

Armalite's semi-automatic AR-15 didn't make it to the civilian market until 1964, after Colt bought the design. Characters therefore wouldn't be able to use an AR-15 until 1964, even though the design had been around for six years.

The AR-15 exploded in popularity in 2004, when the federal Assault Weapons Ban expired. It's since been the flag bearer for modern sporting rifles used in shooting competitions and hunting. Characters might also use it for defensive or tactical purposes.

Keep in mind the AR-15 uses a detachable magazine, not a clip. It's effective out to 200 yards or so, depending on the shooter.

With its low recoil and modern features, the AR-15 is generally a breeze to shoot. Characters of all stripes could use it after a brief rundown.

The AR-15 also lends itself well to customization. Writers needing a rifle with special add-ons may likely go with the AR-15.

Given the widespread imitation of the AR-15 by companies other than Colt, it's acceptable to write *AR-15* or *AR-style rifle* generically. However, when referring to both the manufacturer and the model specifically, write *Colt AR-15*. For example, Maynard might carry an AR-15 in a scene and I'd never mention the manufacturer of the firearm. But when Maynard specifically identifies a firearm as an AR-15 as a critical detail, it'd be a Colt AR-15.

Ruger 10/22

The Ruger 10/22 is an ideal default for a character's semi-automatic .22 rifle. (Photo courtesy of *Gun Digest*.)

- **TYPE:** semi-automatic rifle
- **CALIBER:** .22
- **CAPACITIES:** 10, 25, others depending on magazine
- **YEAR INTRODUCED:** 1964; still produced today
- uses a detachable magazine (not a clip)

The Ruger 10/22 is an excellent choice when writing about a .22 rifle. As one of the most popular rifles of all time, it's a classic that Grandpa would appreciate, yet is timeless enough to appeal to new shooters.

Characters of all firearm skill levels would be able to operate the 10/22 without much difficulty. It's one of the easiest rifles to shoot. As a semi-automatic, firing is as easy as pulling the trigger. No need to pump anything or to work a bolt-action.

The .22 doesn't offer much in the way of firepower. Writers might find that ten (or twenty-five) well-placed shots can make up for the difference, though.

Winchester Model 70

Don't be fooled by appearances. The Winchester Model 70 is as at home in the deer stand as it is in a SWAT operation. Writers searching for an all-purpose, bolt-action rifle to pop into a scene can stop looking. The Model 70 is it. (Photo courtesy of *Gun Digest*.)

- **TYPE:** bolt-action rifle
- **CALIBERS:** .22, .223, .243, .250-3000, 7mm, .257, .264, .270, 7 × 57mm, .300, .30-06, .308, .338, .35, .358, .375, 9 × 57mm, 7.65mm, others
- **CAPACITIES:** three (magnum ammunition), five (standard)
- **YEAR INTRODUCED:** 1936
- uses an internal magazine built into the firearm, not a detachable one

Writers in need of a bolt-action rifle, look no further. The Model 70 is the standard for bolt-action rifles. Scores of variations manufactured over the decades make it an appropriate choice for civilian, law enforcement, and military characters. It's an excellent all-around rifle that writers can use as a default for their characters.

Characters would not use a detachable magazine to load the Model 70. Instead they'd open the bolt action and manually insert cartridges one at a time into the internal magazine. A safety switch would be disengaged to fire. Characters would work the bolt action between each shot.

Feel free to modify this rifle with accessories depending on the character, but don't up the ammo capacity.

Winchester Model 94

The Winchester Model 94 is an iconic lever-action rifle. It's what comes to most readers' minds when they picture that type of rifle. Writers can take advantage of that popularity and look knowledgeable at the same time by writing in one. (Photo courtesy of U.S. Repeating Arms Company for *Gun Digest*.)

- **TYPE:** lever-action rifle
- **CALIBERS:** .30-30, .44 mag., others
- **CAPACITIES:** six to eight depending on magazine/barrel length
- **YEAR INTRODUCED:** 1964
- uses a tube magazine that runs underneath the barrel
- uses an external hammer

Sometimes a scene just isn't complete without a lever-action rifle. In those cases, writers should jump right to the Model 94.

Winchester introduced this firearm in 1964 as an update of its popular Model 1894, which traces its history back to the "gun that won the West," the Model 1873 (feel free to use those guns as you would the Model 94 for earlier settings). All that history might not matter for whatever you're writing, but the Model 94's lineage is impressive nonetheless.

The Model 94 finds most of its use today with hunters and hobbyists, but it wouldn't look out of place for characters involved in other activities.

Ammunition is loaded one at a time into the side of the firearm above the trigger. The cartridges feed into a magazine tube, sort of like a shotgun's.

To fire, a character would work the lever to chamber a cartridge. Doing so would simultaneously cock the external hammer. The rifle would be ready to fire. The character would pull the trigger, then work the lever to simultaneously eject the spent cartridge out the top of the firearm.

That external hammer acts as the safety. A character could load a cartridge into the chamber, then manually move the hammer forward into the safe position. When it's time to shoot, the character could manually cock the hammer back, then fire.

TOP FULLY AUTOMATIC FIREARMS FOR MILITARY CHARACTERS AND MORE

Remember that machine guns use rifle ammunition and submachine guns use handgun ammunition. It's better not to use the terms interchangeably.

AK-47

AK-47s don't always have to be written into the hands of antagonists. Setting has more to do with their use in a story. Eastern countries, former or current communist countries, and the developing world are more likely to see use of the AK-47 across all character types. (Photo courtesy of *Gun Digest*.)

- **TYPE:** fully automatic machine gun
- **CALIBER:** 7.62 × 39mm
- **CAPACITY:** thirty
- **YEAR INTRODUCED:** 1947
- appropriate to refer to as an *assault rifle*, but not *assault weapon*
- formally introduced in 1947

When the Soviet Union unofficially introduced the AK-47 during its "Great Patriotic War" of 1941–1945, it changed the world of firearms forever. The firearm's fame—or infamy—grew to such heights that it's even featured on the flag of Mozambique.

That should tell writers something. The proliferation of these "Russian bullet hoses" across the planet makes them the default firearm for international characters, usually but not always members of military and criminal organizations. AK-47s are typically found in former or current communist countries and the developing world. They aren't as popular in developed Western countries.

The *AK* in AK-47 stands for *Avtomat Kalashnikov*, the latter word being the last name of its inventor. The 47 stands for the year it was formally introduced, 1947. Writing the AK-47 into a World War II setting is an easy pitfall that you should avoid.

The appeal of the AK-47 is its simplicity. A character unfamiliar with an AK-47 could figure out how to use it in a few minutes. It's also a reliable, hardy weapon even in extreme conditions.

The Writer's Guide to Weapons

The trade-off is that the AK-47 is relatively inaccurate. Cycling ammunition through the firearm is a violent process, throwing off the shooter's aim with each shot. The AK-47 drops off in accuracy beyond about 100 yards.

Scores of variations of the AK-47 exist, often because they were assembled by hand through the years. For writing, go with the standard thirty-round version.

One last note: An updated model appeared in 1974, called the AK-74. Designers tried to improve accuracy. However, it didn't gain nearly as much global popularity as the AK-47.

Colt Model 635

The Colt Model 635 is an off-the-beaten-path pick for submachine guns. It's a great alternative to the Uzi. (Photo courtesy of *Gun Digest*.)

- **TYPE:** fully automatic submachine gun
- **CALIBER:** 9mm
- **CAPACITIES:** twenty or thirty-two
- **YEAR INTRODUCED:** 1990
- can switch to semi-automatic mode (select-fire)
- uses a detachable magazine (not a clip)

The Model 635 is a firecracker of a submachine gun. Colt based the design on the popular M16, knocking down the size and caliber.

The Model 635 fires at a rate of 900 rounds per minute, but that's just for measurement's sake. Keep in mind the magazine would hold thirty-two rounds at most. Reloading would eat up much of that minute.

The 635 never gained much popularity with the U.S. military, but it is used in other countries. However, it's a great pick for criminal characters as an alternative to the Uzi cliché.

Colt M16

The Colt M16 is perhaps the most iconic rifle in the U.S. military. It's been in service since the Vietnam era, so make it a default pick for U.S. military characters. As a select-fire rifle, it can switch between semi-automatic, burst, and fully automatic modes. The civilian version, available only as a semi-automatic, is called the Colt AR-15. (Photo courtesy of *Gun Digest.*)

- **TYPE:** fully automatic machine gun
- **CALIBER:** 5.56 × 45mm (acceptable to write as just 5.56mm)
- **CAPACITY:** twenty
- **YEAR INTRODUCED:** 1962
- can switch to semi-automatic mode or three-round burst mode (select-fire)
- uses a detachable magazine (not a clip)

Are you writing U.S. military characters? The M16 should be the default choice for their machine guns. The M16 can trace its roots back to the 1950s with Armalite's AR-15 rifle (later purchased by Colt). The AR-15 caught the attention of the U.S. military, which formally adopted the rifle as the M16 in 1962.

While the firearm was and is at the frontlines of many conflicts, it became iconic in Vietnam. It's now the go-to machine gun for military characters.

In 2010, the U.S. military announced it was seeking a replacement for the M16, but as of this writing, that hasn't come to fruition.

Note the AR-15 that's available on the civilian market is not the same as the M16. The civilian version is offered only in semi-automatic form. When referencing ammunition used by the civilian AR-15, call it .223 (roughly equivalent to 5.56mm). For the M16, call it 5.56mm (or, to show off even more, 5.56 × 45mm).

Don't forget: M16s are primed for grenade launcher add-ons if writers need them. They'd sit below the barrel, allowing the shooter to continue using the firearm normally.

Colt M4

The Colt M4 is like a smaller version of the iconic M16. Assign it to U.S. military characters from 1994 and later. (Photo courtesy of *Gun Digest*.)

- **TYPE:** fully automatic machine gun
- **CALIBER:** 5.56 × 45mm (acceptable to write as just 5.56mm)
- **CAPACITY:** thirty
- **YEAR INTRODUCED:** 1994
- can switch to semi-automatic mode or three-round burst mode
- uses a detachable magazine (not a clip)

The M4 represents the next step in the evolution of the M16. Colt originally manufactured it for U.S. Special Forces in 1994. It went on to serve in most other areas of the military.

As a carbine, it's basically a smaller version of the M16. Many versions of the M4 exist. For the sake of simplicity, just write it as "M4."

Like the M16, the M4 is a prime pick for U.S. military characters. It's also up for replacement as of this writing.

Fabrique Nationale Herstal Fusil Automatique Leger (a.k.a. FN FAL)

The FN FAL then and now. The FAL is found in nearly every Western country's military and police forces in some capacity. (Photos courtesy of *Gun Digest*.)

- **TYPE:** fully automatic machine gun
- **CALIBER:** 7.62 × 51mm (acceptable to write it simply as 7.62mm)
- **CAPACITY:** twenty
- **YEAR INTRODUCED:** 1953
- uses a detachable magazine
- can switch between semi-automatic and fully automatic modes (select-fire)

More than ninety of the world's militaries (mostly Western countries) adopted the FN FAL after it launched in 1953. As one of the most successful machine guns of all time, the FN FAL (don't bother writing out its formal name) is still in use across the globe.

For writing, think of the FN FAL as the Western equivalent of the AK-47. It's found around the world, fires relatively easy-to-obtain ammunition, and is a real workhorse. Go with the FAL if putting an AK-47 into a character's hands doesn't feel right. When a character does use it, the FAL would be effective at ranges out to 100 yards and beyond.

Just for perspective on that ammunition, 7.62 × 51mm is roughly equivalent to a .308 caliber cartridge.

Heckler & Koch MP5

It's not uncommon for some MP5s to sport a folding stock and suppressor, as shown here. (Photo courtesy of *Gun Digest*.)

- **TYPE:** fully automatic submachine gun
- **CALIBERS:** 9mm (most common), .40, 10mm
- **CAPACITIES:** fifteen or thirty
- **YEAR INTRODUCED:** 1966
- can switch to semi-automatic mode or a burst mode that fires three rounds per trigger pull (select-fire)
- uses a detachable magazine (not a clip)

Militaries across the Western world adopted the MP5 after it was introduced in West Germany in 1966. It's the perfect fit for military characters or individuals with access to this type of weaponry. Law enforcement agencies, including the FBI, use the MP5, too.

Heckler & Koch cranked out many variations of the MP5, and the firearm is still manufactured. Just write it as "MP5" no matter the time frame. It'll get the point across.

Fabrique Nationale Herstal USA Special Operations Forces Combat Assault Rifle (a.k.a. SCAR)

The SCAR is a modern pick for Western characters, especially those in militaries. (Photo courtesy of Shutterstock.)

- **TYPE:** fully automatic machine gun
- **CALIBERS:** 5.56 × 45mm or 7.62 × 51mm (acceptable to write as 5.56mm or 7.62mm)
- **CAPACITIES:** twenty or thirty
- **YEAR INTRODUCED:** 2005
- uses a detachable magazine
- can switch between semi-automatic and fully automatic modes (select-fire)

Is it any wonder this gun goes by *SCAR* instead of its full name? Go ahead and write it that way instead.

The SCAR took over from the M4 in the mid-2000s as the primary rifle for the U.S. Special Forces. However, the SCAR isn't just one rifle. It's a family of firearms, with names like Mk 16, Mk 17, and others.

Spelling out the differences within this family is more suited to technical books like *Gun Digest*. For the sake of writing, pick a caliber and call it a "SCAR." The 5.56mm version (equal to the .223) is lighter, while the 7.62mm (equivalent to the .308 caliber) model is heavier.

The SCAR would pair well with military characters, but don't feel limited. For example, a crime lord with good taste in modern firearms might get ahold of some SCARs to help take care of business.

Steyr Armee Universal Gewehr (a.k.a. Steyr AUG)

The Steyr AUG's bullpup design makes it operable with one hand, although two is best. (Photo courtesy of Shutterstock.)

- **TYPE:** fully automatic machine gun
- **CALIBER:** 5.56 × 45mm (acceptable to write as 5.56mm)
- **CAPACITIES:** thirty or forty-two
- **YEAR INTRODUCED:** 1978
- uses a detachable magazine
- bullpup magazine (magazine is located behind the trigger)
- can switch between semi-automatic and fully automatic modes (select-fire)

For a change-up in the looks department, the Steyr AUG is worth a shot. It's a bullpup, meaning the detachable magazine and action are located a few inches *behind* the trigger, not in front. This allows for a more compact design without downgrading into a smaller caliber. For experienced characters, one-handed operation is possible.

The AUG is a product of Austria, but it's a go-to bullpup for militaries and police forces around the world. Federal agencies in the United States even use it.

Translated out of the metric system, the 5.56mm is equivalent to the .223 caliber.

TOP PICKS FOR MILITARY FIREARMS OF YESTERYEAR

Browning Automatic Rifle (Model 1918)

Allied characters from World War I and II would've been familiar with the BAR (Browning Automatic Rifle). When used by the U.S. military, this firearm is called the M1918 or Model 1918. (Photo courtesy of Jim Thompson for *Gun Digest*.)

- **TYPE:** fully automatic machine gun
- **CALIBER:** .30-06
- **CAPACITY:** twenty
- **YEAR INTRODUCED:** 1917
- uses a detachable magazine
- can switch between semi-automatic and fully automatic modes (select-fire)

Two firearms go by the Browning Automatic Rifle name. One is for hunting; the other is for the military. I've already discussed the former; this is the latter.

Colt, Marlin, and Winchester all produced the BAR (it's acceptable to use the abbreviation) from 1917 to 1945. The firearm saw service through the Korean War, too, before phasing out. It wouldn't be out of place for military characters through the Vietnam War to use one.

The BAR is ideal for U.S. and allied military characters during those time periods. Civilian and criminal characters might also use it, especially after World War I through 1934. That's when the National Firearms Act when into effect, making it more difficult to obtain the BAR.

Weighing around 18 pounds, the BAR is on the heavy side. The benefit of laying down a hard cloud of .30-06 makes it worth the effort.

The Writer's Guide to Weapons

Springfield Armory M1 Garand

The M1 Garand represents one of the few firearms for which it's accurate to write *clip* instead of *magazine*. (Photo courtesy of *Gun Digest*.)

- **TYPE:** semi-automatic rifle
- **CALIBER:** .30-06
- **CAPACITY:** eight
- **YEAR INTRODUCED:** 1936
- uses a clip (not a detachable magazine)

Well, well, well, take a look at that. It's a firearm that uses a clip instead of a detachable magazine. Yes, writers, this is one firearm where writing *clip* is actually the preferred term.

The M1 Garand's clip would be loaded with eight .30-06 rounds. The clip would then be inserted into the rifle's internal magazine. The clip would pop out with a familiar, metallic *ping* sound once all eight rounds were fired.

The U.S. military adopted the M1 Garand as its standard-issue rifle from 1936 to 1957. Its significance in World War II and the Korean War can't be overstated. More than 5.4 million were manufactured.

Characters outside the military might use a Garand, too. Its accuracy and reliability made it a favorite for sport and hunting. Writers should feel free to attach a bayonet to the Garand if needed.

SKS

The SKS is the underappreciated cousin of the AK-47. This semi-automatic rifle sports a bayonet that swings outward to deploy. The bayonet is visible in its ready position in this image, located just to the left of the tip of the barrel. (Photo courtesy of *Gun Digest*.)

- **TYPE:** semi-automatic rifle
- **CALIBER:** 7.62 × 39mm (acceptable to write as just 7.62mm)
- **CAPACITY:** ten
- **YEAR INTRODUCED:** 1946
- uses a clip (not a detachable magazine)

Think of the SKS as the Soviet Union's take on the M1 Garand. After World War II, it became a primary semi-automatic rifle for the Soviet Union and its allies. It's perfect for midcentury characters from communist countries, including China.

Like the Garand, the SKS uses a clip (yes, I said *clip*) of ammunition that's inserted into the rifle's internal magazine. The SKS uses a flip-out bayonet that swings open when deployed.

It'd be unlikely for a character from the West to use an SKS prior to the early 1990s, unless the SKS was captured in combat. But one should note that it's a mistake to feature the SKS in World War II–era stories. The SKS arrived one year after the war ended. Soviet characters during World War II might use the semi-automatic Tokarev M1938 (ten-round detachable magazine, fifteen rounds for the select-fire version) or the Tokarev M1940 (semi-auto, ten-round detachable magazine) rifles. Among others, both were common in the hands of Soviet soldiers during that time.

Mauser Model 98

Scores of Mauser Model 98 firearms were produced from the late 1800s through World War II. This variation, a 98K, is from the World War II era. If Nazis are the antagonists in your story, chances are good they're using the 98 as the bolt-action rifle of choice. (Photo courtesy of *Gun Digest*.)

- **TYPE:** bolt-action rifle
- **CALIBER:** 7.92 × 57mm (acceptable to write as 7.92mm)
- **CAPACITY:** five
- **YEAR INTRODUCED:** 1898
- uses a clip (not a detachable magazine)

Germany's military used the Model 98 in both world wars, making it a top pick for Nazi characters.

Loading the Model 98 requires a clip of five rounds inserted into an internal magazine. Again, this is a firearm where writing *clip* is accurate.

The Model 98 also goes by names Gewehr 98, M98, G98, Gew 98, and others. It's acceptable to use any of these when writing.

Characters outside the military and Germany might use the Model 98, too. Countries allied with or occupied by Germany during the world wars certainly would use it. However, after World War II, the Model 98 phased out of service.

TOP SNIPER RIFLES

Any rifle used to take a character out from a distance could qualify as a sniper rifle. For writers looking to really "reach out and touch someone" in a scene, here are some head-splitting considerations.

Armalite AR-30

Why would a character use a sniper rifle in .338 Lapua, the ammunition this AR-30 uses, over pop culture's favorite, the .50 caliber? The .338 Lapua is generally thought to be more accurate. Of course, accuracy ultimately depends on the shooter, but it's a worthy consideration when writing. (Photo courtesy of *Gun Digest*.)

- **TYPE:** bolt-action rifle
- **CALIBER:** .338 Lapua
- **CAPACITY:** five
- **YEAR INTRODUCED:** 2000
- uses a detachable magazine

For nailing characters at distances up to a half mile away, the AR-30 is a great choice. It'll leave an unforgettable mark on its target, easily adhering to the "one shot, one kill" maxim.

That great firepower requires great responsibility, though. This is a rifle for experienced characters only. Being accurate requires a proper shooting position, usually from a flat surface and assisted by a bipod. It also requires some physical dexterity, since the AR-30 is large and heavy.

The AR-30 is available in other calibers, but the .338 Lapua is most beneficial for fiction. It'll plow lead through just about anything.

Barrett Model 82

The updated version of the Barrett Model 82 from the 1980s is called the Model 82A1. Don't worry too much about that detail when writing. Just call it the Model 82. (Photo courtesy of *Gun Digest*.)

- **TYPE:** semi-automatic rifle
- **CALIBER:** .50
- **CAPACITY:** ten
- **YEAR INTRODUCED:** 1982
- uses a detachable magazine

The Barrett Model 82 is what's known as an anti-materiel rifle. This means it's designed to put holes in vehicles, buildings, and anything else that gets in the way. Characters taking hits from the Model 82's massive payload wouldn't just bleed—they'd drop weight.

The 82 didn't gain much popularity until the first Gulf War (1990–1991), when the U.S. Marine Corps made use of it. The 82 punched through Iraqi trucks, aircraft on the ground, and military equipment, as well as soldiers. Since then, military and law enforcement organizations around the world adopted the 82 for any number of scenarios. When the U.S. military uses it, it's actually called the M107 (or M107A1 for more recent years).

For writers, the 82 is the go-to pick for long-distance, heavy-hitting shots anywhere in the world from 1982 onward. Assign it to characters with a lot of firearm know-how, though. This isn't Grandma's rifle, although she could certainly buy one on the U.S. civilian market in places where the law allows.

Keep in mind that this rifle is usually accompanied by a bipod fixed beneath the barrel. Characters would likely shoot the 82 from a resting position.

McMillan TAC-50

The McMillan Tac-50: the Cadillac of modern sniper rifles. (Photo courtesy of *Gun Digest*.)

- **TYPE:** bolt-action rifle
- **CALIBER:** .50
- **CAPACITY:** five
- **YEAR INTRODUCED:** late 1980s
- uses a detachable magazine (not a clip)
- effective to 2,000 yards and beyond

The TAC-50 is the Cadillac of modern sniper rifles. For writing, it can be useful for characters firing at extreme ranges up to a mile or more.

Wait. A mile? Really?

Believe it. The TAC-50 held the record for the longest confirmed sniper kill until 2009. Rob Furlong, a sniper in the Canadian military, made his record-setting shot in Afghanistan at 2,657 yards—or about a mile and a half—in 2002.

Assign the TAC-50 to military, law enforcement, and U.S. civilian characters (check state and local laws, especially in California). The popularity of the TAC-50 also makes it a prime choice for international characters. Characters would need to be expert shooters to make a successful shot. This isn't Grandpa's squirrel rifle.

The TAC-50 is best used with its built-in bipod deployed. The shooter should be in a resting position. Be sure to consider those details when writing.

When the U.S. military uses the TAC-50, it's called the Mk 15 (this designation started in the early 2000s). The Canadian military calls it a C15.

TOP REVOLVERS FOR PRIVATE EYES, GUNSLINGERS, AND MORE

Revolvers occupy a special place in fiction, especially the crime genre. It's often the handgun type of choice for protagonists, perhaps because of its Old West heritage.

Colt Anaconda

The Colt Anaconda, along with its sister model the Colt Python, is a great pick for characters needing a modern revolver that packs a punch. (Photo courtesy of *Gun Digest*.)

- **TYPE:** revolver
- **CALIBERS:** .44 magnum, .45 (not introduced until 1993)
- **CAPACITY:** six
- **YEAR INTRODUCED:** 1990
- double-action (no need to cock the hammer first; just pull the trigger)

The Anaconda makes the list as a revolver with serious firepower that doesn't require the hammer be cocked prior to pulling the trigger. It's a double-action revolver.

Only characters with a strong command of handguns should use the Anaconda. All that firepower can be hard to handle.

The Anaconda continued the reptilian streak Colt started in 1955 with the Python (available in .357 magnum and .38 Special, double-action, external hammer, and six-shooter). Both are solid choices for double-action revolvers.

Colt Single-Action Army (a.k.a. "Peacemaker" or "Colt 45")

Not every Colt Single Action Army revolver is an antique. Colt has continuously produced the handguns since 1873. They all sport an iconic Old West design. (Photo courtesy of *Gun Digest*.)

- **TYPE:** revolver
- **CALIBER:** .45, but also available in nearly all the others
- **CAPACITY:** six
- **YEAR INTRODUCED:** 1873
- single-action (hammer must be cocked manually before each shot)

The "Dirty Harry Revolver" may own the night in much of crime fiction, but no single revolver can come close to the iconic Colt Single-Action Army.

Whether you call it the "Peacemaker," the "Colt 45," or the "Colt SAA," it's the quintessential revolver. As a testament to its popularity, it's still manufactured today. Assign it to any character anywhere in the world from 1873 onward. It'll hurl bullets nicely in any genre, from Westerns and crime fiction to thrillers and steampunk.

The only potential drawback for fiction is in the looks department. Despite many variations, there's no getting around the Old West aesthetics. That appearance could seem out of place depending on the character or setting.

The question sometimes comes up whether an antique Single-Action Army could be fired successfully today. The answer depends on the condition of the firearm. Use your creative license: It's possible to fire an antique today without raising too many eyebrows.

Ruger Blackhawk

Looking for a classic revolver without delving too far into Old West territory? Write in a Ruger Blackhawk. (Photo courtesy of *Gun Digest*.)

- **TYPE:** revolver
- **CALIBERS:** .45, .41, .357, .30
- **CAPACITY:** six
- **YEAR INTRODUCED:** 1962
- single-action (hammer must be cocked manually before each shot)

For a more modern feel to the classic six-shooter, give characters the Ruger Blackhawk. It knocks out heavy-hitting .45 ammunition just like the Colt Single-Action Army does, minus the cowboy spirit.

Ruger Single Six

As a .22, the Ruger Single Six won't give the character shooting it a black eye. (Photo courtesy of *Gun Digest*.)

- **TYPE:** revolver
- **CALIBER:** .22
- **CAPACITY:** six
- **YEAR INTRODUCED:** 1953
- single-action (hammer must be cocked manually before each shot)

Characters don't necessarily need a hand cannon to leave a crater in a target. Sometimes an easy-to-shoot, small-caliber revolver will do the job.

For those situations, write in the Ruger Single Six. As a .22 caliber, it's ideal for characters new to handguns. It sports a longer barrel—5½ inches is a common version—that makes it more accurate, too.

Smith & Wesson Model 27

Introduced in the 1930s, the Smith & Wesson Model 27 is an enduring, classic revolver. It's a prime pick for detective characters. (Photo courtesy of *Gun Digest*.)

- **TYPE:** revolver
- **CALIBER:** .357 magnum, .38 Special
- **CAPACITY:** six
- **YEAR INTRODUCED:** 1935
- double-action (no need to cock the hammer first; just pull the trigger)

Need a go-to revolver for law enforcement characters? Writers could do a lot worse than the Smith & Wesson Model 27. It's still manufactured to this day, although its use by law enforcement isn't as common as it was when FBI Director J. Edgar Hoover kept one at his side.

Civilian characters might also use the Model 27. Unlike other types of firearms, revolvers are subject to fewer restrictions. If law enforcement can use a certain revolver, chances are a civilian can, too. Note that it took until 1948 for this revolver to receive the Model 27 name. For settings from 1935 to 1948, write it as the "Factory Registered .357 Magnum."

Taurus Judge

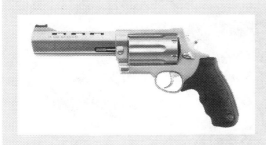

The Taurus Judge can fire .45 cartridges and .410 shotshells. It's a shotgun/revolver hybrid that could make for some interesting scenes. Pictured is the Raging Judge, a magnum version. (Photo courtesy of *Gun Digest*.)

- **TYPE:** revolver
- **CALIBERS:** .45, .410 shotshells
- **CAPACITY:** five
- **YEAR INTRODUCED:** 2007
- double-action (no need to cock the hammer first; just pull the trigger)

Here's a revolver writers can have a lot of fun with, depending on how sinister that "fun" is defined. The Taurus Judge can fire .45 ammunition or .410 shotshells (BBs). It's a shotgun in a handgun. Any combination of ammunition will work, such as two .45s and three .410s or four .45s and one .410.

A character might appreciate a .410 shotshell in self-defense situations. A writer might use it for an off-the-beaten-path firearm depiction. Either way, keep in mind that firing the .410 makes a donut of the shot pattern. Because the barrel is rifled, the BBs spin as they exit the firearm. This creates a donut shape. Depict injuries likewise.

In the real world, the Judge is either loved or loathed. Some see it as a versatile defense handgun. Others question the practicality of a shot pattern that disperses into irrelevancy beyond intimate ranges. Either way, writers are sure to find creative uses for this popular revolver.

TOP PISTOLS FOR LAW ENFORCEMENT AND OTHER CHARACTERS

Keep in mind that individual law enforcement organizations often assign or recommend firearms for its members. There isn't a single "cop gun" out there. What follows are suggestions for law enforcement characters, but it's not a blanket statement. Feel free to assign these firearms to civilians, too.

Beretta 92

The Beretta Model 92 is a perfect choice for law enforcement characters. (Photo courtesy of *Gun Digest*.)

- **TYPE:** semi-automatic pistol
- **CALIBER:** 9mm (don't write this as .9mm)
- **CAPACITY:** ten, fifteen, sixteen, seventeen, twenty
- **YEAR INTRODUCED:** 1975
- double-action (no need to cock the hammer first; just pull the trigger)
- slide-action

Few pistols can come close to the reliability of the Beretta 92. That's probably why so many law enforcement and military organizations worldwide (Beretta is an Italian company) adopted it after its introduction in 1975.

Several variations of the 92 exist. The United States military adopted the 92 in the mid-1980s. When used by military characters, this gun is called the M9. The M9 is nearly identical to the civilian/law enforcement version (the 92).

Just remember: Unlike Glocks, the Beretta 92 has an ambidextrous safety switch to flip off before firing.

Browning Hi-Power

Fiction's fixation on Glocks can cause classics like the Browning Hi-Power to get sidelined. Don't skip this one, writers. The Hi-Power is a versatile pistol ready for use in many settings and scenarios. (Photo courtesy of *Gun Digest*.)

- **TYPE:** semi-automatic pistol
- **CALIBER:** 9mm (don't write this as .9mm)
- **CAPACITY:** thirteen, twenty
- **YEAR INTRODUCED:** 1935
- single-action (hammer must be cocked manually before first shot)
- slide-action

Stories set prior to the advent of the Beretta 92 and Glock 17 aren't out of luck when it comes to police pistols. Before those two giants cast a long shadow over the handgun scene, the Browning Hi-Power (also spelled *Hi Power*) ruled the roost. It still does in many respects.

The Hi-Power hit the market shortly before World War II, which benefitted its popularity. Both the Nazis and the Western Allies used the Hi-Power, which led to its use in militaries and law enforcement organizations around the world.

In his book *Massad Ayoob's Greatest Handguns of the World, Volume II*, the author writes, "No handgun has been so universally accepted by the free world." That goes for police and military forces in South America, Taiwan, the United Kingdom, parts of eastern Europe, and, of course, the United States.

The Hi-Power is a universal pick for writing law enforcement, military, and civilian characters. Just remember to have them thumb off the safety switch.

CZ 75

Characters from communist countries during the Cold War might use the CZ 75, although it was never formally adopted by the militaries of the Soviet Union or Warsaw Pact countries. They've since proliferated across the West. (Photo courtesy of *Gun Digest*.)

- **TYPE:** semi-automatic pistol
- **CALIBERS:** 9mm (most common), .40
- **CAPACITIES:** sixteen, others depending on variation
- **YEAR INTRODUCED:** 1975
- double-action (no need to cock the hammer first; just pull the trigger)
- slide-action

Writers might be interested in the claim CZ posts on its website: "[The CZ 75] is used by more governments, militaries, police, and security agencies than any other pistol in the world."

Manufacturers like to brag in this way, but for the sake of writing it's true enough. The CZ 75 doesn't have the film and fiction presence of other models, but it's a big deal in the real world.

Here's the tricky part about writing the CZ 75. Due to some convoluted patent arrangements, manufacturers in countries around the world were free to make their own clones. These copycats drove demand for the CZ 75 up until trade relations improved after the Cold War. Mention a characters' fake CZ 75 for an added touch of realism.

Glock

It's hard to go wrong giving law enforcement characters, or just about anyone, a Glock. Just remember that *Glock* refers to a brand, even if the word is sometimes treated like the Kleenex of handguns. (Photo courtesy of *Gun Digest*.)

- **TYPE:** semi-automatic pistol
- **CALIBERS:** .45, .357, 10mm, .40, 9mm, .380
- **CAPACITY:** varies
- double-action (no need to cock the hammer first; just pull the trigger)
- slide-action
- no safety switch to thumb off
- despite using plastic components, will not cheat metal detectors

When the term *Glock* is used in fiction, I get the feeling it's a placeholder for "modern-looking semi-automatic pistol." This is a credit to Glock, the company, for making its early 1980s pistols such a success with law enforcement and civilians.

However, the word *Glock* refers to the company, not a particular gun model, of which Glock makes many. The most iconic model is the one that launched the company in 1982, the Glock 17. It's still popular today and is a great choice for civilian or law enforcement characters.

For those who are curious, the Glock 17 holds seventeen rounds of 9mm ammunition, although extended magazines can get up to nineteen or thirty-three. Like all Glocks, it doesn't come with a traditional safety that needs to be switched on or off. Instead it has a trigger safety, which is a small tab on the trigger that must be pressed before the trigger can be pulled.

Glocks also use a slide-action. The slide on top of the firearm must be racked to load the first shell from the magazine into the chamber.

Writers unsure of what kind of Glock a character is using should go straight to the Glock 17. For accuracy's sake, it's hard to go wrong. Glocks from the 1980s are still around today, performing as well as they did when first introduced.

Here's a bit of Glock trivia that could come in handy: The company actually made a fully automatic pistol for law enforcement and military organizations. It's called the Glock 18. Although its best use may be as forum fodder online, it could be the perfect match for a character in fiction.

Also, the 1988 Undetectable Firearms Act (UFA) passed into federal law largely in response to the Glock 17's plastic components. Some thought the Glock 17 was able to cheat metal detectors or that its plastic parts marked a forthcoming undetectable handgun. History showed that wasn't true. Read the section on improvised and custom firearms for more perspective on the UFA.

Sig Sauer P226

The Sig Sauer P226 is used in some capacity by just about every military and law enforcement organization in the U.S. (Photo courtesy of *Gun Digest*.)

- **TYPE:** semi-automatic pistol
- **CALIBERS:** 9mm, .40, .357
- **CAPACITY:** fifteen or twenty (9mm), ten or twelve (.357 and .40)
- **YEAR INTRODUCED:** 1983; .357 version introduced in 1996
- double-action (no need to cock the hammer first; just pull the trigger)
- slide-action

Most of the pistols on this list are in 9mm. Writers looking for a little variety might go with the Sig Sauer P226 to change things up. The .40 and .357 versions offer a bit more bite than the 9mm.

The P226's main appeal is in its ergonomics. It's a larger handgun that's not too clunky to hold.

Assign the P226 to military and law enforcement characters. The Sig Sauer website lists the Texas Rangers, Ohio Highway Patrol, Michigan State Police, and the U.S. Navy Seals as just a few of the agencies using the P226.

TOP HANDGUNS FOR SPIES

Spy characters could use any number of handguns. For the purposes of this guide, it's assumed spies need small firearms that are easy to hide on (or in) the body. These small handguns are typically known as *derringers*, *mouse guns*, or *pocket pistols*.

Beretta Model 418

Before James Bond famously started using the Walther PPK, Ian Fleming outfitted him with a .25 caliber Beretta Model 418. (Photo courtesy of *Gun Digest*.)

- **TYPE:** semi-automatic pistol
- **CALIBER:** .25
- **CAPACITY:** eight
- **YEAR INTRODUCED:** 1947
- single-action
- slide-action
- known as the "Bantam" in the U.S. market

Ian Fleming's early James Bond novels saw the secret agent carrying this .25 caliber Beretta.

The 418 is the "lady's gun" Bond reader Geoffrey Boothroyd wrote about in a letter to Fleming. He suggested something with more punch. This led to Bond's switch to the Walther PPK.

The .25 is indeed a light caliber, but Fleming—a former secret operative himself—likely put more stock in accuracy than firepower. This led him to eventually settle on the .32 caliber PPK, which isn't much larger than the .25 Model 418.

Characters should take the same approach when using the 418. This is a compact firearm for finesse work. Accuracy definitely matters if a character can't handle a hand cannon. There's nothing disparaging about a character, male or female, with dead-on aim.

Boberg Arms XR45-S

Boberg Arms also makes the XR-9, shown here, which is similar in appearance to the XR45-S but comes in 9mm. (Photo courtesy of *Gun Digest*.)

- **TYPE:** semi-automatic pistol
- **CALIBER:** .45
- **CAPACITY:** seven
- **YEAR INTRODUCED:** 2014
- double-action (no need to cock a hammer before firing; just pull the trigger)

Writers on the cutting edge might choose the Boberg Arms XR45-S for a stealthy character. Billed as the "world's smallest semi-auto .45," it stuffs seven rounds of hard-hitting ammunition into a tiny pistol.

Whether this is a good idea depends on the character using it. The manufacturer's website claims the pistol is "extremely accurate." This would seem to run counter to the longer-barrels-equal-better accuracy rule; more likely it's on target at intimate ranges.

When firing, the character should hang on tight. This pistol's tiny frame will have a tough time managing the recoil of .45 cartridges.

Bottom line: The XR45-S is proof that downsizing doesn't have to mean sacrificing firepower, but accuracy will certainly be compromised.

Bond Arms Texas Defender

Spies and other covert characters might appreciate the compact design of the Bond Arms Texas Defender. Writers may like its unusual aesthetics. (Photo courtesy of *Gun Digest*.)

- **TYPE:** over-under pistol
- **CALIBERS:** .45, .44, .357 magnum, .40, 10mm, 9mm, .32, .22, .410
- **CAPACITY:** two
- **YEAR INTRODUCED:** 1997
- single-action (hammer must be cocked manually before each shot)
- 3-inch barrel

An over-under pistol? The Texas Defender is just that, sporting one barrel on top of the other. Those barrels can be interchanged depending on the caliber used, making it a versatile pick for the well-equipped character.

Firing the Texas Defender requires first cocking the hammer, then pulling the trigger. Repeat to fire the second barrel. If that sounds a little like a revolver, don't be confused. It's still a pistol because the chambers are stationary and don't rotate in a cylinder.

Note that the Texas Defender will fire a .410 shotshell. Like the Taurus Judge, mentioned earlier, it offers shotgun performance in a handgun. Have fun with that, writers.

Iver Johnson Arms Frontier Four Derringer

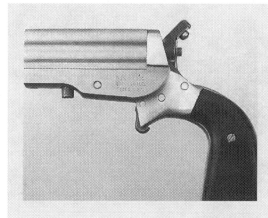

The Iver Johnson Arms Frontier Four is nearly identical to a Sharps four-barrel derringer design from the mid-1800s (shown here). This type of derringer is sometimes called a "pepper-box." Feel free to include one from the 1850s through today. They're great for settling poker disputes. (Photo courtesy of *Gun Digest*.)

- **TYPE:** pistol
- **CALIBER:** .22
- **CAPACITY:** four
- **YEAR INTRODUCED:** 2006
- single-action (hammer must be cocked manually before firing each shot)
- quad-barreled

The Frontier Four stands out for its four barrels. That's not a typo. This derringer (another term for a small pistol) uses a rotating firing pin to shoot .22 ammunition out of four barrels. It's not a revolver, though, because the chambers are stationary. This sounds gimmicky, but it's effective at intimate ranges of a few yards. Because it's a single-action, its hammer must be manually cocked before each shot.

Ruger LCP

As far as compact, modern handguns go, the Ruger LCP is at the front of its class. Between its size and quick use, the LCP is both the cloak and the dagger rolled into one. (Photo courtesy of Ruger.)

- **TYPE:** semi-automatic pistol
- **CALIBER:** .380
- **CAPACITY:** six
- **YEAR INTRODUCED:** 2008
- double-action (no need to cock a hammer before firing; just pull the trigger)
- slide-action
- 2¾-inch barrel

Ruger revived the derringer market in 2008 with the LCP, which stands for *lightweight compact pistol*. It's just that, which makes it a top choice for the modern spy character.

TOP SWITCHBLADES, AUTOMATICS, AND ASSISTED OPENING KNIVES

Note: The classic Italian stiletto switchblade is covered earlier in the Hit List.

KERSHAW LEEK

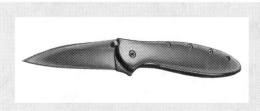

The Kershaw Leek comes in just about any color. The most common is gray, but the flashy, rainbow version is popular, too. (Photo courtesy of *BLADE*.)

- **TYPE:** assisted opening knife
- **BLADE LENGTH:** 3 inches
- **LENGTH CLOSED:** 4 inches
- **LENGTH OPEN:** 7 inches
- **YEAR INTRODUCED:** 1998

As one of the first assisted openers, this knife helped to change the industry in the late 1990s. To the untrained eye, the Leek would appear to operate like a switchblade. The blade swoops open from inside the handle, fast as a blink.

However, the mechanics are nothing like a switchblade. Unlike switchblades, the Leek's blade is biased to stay inside the handle. The user doesn't press a button or switch on the handle to eject the blade. Instead, a part of the blade itself, a tab, is pressed. This opens the blade halfway. Then an "assisting" mechanism takes over and pushes the blade the rest of the way out. The whole thing happens in a fraction of a second.

Legally this means the Leek is not a switchblade. It's an incredibly popular knife in the civilian market for that reason.

Many other assisted openers exist, but this is a go-to model.

SOG Aegis

If the laws of the setting won't allow a character to carry a switchblade or automatic knife, an assisted opener may be a better fit. And if that assisted opener needs to stand up to tough conditions, the SOG Aegis is a prime pick. (Photo courtesy of www.KnifeForums.com.)

- **TYPE:** assisted opening knife
- **BLADE LENGTH:** 3½ inches
- **LENGTH CLOSED:** 4¾ inches
- **LENGTH OPEN:** 8¼ inches
- **INTRODUCED:** early 2000s

For as ubiquitous as the Leek is on the market, it's not cut out for hard use. That can matter in a fight scene.

The SOG Aegis is a great alternative. It's an assisted opener with a tactical brain. It'd work well for any character in need of a quick and effective weapon.

Pro-Tech TR-3

- **TYPE:** automatic knife
- **BLADE LENGTH:** 3½ inches
- **LENGTH CLOSED:** 4½ inches
- **LENGTH OPEN:** 8 inches
- **INTRODUCED:** mid-2000s

If a character in a story set in recent years needs to carry a switchblade, consider outfitting him or her with a modern automatic knife, such as a Protech TR-3. Automatic knives are the modern equivalent of switchblades. They use the latest designs and materials. (Photo courtesy of www.KnifeForums.com.)

Law enforcement and military characters don't need to mess around with assisted openers. They can obtain automatic knives (the term for modern switchblades).

The Pro-Tech TR-3 is a great choice for those modern characters. The character would press a button on the handle to open the blade from the side. Although it's an automatic, the TR-3 is one of the tougher models available. It'd hold up well in a fight scene.

Spyderco Embassy

Assign the Spyderco Embassy automatic knife to law enforcement characters and others able (or just willing) to carry restricted knives. (Photo courtesy of www.Knife Forums.com.)

- **TYPE:** automatic knife
- **BLADE LENGTH:** $3\frac{1}{8}$ inches
- **LENGTH CLOSED:** $4\frac{9}{32}$ inches
- **LENGTH OPEN:** $7\frac{3}{8}$ inches
- **YEAR INTRODUCED:** 2008

From a writing standpoint, the Spyderco Embassy is not all that different from the Pro-Tech TR-3. The Embassy is popular with the law enforcement crowd, so it's worth mentioning.

Benchmade Infidel

No, the name isn't very politically correct. But the Benchmade Infidel is a prime example of an OTF (out the front) knife suitable as a modern alternative to the classic switchblade. (Photo courtesy of www.Knife Forums.com.)

- **TYPE:** OTF (out the front) automatic knife
- **BLADE LENGTH:** $3\frac{9}{10}$ inches
- **LENGTH CLOSED:** 5 inches
- **LENGTH OPEN:** $8\frac{9}{10}$ inches
- **YEAR INTRODUCED:** 2006

The Writer's Guide to Weapons

If vanilla automatic knives or Italian stiletto switchblades just aren't enough, go with the Benchmade Infidel. It's an OTF, or "out the front," automatic. That means the blade comes out the front of the handle instead of the side. The character would need to push a slide forward to release the blade. Getting the blade back inside involves slipping the slide backward.

Military, law enforcement, and criminal characters are more likely than civilians to have an Infidel or any other automatic knife. Civilian characters would have to live in an area that permits switchblades in order to buy one.

TOP FOLDING KNIVES

Buck 110

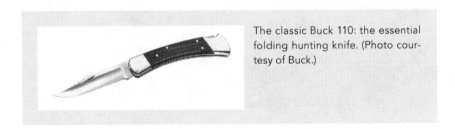

The classic Buck 110: the essential folding hunting knife. (Photo courtesy of Buck.)

- **BLADE LENGTH:** 3¾ inches
- **LENGTH CLOSED:** 4⅞ inches
- **LENGTH OPEN:** 8⅝ inches
- **YEAR INTRODUCED:** 1964

The Buck 110 is the template for folding hunting knives. Give it to outdoorsy characters or any character in need of a simple, reliable folding knife. Few folders can match the popularity of the Buck 110.

However, the Buck 110 isn't the best choice for fighting. It's a great knife, but it's meant for use outdoors and for everyday tasks.

Emerson CQC

- **BLADE LENGTH:** $3^1/_3$ inches
- **LENGTH CLOSED:** $4^2/_3$ inches
- **LENGTH OPEN:** 8 inches
- **YEAR INTRODUCED:** 1994

The Emerson CQC (close-quarters combat) is a true tactical folding knife. Its designer, Ernest Emerson, helped launch tactical folding knives in the 1980s. Any character anticipating a fight could confidently carry one.

Many variations of the CQC exist. The specs listed are for the CQC-7, which is one of the most popular.

Writers needing a knife similar to the CQC-7 but in a slightly earlier time period might check out the CQC-6, introduced in 1989.

The Emerson CQC has "close-quarters combat" built into its name. Characters might use it for just that. (Photo courtesy of *BLADE*.)

Gerber LST

The Gerber LST is an all-purpose folding knife for characters from the 1980s and beyond. It's nothing too fancy but might be worth writing instead of a generic folding knife if it matters to the story. (Photo courtesy of Gerber for *BLADE*.)

- **BLADE LENGTH:** $2^2/_3$ inches
- **LENGTH CLOSED:** $3^2/_3$ inches
- **LENGTH OPEN:** $6^1/_{10}$ inches
- **YEAR INTRODUCED:** 1980

The Gerber LST is a great choice for stories set in the Reagan years. It fills the gap between the old school Buck 110 of 1964 and Spyderco's Delica/Endura models in the 1990s. It's mentioned here for that reason, so heads up 1980s writers.

Performance-wise, this is an all-around knife with a smart design. It would go well with a similar kind of character.

Spyderco Delica/Endura

- **DELICA BLADE LENGTH:** 2⅞ inches
- **DELICA LENGTH CLOSED:** 4¼ inches
- **DELICA LENGTH OPEN:** 7⅛ inches
- **ENDURA BLADE LENGTH:** 3¾ inches
- **ENDURA LENGTH CLOSED:** 5 inches
- **ENDURA LENGTH OPEN:** 8¾ inches
- **YEAR INTRODUCED:** 1990

The Spyderco Endura (top) and Delica (bottom) are two popular folding knives. (Photo courtesy of *BLADE*.)

The Spyderco Delica and Spyderco Endura are two of the most popular and successful folding knives. They're used across the board in nearly every occupation and around the world.

Either is a good pick for a character after 1990, the year they were introduced. They sport a modern look and come in many variations.

Like the Buck 110, they are default knives for writers. Unlike the Buck 110, the Delica and Endura would fare better in a fight. They're not tactical knives per se, but neither would be the worst choice.

TOP FIXED BLADE COMBAT KNIVES

Fairbairn-Sykes Fighting Knife

The Fairbairn-Sykes could also be abbreviated as the F-S. Just spell it out the first time you reference it. (Photo courtesy of www.KnifeForums.com.)

- **TYPE:** dagger (sharpened on both sides)
- **BLADE LENGTH:** 7 inches
- **OVERALL LENGTH:** 11½ inches
- **YEAR INTRODUCED:** 1943

Great Britain scrambled to put a decent knife into the hands of its special operations units in World War II. After several attempts, the Fairbairn-Sykes Fighting Knife (also known as the British Commando Knife) made it to frontlines in 1943.

Several incarnations of this knife exist, but feel free to write it with a 7-inch blade. Military characters from the United Kingdom in the 1940s through today could carry this knife. It's possible characters in other countries might use this knife, too, since it's so popular. This knife proliferated across the globe in World War II, and people on all sides became familiar with it.

However, be careful about outfitting U.K. civilians in stories set in recent years with the Fairbairn-Sykes. Knife laws in that country severely restrict anything resembling a "fighting knife."

Applegate-Fairbairn Fighting Knife

- **TYPE:** dagger (blade sharpened on both sides)
- **BLADE LENGTH:** 6 inches
- **OVERALL LENGTH:** 10¾ inches
- **YEAR INTRODUCED:** 1980

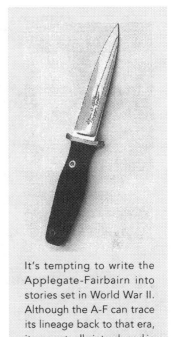

Not to be outdone by their counterparts in Great Britain, the United States responded to the Fairbairn-Sykes Fighting Knife with the Applegate-Fairbairn Fighting Knife. It took only forty years to do it.

What's the difference? Introduced in 1980, the Applegate-Fairbairn (also abbreviated as A-F) sports a more modern feel and updated materials. The late Col. Rex Applegate designed this knife specifically for hand-to-hand military combat. Applegate's techniques and knives survive him.

Here's why Googling this knife will lead writers astray. The A-F can trace its heritage back to World War II, when the first incarnations hit the frontlines. However, Applegate didn't formally introduce the A-F until 1980.

That means the A-F only *sort of* existed in World War II. For the sake of accuracy, write the A-F in stories set in 1980 or later.

It's tempting to write the Applegate-Fairbairn into stories set in World War II. Although the A-F can trace its lineage back to that era, it was actually introduced in 1980, according to *BLADE* magazine. (Photo courtesy of *BLADE*.)

Feel free to assign the A-F to Western covert or military characters. The A-F is also available on civilian markets where laws allow (research the setting's blade length laws and dagger restrictions).

Several A-F variations are available from different manufacturers, but a good go-to is the 6-inch blade model made by Boker. Gerber also makes automatic and assisted opening versions of this knife. Blade lengths with those vary from less than 3 inches to 4½.

Benchmade Nimravus Cub II

Sure, this is a shameless endorsement of a product I happen to like. But the Benchmade Nimravus Cub II really is the perfect portable, do-it-all fixed blade knife. Give it to military, outdoors-y, law enforcement, civilian, and criminal characters. (Author's photo.)

- **TYPE:** fixed blade
- **BLADE LENGTH:** $3\frac{1}{2}$ inches
- **OVERALL LENGTH:** $7\frac{22}{25}$ inches
- **INTRODUCED:** mid-2000s

The "Nim Cub," as it's often called, doesn't pack the history of the other knives on this list. It didn't revolutionize combat knives. In fact, it's pretty vanilla.

However, it ranks as my favorite fixed blade knife in the real world. It's ergonomic, lightweight, portable, tough, and versatile. No hunting or outdoors trip of mine goes without the Nim Cub.

Benchmade designed this knife for use by airborne military units. The Nim Cub needed to do everything, from tactical to survival. It succeeded in spades. For fiction, this is a top choice for characters in and out of the military.

Cold Steel Tanto

The *tanto* in this Cold Steel Tanto refers to the roughly 45-degree angle at the tip. This makes it ideal for characters needing to plow through tough materials. (Photo courtesy of Cold Steel for *BLADE*.)

- **TYPE:** fixed blade
- **BLADE LENGTH:** 6, $7\frac{1}{2}$, 9, or 12 inches
- **OVERALL LENGTH:** $11\frac{1}{2}$, $13\frac{1}{8}$, $14\frac{5}{8}$, or $17\frac{5}{8}$ inches
- **INTRODUCED:** mid-1980s

The *tanto* term refers to the style at the tip of the blade, where the edge forms a hard angle to meet the point instead of the classic sweeping shape. Tantos are present on the Cold Steel Tanto, as well as many other knives.

This design strengthens the tip of the blade. Characters needing to hack through hard materials, even metal, should consider a Cold Steel Tanto.

Caveat: The character should be familiar with handling knives. The size of some of the models approaches that of a short sword. The version with the 6-inch blade is the most practical in all likelihood.

Of course, a writer surely could think of things to hack to pieces with the 12-incher.

Gerber Mark II

As a dagger, the Gerber Mark II is ideal for quick hit-and-run scenes. (Photo courtesy of Gerber.)

- **TYPE:** dagger (blade is sharpened on both sides)
- **BLADE LENGTH:** 6½ inches
- **OVERALL LENGTH:** 12¾ inches
- **YEAR INTRODUCED:** 1966

Need something to round out that cloak and dagger ensemble? Introduced in 1966, the Gerber Mark II is the ticket.

The U.S. military put the 1966 Mark II to use for the next forty years, so it's a good choice for outfitting your characters. The Mark II is also available on the civilian market (where the law allows).

Like all daggers, the Mark II is best used for stabbing when writing fight scenes. The drawback is that in a struggle, there's twice the number of ways for the character with the knife to cut himself, since the blade is sharpened on both sides.

KA-BAR USMC

Introduced in World War II, the KA-BAR USMC is still issued to U.S. Marines and members of other branches of the military. Pictured is an updated version using modern materials. (Photo courtesy of *BLADE*.)

- **TYPE:** fixed blade
- **BLADE LENGTH:** 7 inches
- **OVERALL LENGTH:** 11⅞ inches
- **YEAR INTRODUCED:** 1942

Few knives are as iconic as KA-BAR's USMC. The U.S. Marine Corps started using this fixed blade knife in late 1942 during World War II. Other services quickly adopted it.

This knife is tough as hell, versatile, easy to grip, and imitated by a number of companies. It's appropriate to write this knife generically as a *KA-BAR* instead of *KA-BAR USMC*.

This is the perfect knife to outfit any U.S. military character up to present time in any conflict or setting. It's also popular on the civilian market.

I place the KA-BAR as the number one pick for characters needing a knife for combat—even outside of the military. It'll handle nearly anything, including a tour of duty through the pages of fiction.

Randall Model 1

The Randall Model 1, knife of the stars. It's been used by everyone from the Army to astronauts. (Photo courtesy of Mike Silvey for *BLADE*.)

- **TYPE:** fixed blade
- **BLADE LENGTH:** 5, 6, 7, or 8 inches
- **OVERALL LENGTH:** approximately 11¾ inches, depending on blade length and style
- **YEAR INTRODUCED:** 1941

World War II cranked out many more iconic knives than just the KA-BAR. The Randall Model 1 "All Purpose Fighter" debuted to incredible demand by U.S. troops. It's since been used in every branch of service up through today, as well as "astronauts, government agents, celebrities, statesmen, and royalty," according to information found at www.RandallKnives.com.

The Model 1 is not as well known to the general readership, but including it will make the writer look pretty sharp. Plus, the variety of blade lengths offers versatility when the story calls for it.

TOP SURVIVAL KNIVES AND MULTI-TOOLS

Famar's USA SRT Survival Knife

- **TYPE:** folding knife
- **BLADE LENGTH:** 3½ inches
- **LENGTH CLOSED:** 5⅛ inches
- **LENGTH OPEN:** 8⅝ inches
- **YEAR INTRODUCED:** 2013

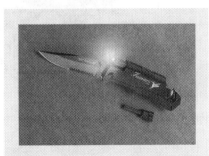

Famar's USA SRT Survival Knife comes with everything but the plot. (Photo courtesy of *Living Ready*.)

For characters with more inner "Inspector Gadget" than "MacGyver," there's the Famar's USA SRT Survival Knife.

The SRT comes with a built-in LED light, a fire-starting rod, a glass breaker (a stud on the bottom of the handle, called the pommel), and a razor belt cutter. Oh, and a half-serrated blade.

Will it keep a character on an adventure alive in a pinch? Yes. Does it pass scrutiny in real life? It depends. Either way, writers should feel free to use the SRT for the fiction its designers must have had in mind.

Leatherman

- **TYPE:** multi-tool
- **LENGTH:** varies
- **YEAR INTRODUCED:** 1983
- has various blades and accessory tools

The original Leatherman multi-tool came to the market in 1983. It's now become a generic term for a pliers platform with knives and other tools folded inside, and it's acceptable to write it that way.

If a character needs a multi-tool prior to 1983, write in a Swiss army knife.

The Leatherman started as a glorified pair of pliers. It's perfect for bringing out the MacGyver in any character. (Courtesy of Leatherman Tool Group for *BLADE*.)

SOG Trident Tanto TF-7

Why would a knife need a built-in seat-belt cutter? In an emergency, a character could cut straps or other material without unfolding the blade first. The seat-belt cutter is located in the notch near the end of the handle on this SOG Trident. (Photo courtesy of www.Knife Forums.com.)

- **TYPE:** assisted opening knife
- **BLADE LENGTH:** 3¾ inches
- **LENGTH CLOSED:** 4¾ inches
- **LENGTH OPEN:** 8½ inches

The Trident would be categorized as yet another assisted opening tactical knife, except for one important difference: There's a seat-belt cutter in the handle.

It may seem redundant to include a separate seat-belt cutter in a knife, but this small slot with a blade inside makes it much easier to cut a seat belt after a wreck. The knife doesn't need to be open.

This isn't a feature exclusive to the Trident. It's just that this is a great example of a knife with a belt cutter. This knife is perfect for first-responders (EMT, firefighter, police officer) or simply well-prepared characters.

Spyderco Assist

- **TYPE:** Folding knife
- **BLADE LENGTH:** 3$\frac{7}{10}$ inches
- **LENGTH CLOSED:** 4$\frac{7}{8}$ inches
- **LENGTH OPEN:** 8$\frac{3}{8}$ inches
- **INTRODUCED:** around 2008

Knife handles don't always have to be black. The highly visible blaze orange on this Spyderco Assist complements its intended purpose. It's an off-the-beaten-path choice for characters in maritime or emergency scenarios. (Photo courtesy of www.KnifeForums.com.)

Several features of this knife make it ideal for a first-responder or marine-centric character.

The Spyderco Assist lacks a tip, which allows for close work next to skin or other sensitive materials. Think freeing someone from a wrecked car. Small serrations along the blade come in handy for this purpose, too.

Rounding out the knife is a wavy pattern along the handle, a feature that assists in cutting rope. The rope is placed inside one of the indentations in the handle before the blade is folded down and closed on top of it. This action cuts the rope cleanly without having to saw away at it.

Victorinox/Wenger Swiss Army Knives

- **TYPE:** multi-tool
- **LENGTH:** varies
- **INTRODUCED:** 1880s
- tools vary

A certain irony coincides with the fact that a country known for neutrality is also the home of one of the most famous "army knives" in existence. Swiss army knives hit the scene in the 1880s and are now found across the globe.

While there are scores of imitators, those made by Victorinox and Wenger are the granddaddies of them all. While it's acceptable to write *Swiss army knife* generically, mention either brand to amp up a manuscript's authenticity.

A Victorinox Swiss Army Knife is great for getting characters in and out of trouble. (Photo courtesy of Victorinox for *BLADE*.)

What's the difference between the two brands? Not much. Both played a part in introducing the knife to the Swiss army in the 1880s. Both are located in Switzerland. The only difference is Wenger came from a French-speaking area, while Victorinox hailed from a German-speaking area. The Swiss government bought from both companies to supply its military.

TOP MACHETES

Cold Steel Bowie Machete

For a size comparison, the Cold Steel Bowie Machete (second from bottom) is pictured next to full-sized machetes. Note how the Bowie Machete sports a more compact design. It straddles the line between a standard fixed blade knife and a machete. This middle ground can come in handy when a scene needs an exceptionally beefy blade but a machete doesn't make sense. (Photo courtesy of www.KnifeForums.com.)

- **BLADE LENGTH:** 12 inches
- **OVERALL LENGTH:** 17⅝ inches

The large size of a machete makes it difficult to control. For something more practical, go with the Cold Steel Bowie Machete. It takes the tried-and-true design of a classic Bowie knife and adds a few inches.

This is as small as machetes get without becoming regular fixed blade knives. Give it to a character with a flair for style while hacking things to pieces.

As far as a year of introduction for this specific model, the earliest I could confirm was 2013.

Cold Steel Two-Handed Katana Machete

Sometimes, a mere machete just won't do. This Cold Steel Two-Handed Katana Machete can pull triple duty as a machete, sword, and throwing spear. I couldn't mention this little number without directing you to an equally over-the-top, tragicomic video demonstration. Don't view before eating. tinyurl.com/katana-machete (Photo courtesy of Cold Steel.)

- **BLADE LENGTH:** 24 inches
- **OVERALL LENGTH:** 40½ inches

Here's an over-the-top twist on any standard machete. The Cold Steel Two-Handed Katana Machete's handle takes up almost half of its overall length. Why? It's meant to be thrown.

That's right. It's a machete the length of a sword designed to be thrown like a spear. Two hands are recommended—for safety, of course.

The Katana Machete can be used for standard slashing and hacking, too. But the fact it's designed for throwing may prove too tempting for fiction.

The earliest I could confirm this machete was available was 2010.

Condor Tool & Knife El Salvador

The El Salvador machete sports a classic design. It's an easy choice for characters slashing through brush, zombies, or whatever else is in the way. (Photo courtesy of Condor Tool & Knife.)

- **BLADE LENGTH:** 18 inches
- **OVERALL LENGTH:** 23½ inches
- **YEAR INTRODUCED:** 2004

For a machete with a classic look, the Condor Tool & Knife El Salvador is the ticket. It's the perfect first choice when outfitting a character from 2004 onward. It's inexpensive—around $75.

Remember that it's perfectly acceptable to write *machete* generically. But if you need the name of a classic-looking machete, the El Salvador is it.

Gerber Gator Sawback

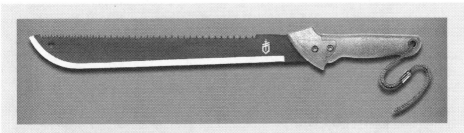

Other than the teeth along the spine of this machete, the Gator's other advantage is its ubiquity. It's a staple at sporting goods stores across the U.S., increasing the chances your character might own it. (Photo courtesy of Gerber Gear.)

- **BLADE LENGTH:** 18 inches
- **OVERALL LENGTH:** 25 $7/10$ inches
- **INTRODUCED:** early 1990s

For a sadistic twist, outfit a character with the Gerber Gator Sawback. It sports a saw along the spine of the knife. Controlling the saw teeth is a challenge, since pressing down on the sharpened edged on the opposite side of the blade will guarantee a gaping hand wound.

Then again, maybe a slow, clumsy saw is just what the scene ordered.

TOPS Knives Armageddon

Designers had tactical uses in mind when crafting the Armageddon machete (top) instead of utilitarian outdoors work. It could be dropped into any setting, though. (Photo courtesy of www.KnifeForums.com.)

- **BLADE LENGTH:** 10$5/8$ inches
- **OVERALL LENGTH:** 16$1/2$ inches

Most machetes aren't designed for combat, but this is the exception. The TOPS Knives Armageddon is considered a *tactical machete*, and it's ideal for characters who are expecting trouble.

The key difference lies in the thickness of the blade. Most machetes use thinner blades compared to knives. The Armageddon uses a quarter-inch-thick blade. This allows it to handle tougher cutting jobs like a knife while maintaining the oversized utility of a machete.

The earliest I could confirm the Armageddon's existence was 2006.

TOP BOOT KNIVES

A.G. Russell Sting Boot Knife

Since the mid-1970s, the Sting set the standard for boot knives. Writers would do well to slide it into a character's boot as a backup knife. (Photo courtesy of www.KnifeForums.com.)

- **TYPE:** dagger (blade is sharpened on both sides)
- **BLADE LENGTH:** 3⅛ inches
- **OVERALL LENGTH:** 6⅞ inches
- **YEAR INTRODUCED:** 1975

The AG Russell Sting is one of the most popular boot knives on the market. It's perfect for slipping inside a sheath in a boot, or for everyday tasks that don't involve concealment. The Sting is a tough little number ready for a character's last-ditch defense.

Like all boot knives, the Sting isn't necessarily carried in the boot. A *boot knife* refers more to a style than a specific function. The Sting could be used like any other knife.

Columbia River Knife & Tool (CRKT) manufactures the Sting today.

Gerber Guardian

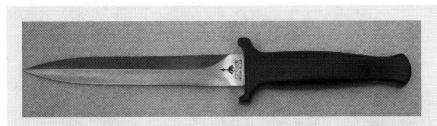

For a boot knife that also functions well as a classic dagger, write in the Gerber Guardian. (Photo courtesy of www.KnifeForums.com.)

- **TYPE:** dagger (blade is sharpened on both sides)
- **BLADE LENGTH:** 3²⁄₅ inches
- **OVERALL LENGTH:** 7¹⁄₃ inches
- **YEAR INTRODUCED:** 1981

The Gerber Guardian ranks up there with the Sting as a popular boot knife. The two knives are quite similar, although the Guardian sports a more classic dagger design.

When a character needs a boot knife, use either the Sting or the Guardian. Both are no-fail picks.

TOP BUTTERFLY KNIVES

Benchmade 42 Bali-Song/Bali-Song, Inc. Wee Hawk

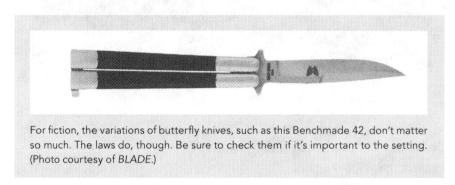

For fiction, the variations of butterfly knives, such as this Benchmade 42, don't matter so much. The laws do, though. Be sure to check them if it's important to the setting. (Photo courtesy of *BLADE*.)

- **BLADE LENGTH:** $4\frac{1}{5}$ inches
- **CLOSED LENGTH:** $5\frac{1}{5}$ inches
- **OPEN LENGTH:** $9\frac{2}{5}$ inches
- **INTRODUCED:** late 1970s

The go-to butterfly knife for fiction is the Bali-Song, Inc. Wee Hawk. It was first introduced in the late 1970s and ended production in the late 1990s, but many remain in circulation.

The design proved incredibly popular and is still considered by many to be the ultimate butterfly knife. It lived on as the Benchmade 42 Bali-Song (write it as *Benchmade 42*), produced from the early 2000s to 2010. Keep those brand names—Benchmade and Bali-Song, Inc.—in mind if such things matter to the year the story takes place. Also consider applicable laws for the setting, because this knife is often restricted.

Other Butterfly Knives

The Bradley Cutlery Kimura series, models from Bear & Son Cutlery, and standards like the Spyderco SpyderFly could all have their own separate entries—but they're not getting them. Why not?

Here's the thing. When writing fiction, butterfly knives don't need to vary too much. They're used for intimidation and light cutting jobs. That's about it. The differences between the go-to Benchmade 42 and these others begin to dissolve because of that narrow usage.

As a shortcut, remember it's acceptable to use *butterfly knife* or *balisong* generically. *Bali-Song* is a registered trademark of Benchmade. That hyphen makes a difference.

TRUE CRIME STORIES FROM REAL CRIME WRITERS

Maynard Soloman, gal-damn detective, provided most of the examples in this guide. It's time to give him a break before gangrene hits. Let's shift to the real world.

What follows are true crime stories from real crime writers. Use their perspective for writing firearms and knives in fiction.

WHAT IT'S LIKE TO BE SHOT

Joseph Brennan, author of *Superdollar*, is a crime writer from Northern Ireland. During the Troubles of the 1970s, he became involved with the Irish Republicans, a group fighting with the Loyalists. He's since left that violence in the past.

British troops shot Brennan during an encounter in 1972. Here's his description of how that felt. Note how the type of ammunition affected the injury.

> I had nearly reached the end of the street and the safety of a corner when I believe that one of the soldiers realised that my gun was empty. The ground just to my left spat up at me as I heard the two high-velocity cracks a split second later. The next round spun past my head. I heard it. I then stumbled as I ran, and it was then that I was hit.
>
> If I had not stumbled when I did, I would most likely have died. My head jolted to the side and my shoulder went up and that's when the round went through my shoulder. It was a minor explosion as blood and fibres from the padding in my jacket formed a crazy mist around the right side of my face.
>
> I was aware of the pain but was somehow able to ignore it, if that makes sense. I also felt relief because I knew there and then I had survived it.
>
> The impact of the bullet spun me round as I hit the ground, and I could see the soldier who had fired raise a clenched fist in triumph. He thought I was down. I rolled with the force and the momentum and got to the corner.
>
> I ran for around three minutes through the maze of side streets before collapsing. I was still conscious, but my head was spinning and I could see the faces of the two men and a woman who picked me up and carried me to a Black Hackney Cab and safety.
>
> In the end the wound was not so serious. The round hit me in the back about two

or three inches from the top of my shoulder blade. … The entry wound was so neat and measured about one millimetre more than the 7.62mm [roughly equivalent to the .308 rifle caliber] of the round itself. The exit wound was less neat and around 20 millimetres and slightly oval shaped.

The doctor who treated me told me that if it had been a low-velocity round, things would have been more serious, as it would most likely have exploded upon hitting the bone. However, the full metal jacket round stayed intact and ploughed neatly on through.

WHAT IT'S LIKE TO BE IN A GUNFIGHT

In his memoir, tentatively titled *Adrenaline Junkie* as of this writing, crime writer and Writer's Digest Books author Les Edgerton recalls his wilder years running with rough crowds. Here's his depiction of trading shots in a gunfight, as excerpted with permission from the memoir. Watch for how the encounter confused Les as he traded shots, unlike in the clear-cut action of fiction.

One night, cruising around back roads and stopping every so often to break into these country bars, which were everywhere around South Bend, Rat and I passed a junior high school stuck way out in the boonies south of town.

We'd never robbed a school before and didn't know whether they kept money in the office, but it looked like an easy hit so we pulled in and broke into the front door. It was just Rat and me.

We were walking down the main hallway, big as shit, figuring we had all the time in the world since nobody's going to be in a schoolhouse at 2 a.m., when all of a sudden somebody at the other end of the corridor jumped out and fired a shot at us. It sounded like a cannon going off in that empty school.

Rat and I each jumped into a room on either side of the hallway and yanked our pieces out and started firing at the other end where the gunfire had come from. We were whispering back and forth, and came up with this master plan that we would trade fire with the cops—that's what we figured they were—and then we'd run for the car and try and outrun them. I had my T-Bird then and there wasn't much could catch it.

We'd each shot four or five shots and were just about to make our break when this voice yelled, "We give up!" I looked over at Rat and he at me and I said, "Cops don't give themselves up, do they?" He started laughing and said, "Fuck no."

"You cops?" we both yelled down the hall.

"No!" came a voice back. "Are you?"

It was two other guys with the same idea who had broken into the other end at about the same time we had.

We talked to each other a few minutes, and then Rat and I said we were going to get the hell out of there. Even though the school was way out in the boonies we figured maybe some farmer had heard the shots and might be calling the cops. The other two guys said they were going to go ahead and check it out, see if there was any money. Rat and I got in my car and booked. I don't know whether those other guys ever got busted or not. I didn't buy newspapers in those days, and we didn't have a TV. I hope they made it. They seemed like nice guys once they "gave up."

In an e-mail, Edgerton said, "Rat had one of those pesky little Raven .25 calibers, and I had a .38 revolver. I kept telling him to get rid of that little toy. If he ever shot anyone with it, it was just going to piss them off, plus it left [empty casings] lying around."

WHAT IT'S LIKE TO BE IN A KNIFE FIGHT

The colorful stories from Edgerton's memoir keep coming. Here's an example involving a fight with a switchblade.

Note how the blade doesn't stand up to the rigors of the melee. Despite the way they're depicted in fiction, switchblades can't take a lot of abuse. Fixed blade knives, modern assisted opening knives, and even standard folding knives benefit from better designs and technology.

Also pay attention to Rachelle's reaction after getting stabbed. She had no idea it had happened.

Rachelle was so tiny I knew she wasn't any match for Cat. If Rachelle topped the scales at 90 pounds I'd be surprised. I ran back to the stairs, took them two at a time, and flew around the corner of the building to the lot. Just as I came around the corner, I saw Cat raise her arm and smack Rachelle, who ducked, catching the blow on her back.

I ran as fast as I could, arriving there just as Cat was raising her arm to strike again, and that was when I saw she had the switchblade in her hand. She'd already stabbed her once, but neither Rachelle nor I realized that at this point.

As Cat was coming down with the knife, I grabbed her wrist with one hand and Rachelle with the other and shoved them apart as hard as I could. Cat went down on her hands and knees, then snarled and lunged at me, trying to catch me in my stomach with the knife. I ducked and at the same time grabbed her hand as it was coming across and smashed it as hard as I could on my knee, which made her lose control, and the knife clattered to the pavement.

My first thought was to find the knife before she did, that without it she couldn't do much damage. It was pitch-black, so it took a few seconds before I felt it with my foot.

When Cat saw I had the knife in my hand, she snarled and took off running for the other parking lot, cutting back through the pool area. I stood there with the knife in my hand until I heard her car start and squeal out of the lot. I tried to fold it, but the blade was bent in two places and wouldn't go back.

I walked over to Rachelle, who was standing up against her car. She looked all right, but I wanted to be sure.

"You okay?" I asked.

"I think so," she said. Just then, I noticed tiny speckles of bright crimson all over her white silk blouse. It looked like sprinkles of Tabasco sauce.

"Oh, man," I said. "She hit you in the nose. You've got a nose bleed."

I'm standing there, the knife in my hand, I've just seen Cat hit her with it the instant before I could get there, Cat had tried to disembowel me … and it still didn't dawn on me that she'd stabbed Rachelle. It hadn't dawned on Rachelle either. It just all happened too fast, and I'd guess we were both in shock.

"No," she said. "She didn't hit me in the nose. I ducked, and she hit me in the back."

"Turn around," I said.

The entire back of her blouse was solid red, and a crimson stain was spreading down her white pants.

"Jesus," I said. "You've been stabbed."

"I have?" Rachelle said.

"Yeah. Can you walk?"

She could. We walked over to the pool area, which was better lit. I slipped down her blouse a little to see the puncture. Blood had quit running except for little dribbles that came out when she moved, kind of bubbly stuff.

"You need to go to the hospital," I said.

"No," she said. "I'll be all right. I'll just go home and have my mom look at it. I don't think it's that bad."

Just then, a guy came through the breezeway from the far parking lot. I called out to him.

"Hey! I've got a girl here who's been stabbed. You know if there's a doctor in the complex?" That was a stupid question. I lived in Drug Central, home of drug dealers and prostitutes and house creepers. And me.

He came over.

"Man!" he said when he saw all the blood. "I think the lady that lives there is a nurse," he said. He pointed to a ground-floor apartment on the other side of the pool from where we stood. I left Rachelle and ran over and knocked and knocked, but no one came to the door. I went back to Rachelle, and she said, "I'm starting to feel a little dizzy. Let's go up to your room where the light's good so you can take a better look at it."

I held her elbow and we walked up the stairs and down the walk to my apartment, and once inside I removed her blouse. Not much blood was coming out by now. It was just bubbling a little when her muscles flexed, but her entire back was covered with sticky-tacky, drying blood.

IMITATING HOLLYWOOD COULD GET SOMEONE KILLED

Fiction sometimes depicts knives or guns being shot out of hands. As this story from retired law enforcement officer and writer Leroy Vaughn details, doing so is difficult. Here's his story about "Glen," a fellow officer, in an encounter with a machete-wielding man. It was originally published in the online 'zine *Fingerprints* (fingerprintsjournal.blogspot.com).

Pay attention to how hard it is to hit anything with a handgun, even for a police officer.

Glen was one of those cops who wanted to be a peace officer. He was going to do everything he could to get the little man to drop the machete. He asked the man several times to put the weapon down and place his hands on his head. He wasn't sure the man could understand him, but he knew that pointing a pistol at him would get his point across.

The man screamed, and Glen assumed that the man was cussing at him, but the man could not or would not speak English. The man was now less than seven feet from Glen. Glen knew he had no choice. He was going to have to shoot the man to stop him, or Glen would be dead.

Glen was a big fan of cowboy movies, and he thought that at that distance he could shoot the machete out of the man's right hand. The man started to swing the machete as he moved closer. Glen fired one round from his .38 revolver at the man's hand.

Glen was surprised when the man went down. Glen kicked the machete out of the man's hand as he lay bleeding on the sawdust covered floor. Glen bent down to check the man as the bartender came over to look at the man on the floor. Glen looked at the bartender and told him the man was dead, having felt for a pulse on the man's carotid artery.

"Where did you hit him? I thought you went for his hand," I told him as he lit another cigarette. "I did aim for the hand, but I was the worst shot in my class at the academy. I couldn't hit an elephant with a bazooka. There was a coroner's inquest the next week, and I was told that I had shot him right through the heart."

TACTICS USED BY LAW ENFORCEMENT AND THE MILITARY

It would take another book to cover all the points of police and military tactics. Here are a few key concepts for writing characters inside these organizations.

SEND IN THE SWAT TEAM

Characters on a special weapons and tactics (SWAT) team are often written in during an intense standoff, raid, or other high-stakes encounter. In some communities and organizations, these are also called SRTs (special response teams).

Former law enforcement officer Lee Lofland writes about this subject extensively in his excellent book, *Police Procedure & Investigation*, published by Writer's Digest Books. The following information originates in that title.

A SWAT entry team usually consists of six to ten officers, all packing tech, weapons, and well-timed one-liners (okay, that's only in fiction). One officer takes out the door with a battering ram, then steps aside while the others file into the building.

A flash-bang grenade may be tossed into the building prior to their entry. The grenade uses noise and smoke to disorient occupants. The entry team then goes about the building to clear each room.

As the entry team piles in through the door, other SWAT team members simultaneously "rake and break." This involves breaking in through other windows and doors. The rake-and-break crew orders anyone inside to hit the ground. The occupants are held at gunpoint until the entry team arrives and cuffs them.

Once the SWAT team gives the all clear, the investigation starts. Detectives and other officers gather evidence, make arrests, conduct interviews, etc.

SWAT Snipers

SWAT snipers typically use bolt-action rifles because of their reliability and accuracy. The models vary, so check the listings accompanying this guide. Most would use .223 caliber rifles or higher.

Lofland cites 860 yards (about a half mile) as the maximum range for SWAT snipers.

TRAFFIC STOPS

Many steps take place before an officer asks for the prototypical "license and registration, please" during a traffic stop. Before or after pulling a vehicle over, the officer:

- tells dispatch the license plate number.
- checks the vehicle and driver against the FBI's National Crime Information Center (NCIC) database.
- calls in for backup, if necessary.

Before approaching the driver, the officer typically:

- feels that the trunk is secure by placing a hand on it (to check for ambushes).
- visually scans the interior of the vehicle.

Then the officer proceeds to speak with the driver. It may become necessary for the driver to step outside for the sake of the officer's safety. The officer may also return to her car and run the driver's license number for additional information.

Somewhere around this point in the process, fiction usually depicts a wanted character peeling off in the car. If you go this route, remember that having the officer fire shots in response doesn't always make sense. In rural areas, it might be okay. But in urban or high-traffic settings? Consider collateral damage.

STOP AND FRISK

An officer can initiate an on-the-spot pat down, or "stop and frisk," if there's reason to believe someone is carrying a weapon. This doesn't require an arrest, but "officers must have facts to conduct a search, not merely a hunch, a gut feeling, or even a really good guess," as Lofland writes.

This stop and frisk, Lofland continues, "must be quick, and the officer may only perform it to search for weapons. Any other items discovered during this brief search may not be used as evidence, since their seizure would be considered the fruit of an illegal search, even if those items were later determined to be key items of evidence in a major case. Even if officers found a key piece of evidence that solved a string of murders, it couldn't be used."

Puts a damper on most *Law & Order* episodes, doesn't it?

MAKING AN ARREST AND THE USE OF FORCE

The use of force when making an arrest is supposed to be proportionate to the suspect's level of compliance. Lower compliance equals greater force, and vice versa. "Police brutality" occurs when that balance is out of proportion in the eyes of the law (or, sometimes, the public eye).

Officers can use a variety of nonlethal, or less lethal, tools when applying force.

- **ASP EXPANDABLE BATONS:** More portable and concealable than the standard baton, these can collapse down to a few inches.
- **BEANBAG PROJECTILES:** Ever been in a riot? These are what stung so much the next day. Beanbag projectiles are exactly what they sound like: cloth filled with BBs blasted from shotguns.
- **ELECTRIC POLICE JACKET:** These jackets, typically sported during riots, shock anyone who touches them.
- **FREEZE PLUS P SPRAY:** "A combination of pepper spray and tear gas (orthochloroben-zalmalononitrile). This combination creates a synergistic effect, with each chemical magnifying the other. Freeze Plus P will penetrate wet or greased skin, as well as entering the body through inhalation," Lofland says.
- **NOISE- OR SOUND-IMPULSE DEVICES:** These devices blast irritating noises or music until a person submits to law enforcement. They might include speakers blaring Justin Bieber, although that might border on police brutality.
- **PEPPER SPRAY (OLEORESIN CAPSICUM):** The classic tearjerker.
- **RUBBER BULLETS:** These fall under the less lethal category, since they can cause death at close ranges.
- **SHOCK STICKS:** Also known as electric batons, these are the equivalent of a cattle prod for human hamburgers.
- **STUN BELT:** "[This is a] device placed around the waists of prisoners to prevent combative behavior. Officers carry a remote-control device that, when activated, delivers a debilitating electric shock to the prisoner. This device is often used on jail and prison inmates, or by police officers when transporting violent suspects," says Lofland.
- **TWO-HANDED BATONS:** In an intense situation, when a standard baton just isn't enough, officers might use a two-handed version roughly 36 inches in length.

A CRASH COURSE IN MILITARY TACTICS

Military tactics vary widely according to the branch of service, treaties, equipment, historical setting, and more. That can make writing military characters, especially those engaged in combat scenes, difficult.

The temptation, in stories set at the advent of the Tommy gun through today, is to let military characters open up with fully automatic firearms. The character spots a target, takes aim, and unloads, hosing the scene with leaden death nuggets. The more bullets flying through the air, the better chance of hitting the target character, right?

Well, sort of.

Remember that military characters, just like any other in a story, need to lug around all that ammunition. It gets heavy in a hurry. Given it takes mere seconds to empty a magazine in a full-auto, it's probably premature to toss out that volume of ammo. A character could be up crap creek in a hurry. The quality of shots, not quantity, counts the most in combat.

That's why modern military tactics, depending on the scenario, might use full-auto gunfire to force the target into a less favorable position or to take cover. Another shooter, likely with a rifle suited for precision, would make the actual kill shot.

Again, tactics vary, but statistics seem to back up this high shot-to-kill ratio. A July 2005 Government Accountability Office report, GAO-05-687, stated U.S. forces in Iraq and Afghanistan required 1.79 billion small caliber and 21.5 million medium caliber rounds in fiscal year 2005 alone. An analysis by John Pike of www.GlobalSecurity.org, a military research group, estimated that 250,000 to 300,000 rounds were used per enemy combatant killed in those countries.

Those figures include training outside combat, but the point is still valid. It takes a target character's weight in lead to kill him.

This makes for interesting trivia, but many writers will likely gloss over the shots that don't make contact. That's okay. Just be aware that militaries train for a reason.

GLOSSARY

ACTION: The mechanism that moves ammunition in and out of a firearm's chamber (the place where a cartridge is seated to be fired).

ANKLE HOLSTER: A type of handgun holster worn around the ankle, usually underneath a pant leg.

ARMOR-PIERCING AMMUNITION: A type of ammunition that has a bullet that is either coated in Teflon, made of hardened metals, or both. Whether such a bullet actually penetrates armor depends on many factors.

ASSAULT RIFLE: Not to be confused with *assault weapon*. As Patrick Sweeney writes in *The Gun Digest Book of the AK & SKS*, an assault rifle is "a shoulder-fired, select-fire weapon used by an individual soldier, firing a cartridge of intermediate rifle caliber, with a detachable, high-capacity magazine." *Select-fire* means the rifle can switch between fully automatic and semi-automatic modes.

ASSAULT WEAPON: A consistent definition does not exist for this term. Federal, state, and local laws each define it differently, and each of those definitions changes with the times. Use *tactical rifle*, *automatic rifle*, *machine gun*, *submachine gun*, *assault rifle* (see its separate entry for the distinction), or something generic (or brand specific) instead.

ASSISTED OPENING KNIFE: This knife has a swinging blade concealed inside the handle that is biased to stay put. It is opened when the operator pushes on a thumb stud, disc, hole, or tab connected to the blade. At about halfway open, a spring or torsion bar in the knife "assists" the blade into its open position. Not to be used interchangeably with *switchblade*.

AUTOMATIC KNIFE: Another term for *switchblade*, but in the modern sense. It's more accurate to use *automatic knife* when referring to switchblades used by law enforcement and military characters after 1958. Automatic knives are built with the latest materials and technology and are designed for hard use. Some open from the side like a traditional switchblade. Others open and close from the front. Those are called OTF (out the front) knives.

AUTO LOCK HOLSTER: A type of pistol holster that uses a locking mechanism to secure the firearm. It must be unlocked, usually by pressing with a thumb, in order for the firearm to be drawn. Not used with revolvers.

BACK SHEATH: A type of knife sheath worn across the back, usually secured to the shoulder.

BALISONG KNIFE: Another term for *butterfly knife*. The plural form may be written as *balisongs*. Bali-Song is a registered trademark of Benchmade, so don't spell it that way unless referring specifically to those knives.

BALLISTIC KNIFE: A device, usually homemade, that launches a knife or sharp object from a cylinder. Often restricted by state or local laws.

BALLISTICS: The science of how a bullet or other projectile travels.

BBs: Spherical projectiles of lead, steel, or other metal inside a shotshell. Not to be used interchangeably with *bullets*.

BLOOD GROOVES: Also called *fullers*. Despite their name, these long indentations along a knife's blade aren't actually used for channeling blood from a wound. They don't make it easier to remove the blade from a body, either. They reduce the weight of the blade. That's about it. Knife designers use them to achieve a certain balance or look.

BOLT-ACTION RIFLE: A rifle that uses a sliding metal cylinder (bolt) to move shells in and out of the chamber. The shooter manually operates the bolt to cycle ammunition. The rifle can't fire unless the bolt is in a forward-down position, even if the safety is off.

BOOT KNIFE: A short, slender fixed blade knife. Despite the name, it's not always carried in a boot. This is a style of knife.

BOOT SHEATH: A type of knife sheath designed for securing inside footwear, usually but not always a boot.

BOWIE KNIFE: A style of fixed blade knife popularized by Jim Bowie and the infamous Sandbar Fight of 1827. A Bowie knife is characterized by a large blade whose tip is lower than the top of the handle, as if part of the spine had been clipped out. This is referred to as a *clip point*. One person or company does not own this design—it's just a style.

BREAK-ACTION: A kind of hinged firearm mechanism that opens with a lever or release to expose the chamber. The operator places shells directly into the chamber, then closes the action to fire. Emptying the chamber involves reopening the action and manually removing the shells. This type of action is most common with single-shot and double-barrel shotguns.

BUCK KNIFE: When written as *buck knife*, it's a generic term for any hunting knife. A *Buck knife* is different. Buck is a brand that makes many kinds of knives. It's more accurate to write *hunting knife* unless specifically referring to knives made by Buck or the iconic Buck 110 knife.

BUCKSHOT: Another term for *00 shot* or *double-ought shot*. It's a shotshell with large BBs. It's usually restricted for civilian use by law and most commonly used for defense purposes.

BULLET: A single metal projectile seated at the top of a cartridge. Not to be used interchangeably with *cartridge*, *round*, or *shell*. It's just the projectile.

BULLPUP: Not a dog at all. This is a type of rifle or shotgun where the action and magazine are positioned behind the trigger instead of in front of it. This makes for a compact design without sacrificing performance.

BUTTERFLY KNIFE: Another term for *balisong*. This is a knife that contains a blade nestled between two handle halves. The handles are hinged into the tang of the blade. In its closed position, none of the blade is exposed. Swinging open one of the handle halves 360 degrees until it meets the other handle half exposes the blade.

CARBINE: A small or light rifle.

CARTRIDGE: Another term for *shell* or *round*, *cartridge* applies to rifle and handgun ammunition. It's technically accurate, but not common, to use this term for shotgun ammunition, too, but it is not to be used interchangeably with *bullet*. A cartridge contains the casing, primer, gunpowder, and projectile(s). It's the whole thing.

CASING/CASE: A component of a rifle, handgun, or shotgun shell. This guide considers *casing* the preferred term. For rifles and handguns, a casing is the metal sleeve (usually brass) that houses gunpowder and a primer. The bullet is seated at the top of the casing. For shotguns, the casing is usually plastic and wraps up all the interior components.

CASTLE DOCTRINE: Under this principle, a person has no obligation to retreat when threatened at home. A lethal act of violence to stop a threat would therefore be justified.

CENTERFIRE AMMUNITION: A rifle, handgun, or shotgun shell designed for a firing pin to strike the center of the primer. This is different from rimfire ammunition, where the firing pin strikes the rim of the casing. The more powerful varieties of rifle and handgun ammunition are almost always centerfire. Lighter calibers, such as the .17 and .22, are rimfire. Shotgun shells are almost always centerfire.

CHAMBER: The spot at the base of the barrel where a shell is seated to be fired.

CHARGING HANDLE: Sometimes called a *cocking handle*. With regard to semi-automatic or fully automatic shotguns and rifles, it's a small tab or knob located near the chamber. The shooter works the cocking handle back to chamber the first shell, then activates a release or lets go so the handle snaps forward. The shell is ready to be fired.

CHOKE: A replaceable, legal modification screwed into the end of a shotgun barrel. It changes the pattern of BBs as they exit the barrel. A permanent choke could also be carved out of the inside of the barrel. This is called a *jug choke*.

CLIP: A term often used incorrectly in place of *detachable magazine*. A clip seats ammunition together for insertion into the magazine of a firearm. Clips are most often used with older firearms. In nearly all cases, use *magazine* instead of *clip*.

CLOSE RANGE: Referring to firearms, a distance typically less than 25 yards.

COCKED: In all instances, *cocked* means the firearm is mechanically ready to fire with the pull of the trigger. With firearms that have hammers, *cocked* means the hammer is back.

COCKING HANDLE: See *charging handle*.

COLLAPSIBLE STOCK: A feature most often associated with semi-automatic or fully automatic rifles, although they could be fitted to any long firearm. Collapsible stocks fold or slide to adjust the length of that part of the firearm.

CONCEALED CARRY: The act of a person hiding a firearm on his or her body. It almost always involves a handgun inside a holster obstructed from view.

COP-KILLER AMMUNITION: A vague term referring either to Teflon-coated bullets designed to penetrate body armor or to hollow-point ammunition. Neither is all that accurate. It's best to avoid this term.

CORDITE: A type of gunpowder used in firearms from the late 1800s to World War II. Cordite is now obsolete.

CROSS DRAW: When referring to handgun holsters, this is when the holster is not on the shooter's strong side. For example, a cross draw holster for a right-handed person would be on the left side.

CROSSHAIRS: The type of scope reticle most commonly found in fiction. It contains two intersecting lines in a cross or plus-sign shape. Some variants include features for ranging.

CUTLERY: Knives used in the kitchen to prep food or for eating. It's redundant to write *kitchen cutlery*.

CUTTHROAT RAZOR: Another term for *straight razor*. It features a shaving blade that folds into a handle.

CUSTOM FIREARM: A firearm customized using manufactured parts and accessories.

DERRINGER: A generic term for a small pistol.

DAGGER: A type of knife that is smaller than a short sword and has a blade that is sharpened on both sides. Designed for stabbing or forward-motion work.

DOUBLE-ACTION HANDGUN: A type of handgun where one pull of the trigger makes the internal or external hammer perform two motions: back (cocked) and forward (firing pin strikes shell). Most modern revolvers and semi-automatic pistols are double-action. The shooter can pull the trigger without cocking a hammer first.

DOUBLE TRIGGERS: A pair of triggers sometimes found on double-barrel shotguns. Each trigger fires a separate barrel.

DROP: In terms of ballistics, it's the distance a projectile, such as a bullet, descends as it travels.

DRUM: A large, pancake-shaped magazine usually associated with submachine guns and machine guns. It rotates cartridges in a circular pattern through the action. Picture a Tommy gun from the Prohibition era.

EDGE: The cutting side of a blade. It's what gets sharpened.

EVERYDAY CARRY KNIFE: A knife designed for carrying in the pocket every day. Designs focus on general utility tasks (opening mail, cutting common materials, etc.) and eye appeal. Often abbreviated as EDC.

EXTENDED MAGAZINE: Referring to shotguns, it's an extra-long tube magazine for carrying additional shells. For pistols and rifles, it's a magazine (not a clip) that holds many more rounds than is standard.

EXTREME RANGE: Referring to firearms, it's a distance between about 300 to 2,000 yards.

FILLET KNIFE: A knife with a thin, flexible blade useful for removing skin from meat. Most often used to process fish, but writers may have more nefarious purposes in mind.

FIRING PIN: The device in a firearm that strikes the primer in a shell. The primer then ignites the gunpowder, which forces the projectile(s) out the barrel.

FIXED BLADE KNIFE: A knife with an immobile blade seated over a handle. The most popular kind of knife.

FIXED CYLINDER REVOLVER: A type of revolver where shells are loaded and unloaded by slipping them in and out of exposed chambers along the side of the firearm. Most common with antique revolvers.

FOLDING KNIFE: A knife with one or more blades that fold in and out of the handle. The operator moves the blades manually. *Pocketknife* is another term for *folding knife*.

FULLY AUTOMATIC RIFLE: A rifle where more than one round will fire so long as the trigger is pulled. Also called a *machine gun*. Acceptable to use *full-auto* in place of the lengthier term.

Don't confuse this with a semi-automatic rifle. Those fire only once per pull of the trigger.

FULL METAL JACKET: A type of handgun or rifle ammunition where the bullet is covered in a layer of hard metal. This makes the bullet more likely to pass through a target.

GAUGE: Shotguns are classified by gauge. The lower the gauge, the more powerful the shotgun. The most popular shotguns are 12-gauge and 20-gauge. Note that the .410 shotgun refers to a caliber, not a gauge.

GINSU KNIFE: This term is sometimes used in place of *chef's knife* or *butcher knife*. Ginsu is a brand. It's more accurate to use generic terms unless you're referring specifically to that brand of knife.

GRAINS: A unit of measurement used for firearm ammunition, such as bullets, slugs, and gunpowder. One grain is equivalent to 64.79 milligrams. One ounce is equal to 437.5 grains. *Grains* is also used in this guide to denote a property of metal in knife blades. That's a separate usage.

GUT HOOK: A curved tool for cutting open animals for processing. Gut hooks are either standalone tools or a part built into knives.

GUNPOWDER: The propellant that launches a projectile out of a firearm. Modern gunpowder does not contain cordite.

HAMMER: A lever located behind the chamber of a firearm that sets and resets the firing pin. They can be internal or external.

HAMMERLESS REVOLVER: A type of revolver that lacks an external hammer.

HIP HOLSTERS: A type of handgun holster that is attached to a belt around the waist.

HOLLOW-POINT BULLETS: A type of rifle or handgun bullet sporting a crater instead of a tip. This design makes the bullet explode upon impact. Hollow-point ammunition is not likely to pass through a target.

HUNTING KNIFE: A knife designed for outdoor activities.

IWB (INSIDE-THE-WAISTBAND) HOLSTER: A type of hip holster designed for wearing on the inside of pants around the waist. Ideal for concealed carry.

IWB (INSIDE-THE-WAISTBAND) SHEATH: A type of knife sheath attached to the waist designed to slip inside the pants instead of outside.

ITALIAN STILETTO: When most people think of a switchblade, they're imagining the long, thin profile of an Italian stiletto.

KARAMBIT: A style of tactical knife with a curved blade and handle. The knife in its entirety makes somewhat of a *C* shape.

KUKRI: A type of knife with a blade that curves inward like a boomerang and is ideal for hacking and slashing. The design is indigenous to Nepal and surrounding areas. Also spelled as *khukri* and about a dozen other ways. Pick one and be consistent.

LASER SIGHTS: A glorified laser pointer attached to a firearm useful for aiming at close ranges. The most popular are red, but green is another option. Not to be confused with red dot sights or scopes.

LEVER-ACTION: A type of firearm action that uses a manual lever to simultaneously eject a shell from the chamber and load a round from a tubular magazine beneath the barrel. This is most common with older-style rifles.

LOCK: A mechanism that keeps the blade in place after it opens from inside the handle of a knife. Commonly found on pocketknives, folding knives, automatic knives, switchblades, and assisted opening knives.

LONG RANGE: Referring to firearms, it's a distance between 100 and 300 yards.

MACHETE: A type of oversized fixed blade knife designed for slashing and hacking.

MACHINE GUN: A fully automatic firearm that uses rifle ammunition. This is different from a submachine gun, which is generally smaller and shoots handgun ammunition. *Fully automatic rifle*, *automatic rifle*, and *tactical rifle* are appropriate synonyms. See the separate entry on *assault rifles* for how to use that term.

MACHINE PISTOL: A submachine gun that's closer in size to a handgun than a rifle.

MAGAZINE: A firearm component that stores shells in reserve until fed into the chamber to be fired. A magazine can be detachable or built into the firearm. If it's detachable, don't confuse it with the term *clip*. A clip seats shells together for insertion into a magazine. However, most magazines don't require separate clips. With shotguns, the magazine is the tube holding reserve shells underneath the barrel. With pistols, the magazine is usually detachable and located inside the handle. A revolver does not have a magazine. It has a cylinder that contains separate chambers. Rifles could have an internal magazine or a detachable magazine depending on the model. Machine guns and submachine guns use detachable magazines. Because of their large capacity, magazines may require clips to replenish them. Just stick to the term *magazine* unless getting technical in this area makes sense. *Mag* is an abbreviated form of this term.

MAGNUM: Magnum ammunition contains extra gunpowder and/or a larger projectile. It is therefore more powerful than regular ammunition. There isn't a set industry definition, though. Manufacturers set their own standards for what qualifies as magnum. With shotshells, magnum ammunition may also contain extra BBs.

MIDRANGE: Referring to firearms, a distance between about 25 and 100 yards.

MOON CLIP: Similar to a speed loader, except it's a thin frame that holds shells together for insertion into the chambers of a revolver. It's best to use *moon clip* instead of just *clip*, since *clip* is misused so often.

MOLLE: Stands for "modular lightweight load-carrying equipment." It's a customizable harness used by military and law enforcement organizations for carrying tactical gear, such as pouches, sheaths, and holsters. Available on the civilian market, too.

MOUSE GUN: A handgun of exceptionally small size.

MUZZLE: The end of the barrel where projectiles exit the firearm.

NECK SHEATH: A type of knife sheath with a lanyard for wearing around the neck.

OPEN CARRY: The act of carrying a firearm in full view. It's basically the opposite of concealed carry.

OTF (OUT THE FRONT) KNIFE: A type of automatic knife. Blades open and close from the front of the knife handle instead of the side.

OVER-UNDER: A type of firearm, usually a double-barrel shotgun, where two barrels are stacked vertically.

PATTERN: The cloud of BBs that exits the barrel of a shotgun.

PISTOL: A handgun that uses a stationary chamber. Not the same as a revolver, which uses several chambers inside a rotating cylinder.

POCKET CLIP: A metal clamp on the handle of a knife that hooks onto the top of a pocket. This makes the knife easier to carry. Pocket clips first became popular in the 1980s.

POCKET HOLSTER: A type of handgun holster designed to slip inside a pocket.

POCKET PISTOL: A small pistol.

POCKETKNIFE: A knife with one or more blades that fold in and out of the side of the handle. The operator moves the blade(s) manually. *Folding knife* is another term for *pocketknife.*

POMMEL: The bottom of a knife handle. Some are designed for looks, while others sport studs intended for striking opponents or breaking windows.

PRIMER: A component of a cartridge or shell. When struck by a firing pin, it ignites the gunpowder in the cartridge.

PROJECTILE: In firearms, this refers to whatever is being launched out the barrel. It could be a bullet, a BB, a shotgun slug, a less-lethal item, or something else.

PROPELLANT: Another term for gunpowder.

PUMP: The back-and-forth motion that works the slide on a pump-action shotgun or pump-action rifle.

PUMP-ACTION RIFLE: A type of rifle where the operator pumps a sliding mechanism underneath the barrel to work the action. The backward motion ejects a shell from the chamber. The forward motion loads a shell from the magazine into the chamber.

PUMP-ACTION SHOTGUN: A type of shotgun where the operator pumps a sliding mechanism underneath the barrel to work the action. The backward motion ejects a shell from the chamber. The forward motion loads a shell from the magazine into the chamber.

PUSH DAGGER: A type of dagger with a T-shaped handle designed for defense purposes. When the dagger is held, the operator's hand makes a fist. Also called a *punch dagger*. Instead of a solid handle, it may have a hole for slipping a finger through.

RACK THE SLIDE: Pertaining to slide-action pistols, this phrase means the slide is manually pulled back and released to chamber a round from the magazine. It's a good term to use when a character loads the first round in a semi-automatic pistol.

RED DOT SCOPE OR RED DOT SIGHT: A tube used for aiming, similar to a traditional scope. However, it uses a red dot instead of the classic crosshairs. If this tube magnifies the target, it's a red dot scope. If it doesn't, it's a red dot sight. Not to be confused with laser sights, which project a red dot onto a target.

RESCUE KNIVES: A general term for knives with features for freeing people in survival situations. Features could include seat belt cutters, dull tips for working the blade near flesh, window breakers, LED lights, and whistles.

RETICLE: Lines inside a scope used for aiming. The classic crosshairs are a type of reticle, although there are many variants.

RETENTION HOLSTERS: A type of handgun holster that uses a snug fit to secure the firearm. Used for both pistols and revolvers.

REVOLVER: A handgun that uses multiple chambers in a cylinder that rotates as the firearm is fired. Not the same thing as a pistol.

RIFLED SHOTGUN BARREL: A specialized shotgun barrel with twisting grooves on the inside. These grooves cause a shotgun slug to spin as it exits the barrel, increasing its accuracy. A rifled shotgun barrel would not be used with BBs (shotshells).

RIMFIRE AMMUNITION: A type of cartridge where the firing pin strikes the rim of the brass casing to ignite the gunpowder. A thinner casing is used, which can support less pressure and therefore less firepower than centerfire ammunition. Rimfire ammunition is most often used in lighter rifles and handguns, such as the .22 and .17.

ROUNDS: A generic term for rifle, shotgun, and handgun ammunition. Interchangeable with *shells* and *cartridges*.

SADDLE: Plastic clips that hold three to five shells and that are secured to a shotgun. This is a way for shotgun users to carry extra ammunition.

SAFETY: A switch or button that prevents a firearm from firing. When the safety is off, the firearm can be fired.

SAWED-OFF SHOTGUN: A modified shotgun with a barrel shortened to less than 18 inches.

SCOPE: A telescoping lens in a tube mounted on a firearm used for aiming.

SEAT-BELT CUTTER: A feature on rescue knives or tools used for quickly cutting seat belts and other material. This is usually a notch in the handle with a sharpened edge inside.

SELECT-FIRE: A type of firearm that can switch between semi-automatic and fully automatic functionality.

SEMI-AUTOMATIC RIFLE: A type of rifle where the action captures force from the recoil generated by shooting the firearm. It uses this force to simultaneously eject and load shells. These rifles fire once per trigger pull.

SEMI-AUTOMATIC SHOTGUN: A type of shotgun where the action captures force from the recoil generated by shooting the firearm. It uses this force to simultaneously eject and load shells. These shotguns fire once per pull of the trigger.

SHANK: An improvised knife fashioned from mundane materials. Also called a *shiv*.

SHELL: Another term for *round* or *cartridge* of ammunition.

SHIV: A type of improvised knife made from mundane materials. Also called a *shank*.

SHOT PLACEMENT: The spot where a projectile hits a target. Good shot placement means the shooter is accurate.

SHOTSHELLS: A shotgun shell that fires BBs.

SHOULDER HOLSTER: A type of handgun holster that straps to the shooter's shoulder and positions the firearm against the ribs.

SHOULDER SHEATH: A type of knife sheath with a harness that secures to the shoulder.

SIDE-BY-SIDE: A type of firearm, usually a double-barrel shotgun, where two barrels are positioned next to each other horizontally.

SIGHT: Hardware attached to the barrel of a firearm used for aiming. Use *scope* if that hardware includes a telescoping lens.

SILENCER: A cylindrical modification attached to the muzzle of a firearm to muffle the sound of gunfire. The more accurate but less-known term is *suppressor*.

SINGLE-ACTION HANDGUN: A type of handgun where the hammer must be cocked before each shot, either manually or automatically. With single-action revolvers, the hammer must be manually cocked before each shot: Cock, pull the trigger, cock, pull the trigger, etc. Single-action semi-automatic pistols are different. An external hammer must be cocked before the first shot. This is accomplished automatically when the first round is chambered by racking the slide. Subsequent shots do not need to be manually cocked: Rack the slide, pull the trigger, pull the trigger, etc.

SLIDE-ACTION PISTOL: A type of pistol that uses a sliding mechanism above the barrel. Moving this slide works the action, which cycles shells in and out of the chamber. Manually working the action to chamber the first shell is called "racking the slide." Most modern pistols are slide-action semi-automatics.

SLIDE-ACTION RIFLE: Another term for *pump-action rifle*.

SLIDE-ACTION SHOTGUN: Another term for *pump-action shotgun*.

SLUG: A shotgun shell that contains a single lead projectile instead of BBs. The projectile is also called a *slug*. It's accurate to use *slug* to refer to the shell or the projectile.

SMALL OF BACK HOLSTER: A type of handgun holster attached to a belt around the waist and placed at the back of the shooter.

SNUBNOSE: A revolver with a short barrel.

SPEED LOADER: A device that quickly drops shells into the chambers of a revolver.

SPEED STRIP: When referring to revolvers, it's a length of flexible material that holds ammunition in a single file line. Shells can be thumbed into the chambers two or three at a time.

STAND YOUR GROUND LAWS: A blanket term for laws that extend the Castle Doctrine outside the home.

STOCK: The solid part of a shotgun or rifle that is held to the shooter's shoulder.

STOPPING POWER: The amount of force a projectile exerts on a target upon impact.

STRAIGHT RAZOR: A shaving blade that folds into a handle. Sometimes called a *cutthroat razor*.

STRONG SIDE: The side of the body with the dominant hand. The right side of the body is the strong side of a right-handed person.

SUBMACHINE GUN: A fully automatic firearm that uses pistol ammunition. Not to be confused with machine guns, which use rifle ammunition.

SUBSONIC AMMUNITION: Firearm ammunition designed for velocities below the speed of sound, which is 1,126 feet per second. A subsonic bullet will not break the sound barrier. When paired with a suppressor (aka silencer), this ammunition will make little noise.

SUPPRESSOR: A cylindrical modification attached to the muzzle of a firearm to muffle the sound of firing. Also called a "*silencer*," though "*suppressor*" is technically more accurate.

SWING-OUT CYLINDER REVOLVER: The most popular kind of revolver, in which the cylinder swings out from the handgun to the side. This allows access to the chambers for loading and unloading. It's what most people think of when they imagine a revolver.

SWITCHBLADE: A knife where the blade concealed inside the handle is biased to open. A switch or button on the handle is pressed to release the blade. Not the same as an assisted opening knife. Modern switchblades are called *automatic knives*. They are made for members of law enforcement and military organizations, as well as civilians where legal.

TACTICAL KNIFE: A knife with features suitable for military, defensive, or first responder purposes.

TACTICAL RIFLE: A more accurate term for *assault weapon*. Tactical rifles contain features useful for engaging in combat.

TACTICAL SHOTGUN: A shotgun with features suitable for use in combat or defensive scenarios.

TANG: An extension of the blade that runs into the inside of the handle of a knife. It offsets pressure in the blade during use. Long (or full) tangs, such as the ones often used in fixed blade knives, are better for hard use than the short or absent tangs common to knives with blades that fold out of a handle.

TERRY STOP: When a law enforcement officer conducts a limited search of a person's clothing on the suspicion that he or she has a weapon.

THIGH HOLSTERS: A type of handgun holster secured to the thigh for wearing inside or outside clothing.

THROWING KNIFE: A fixed blade knife designed for throwing at targets.

THROWING SPIKES: A spike designed for throwing at targets.

TOGGLE-LOCK ACTION: A type of semi-automatic pistol action. It uses arms and levers to capture the force from recoil to move shells in and out of the chamber. It is more common with older pistols.

TOMMY GUN: When people picture a submachine gun from the Prohibition era, they're likely picturing a Tommy gun. It has a fully automatic action and sometimes uses high-capacity magazines. *Tommy* is short for *Thompson*, the last name of its inventor.

TOP BREAK REVOLVER: A type of revolver in which the cylinder sits on a hinge. It can be tipped forward to access the chambers. This is more common with older revolvers.

TRAJECTORY: The path a bullet or other projectile travels.

TRIGGER SAFETY: A small tab on the trigger that must be pressed before the trigger can be pulled.

WAD: A component of a shotshell that seats BBs inside the cartridge.

ZIP GUN: An improvised firearm assembled using mundane objects.

The Writer's Guide to Weapons

BONUS DOWNLOAD
EXHAUSTIVE WEAPONS LISTINGS

Looking for a quick way to research firearms and knives? Be sure to get the exhaustive firearm and knife listings download available at **www.WritersDigest.com/guns-knives**. It's the essential companion to this guide.

The download contains firearms cataloged from 1873 through today, organized by type and year introduced. Find ammunition capacities, historical trivia, manufacturing dates, and more. I highly recommend this download for selecting a character's firearm.

Many common knives on the market today are also included in the download. Use it to get an idea of what's available.

The download is free and exclusive to those who purchased this guide. Don't miss it.

BIBLIOGRAPHY

Adams, Chad. *Complete Guide to 3-Gun Competition*. F+W Media, 2012. Print.

Ayoob, Massad. *Gun Digest Book of Concealed Carry*. F+W Media, 2008. Print.

Ayoob, Massad. *Gun Digest Book of Concealed Carry*. 2nd ed. F+W Media, 2012. Print.

Ayoob, Massad. *Massad Ayoob's Greatest Handguns of the World*. F+W Media, 2010. Print.

Ayoob, Massad. *Massad Ayoob's Greatest Handguns of the World, Volume II*. F+W Media, 2012. Print.

Barnes, Frank C. *Cartridges of the World: A Complete Illustrated Reference for More Than 1,500 Cartridges*. 13th edition. Ed. Richard A. Mann. F+W Media, 2012. Print.

Belmas, Andy, and Kevin Michalowski, eds. *Gun Digest* Nov. 8, 2010. F+W Media. Print.

Brezny, L.P. *Gun Digest Book of Long-Range Shooting*. F+W Media. 2007. Print.

Card, James, and Doug Howlett, eds. *Gun Digest* March 6, 2014. F+W Media. Print.

Card, James, ed. *Living Ready* Summer 2013. F+W Media. Print.

Card, James, ed. *Living Ready* Winter 2013. F+W Media. Print.

Cunningham, Grant. *12 Essentials of Concealed Carry*. F+W Media. 2013. E-book.

Cunningham, Grant. *Gun Digest Book of the Revolver*. F+W Media, 2011. Print.

Cutshaw, Charles. *Tactical Small Arms of the 21st Century*. F+W Media, 2006. Print.

Fessenden, David. *Defensive Handgun Skills: Your Guide to Fundamentals for Self-Protection*. F+W Media, 2010. Print.

Flayderman, Norm. *Flayderman's Guide to Antique American Firearms*. 9th ed. F+W Media, 2011. Print.

Haskew, Mike. *Living Ready* Winter 2013 issue. F+W Media, 2013. Print.

Hayes, Gila. *Concealed Carry for Women*. F+W Media. 2013. Print.

House, James E. *Customize the Ruger* 10/22. F+W Media, 2006. Print.

Kertzman, Joe, and Steve Shackleford, eds. *Best Custom Knives*. F+W Media, 2014. PDF.

Kertzman, Joe, and Steve Shackleford, eds. *Best Factory Knives*. F+W Media, 2014. PDF.

Kertzman, Joe, and Steve Shackleford, eds. *BLADE* April 2014. F+W Media. Print.

Kertzman, Joe, and Steve Shackleford, eds. *BLADE* June 2014. F+W Media. Print.

Kertzman, Joe, and Steve Shackleford, eds. *BLADE* May 2014. F+W Media. Print.

Kertzman, Joe, and Steve Shackleford, eds. *BLADE* November 2006. F+W Media. Print.

Kertzman, Joe, and Steve Shackleford, eds. *BLADE* November 2013. F+W Media. Print.

Kertzman, Joe, and Steve Shackleford, eds. *BLADE* October 2013. F+W Media. Print.

Kertzman, Joe, and Steve Shackleford, eds. *BLADE* September 2013. F+W Media. Print.

Kertzman, Joe, ed. *Knives 2013.* F+W Media, 2012. Print.

Kertzman, Joe, ed. *Knives 2014.* F+W Media, 2013. Print.

Lee, Jerry, ed. *2013 Standard Catalog of Firearms.* 23rd edition. F+W Media, 2012. Print.

Lee, Jerry, ed. *2014 Standard Catalog of Firearms.* 24th edition. F+W Media, 2013. Print.

Lee, Jerry, ed. *Gun Digest 2013.* 67th ed. F+W Media, 2012. Print.

Lee, Jerry, ed. *Gun Digest 2014.* 68th ed. F+W Media. 2013. Print.

Lee, Jerry, ed. *Standard Catalog of Handguns.* F+W Media, 2012. Print.

Lofland, Lee. *Police Procedure & Investigation: A Guide for Writers.* F+W Media. 2007. Print.

Peterson, Phillip, ed. *Gun Digest Book of Modern Gun Values.* 16th ed. F+W Media, 2011. Print.

Peterson, Phillip. *Gun Digest Buyer's Guide to Tactical Rifle.* F+W Media, 2010. Print.

Peterson, Phillip. *Standard Catalog of Military Firearms.* 6th ed. F+W Media, 2007. Print.

Peterson, Phillip. *Standard Catalog of Military Firearms.* 7th ed. F+W Media. 2013. Print.

Shackleford, Steve, ed. *BLADE* September 1994. American Blade. Print.

Shideler, Dan, ed. *Gun Digest 2012.* 66th edition. F+W Media, 2011. Print.

Shideler, Dan. *Gun Digest Book of Classic Combat Handguns.* F+W Media, 2011. Print.

Shideler, Dan, and Derrek Sigler. *Gun Digest Book of Tactical Gear.* F+W Media, 2008. Print.

Shideler, Dan. *Guns Illustrated 2011.* 43rd ed. F+W Media, 2010. Print.

Shideler, Dan. *Standard Catalog of Remington Firearms.* F+W Media. 2008. Print.

Stewart, Creek. *Build the Perfect Bug Out Bag.* F+W Media. 2012. Print.

Sweeney, Patrick. *1911: The First 100 Years.* F+W Media, 2010. Print.

Sweeney, Patrick. *Gun Digest Big Fat Book of the .45 ACP.* F+W Media, 2009. Print.

Sweeney, Patrick. *Gun Digest Book of the AK & SKS.* F+W Media, 2008. Print.

Tarr, James, ed. *Standard Catalog of Colt Firearms.* 2nd edition. F+W Media, 2013. Print.

Van Zwoll, Wayne. *Gun Digest Shooter's Guide to Rifles.* F+W Media, 2012. Print.

Wagner, Scott. *Gun Digest Book of Survival Guns.* F+W Media, 2012. Print.

Wagner, Scott. *Gun Digest Book of the Tactical Shotgun.* F+W Media, 2011. Print.

Wagner, Scott. *Own the Night: Selection & Use of Tactical Lights & Laser Sights.* F+W Media. 2009. Print.

Watson, David. *ABCs of Rifle Shooting.* F+W Media, 2014. Print.

Wieland, Terry. *Gun Digest Book of Classic American Combat Rifles.* F+W Media, 2011. Print.

Wood, J.B. *Gun Digest Book of Firearms Assembly/Disassembly Part IV: Centerfire Rifles.* F+W Media, 2003. Print.

www.agrussell.com. Jan. 2013.
www.akti.org. 2013.
www.armalite.com. Jan. 2013.
www.atf.gov. Jan. 2013.
www.auto-ordnance.com. Jan. 2013.
www.berettausa.com. Jan. 2013.
www.blademag.com. Jan. 2013.
www.bobergarms.com. Feb. 2014.
www.browning.com. Jan. 2013.
www.buckknives.com. Nov. 2013.

www.cnn.com. Nov. 2013.

www.coldsteel.com. Jan. 2014.

www.cz-usa.com. Jan. 2014.

www.fbi.gov. Jan. 2013.

www.gao.gov. March 2014.

www.gerbergear.com. Jan. 2014.

www.globalsecurity.org. March 2014.

www.glock.com. Jan. 2013.

www.gundigest.com. Jan. 2013.

www.gundigeststore.com. Jan. 2014.

www.handgunlaw.us. Nov. 2013.

www.history.com. Jan. 2013.

www.howstuffworks.com. Nov. 2013.

www.innerbody.com. Nov. 2013.

www.ka-bar.com. Jan. 2014.

www.knifecenter.com. Jan. 2013.

www.knifeforums.com. March 2014.

www.leatherman.com. Dec. 2013.

www.lesbaer.com. Jan. 2013.

www.militaryfactory.com. Jan. 2013.

www.medscape.com. Nov. 2013.

www.mcmfamily.com. Feb. 2014.

www.mossberg.com. Jan. 2013.

www.policemag.com. Nov. 2013.

www.princeton.edu. April 2014.

www.randallknives.com. Jan. 2014.

www.remington.com. Jan. 2013.

www.ruger.com. Jan. 2013.

www.shopblade.com. March 2014.

www.sigsauer.com. Feb. 2014.

www.smith-wesson.com. Jan. 2013.

www.startribune.com. Dec. 2013.

www.swissarmy.com. Jan. 2014.

www.tactical-life.com. Feb. 2014.

www.usacarry.com. Nov. 2013.

www.wengerna.com. Jan. 2014.

www.winchester.com. Dec. 2013.

www.winchesterguns.com. Jan. 2013.

www.world.guns.ru. Jan. 2013.

www.yale.edu. July 2014.

HAVE A QUESTION? ASK THE AUTHOR

Writers with specific questions about firearms and knives should go to CrimeFictionBook. com and contact me. The most common question I receive is, "What kind of gun/knife would a XYZ character from Such & Such use?" If I can't answer it, I'll find someone who can.

CrimeFictionBook.com includes the tips on firearms and knives that couldn't fit in this guide. People tell me the free e-newsletter there is pretty keen, too.

I'm also on Facebook, Twitter, Google Plus, and Goodreads, where I'm happy to talk guns, knives, writing, and all things fancy striking.

GET MORE MAYNARD

Despite the demands of this guide, Maynard Soloman, gal-damn detective, is alive and well. He's in his beloved RV, parked somewhere in the short story collection *8 Funny Detective Stories with Maynard Soloman, Gal-Damn Detective*. The e-book is available through all fine e-book retailers. Be sure to write to Maynard on Facebook (facebook.com/crimenovel) and Twitter (@MaynardSoloman), too.

More about Maynard can be found at CrimeFictionBook.com.

INDEX

Printed in the United States
by Baker & Taylor Publisher Services